FIVE FOR FREEDOM
A Study of Feminism in Fiction

FIVE FOR FREEDOM

A Study of Feminism in Fiction

Geoffrey Wagner

London · George Allen & Unwin Ltd
Ruskin House   Museum Street

ISBN 0 04 801014 6

Printed in Great Britain
in 12 *point Fournier type*
by Unwin Brothers Limited
Woking and London

For Colleen
who liberated me
... gently

Contents

Das Ewig-Weibliche
Zieht uns hinan.
FAUST II

I

INTRODUCTION

'What a misfortune to be a woman! And yet the misfortune, when
when one is a woman, is at bottom not to comprehend that it
is one.'
Søren Kierkegaard

In probably one of the wisest works on woman Simone de
Beauvoir wrote: 'Enough ink has been spilled in the quarrelling
over feminism now practically over.'[1] She must surely have been
surprised to see feminism's flames fanned to full fury again in –
of all places – America of the past decade, more especially since
so many current arguments (notably the thesis of woman's
position as analogous to a racial minority) seem to have been
borrowed rather directly from her clever and closely argued pages.

But of course the literature on this subject is already voluminous and anyone sampling it, even cursorily, is soon surprised to
find the vehemence we meet in the American press of the moment
almost tame in comparison with books published in England in
the 1850s. De Beauvoir cites Léon Richier, author of a work on
women's rights in 1869, as 'the true founder of feminism', but
one can find dozens of similar English writers before this date.
The emancipation of women was a driving theme of the great
Victorians, especially, of course, John Stuart Mill, though his
The Subjection of Women did not come out until 1869. A retro-
spective conspectus, like W. Lyon Blease's *The Emancipation of
English Women* of 1910, shows how rich in all the arguments our

[1] Simone de Beauvoir, *The Second Sex*, translated and edited by H. M.
Parshley, New York: Bantam Books, 1970, p. xiii. London: Cape, 1968.
This famous study was first published in two volumes in France in 1949.
In it Mlle de Beauvoir pays tribute to the emancipation of women in Ameri-
can offices, which would receive short shrift at the hands of Fem Lib today.

very early feminists were. New Zealand, after all, granted full women's rights in 1893. And when it is immediately objected that Switzerland did not grant women the vote until recently, there are counter-arguments available here, too. Swiss cantonal voting procedures are still extremely complicated, and at least one book by a Swiss woman has claimed that women there were more free without the vote. Moreover – and this is, of course, the ultimate heresy – not all of them wanted the vote.

Fem Lib . . . women's liberation . . . as slogans these terms are still new. Neither finds a place in Betty Friedan's famous polemic *The Feminine Mystique,* nor Caroline Bird's *Born Female.* Indeed, *The Reader's Guide to Periodical Literature* has only just started to list such categories at all. One quiet woman feminist, indeed, has confessed to alarm that all the selfless work done for more than a century by genuine women emancipators is presently in danger of capture, exploitation and vulgarization by self-seeking and publicity-hungry political activists:

'Women's Liberation is becoming a bandwagon slogan, and I do not choose to be on any bandwagon. I want to be emancipated, independent, delivered from manipulation, and I want the same emancipation for everyone, male and female. I want to be unfettered by attitudes, images, inferred life styles, and all other aspects of a stereotyped label that threatens to dominate and control individuals. The very term "women's liberation" is creating a counter-productive movement.'[2]

Not that the publicity-hunters care. But the time has come to redress a balance, and take a second look at women created out of fact by fiction.

Sexuality is an aspect of being, though perhaps one of the most important. In the General Preface to his *Studies in The Psychology of Sex* (1897) Havelock Ellis wrote, 'I regard sex as the central problem of life.' But sex in 1897 is not sex in 1972 nor even 1949. We are already living – in America, at any rate – in a time when the criterion of sex is uncertain (interested groups

[2] Corinne Geeting, 'The Tyranny of Women's Liberation', *ETC.,* XXVIII: 3 September 1971, p. 359.

have asked for its elimination on passports). Stable physical differences are ceding in such assumptions to the psychological. Trans-sexualism has become virtually recognized, official, in some American cities; a person simply has the sex he or she believes in belonging to. The pathetic transvestite haunting the London underground of a generation ago would not simply not be arrested in modern America, he (or she) would be immediate material for that successful recent revue, the Cockettes.

A professor of psychiatry at the University of Oregon, Dr Ira B. Pauly has described in some detail the case of a physiologically normal female who insisted she was a boy because she felt like one, and later in life had a reasonably happy marriage for three years with a man, avoiding sexual intercourse. By now almost everyone has some favourite story in this respect. De Beauvoir's book concedes the trend in advance – 'Woman is a female to the extent that she feels herself as such.' Again, she confronts, at another point, the sphinx-like difficulty of definition and tells us: 'a fundamental ambiguity marks the feminine being. . . . The fact is that she would be quite embarrassed to decide *what* she *is*; but this not because the hidden truth is too vague to be discerned: it is because in this domain there is no truth.'[3]

What we are certain of in this sphere is simply that we are alive. More or less. A woman exists. And in several species, of course, perpetuation requires no sexual differentiation at all. Secondly, a society gets the kind of classifications it desires. These are under such rapid modification today that, in the sexual realm, they may be endangering rather than enlarging our happiness:

'The problem, as it presents itself to us today, is no longer the question: What are women able to do?, but: What are the limits to which society can go in granting women equality, without endangering its continued existence and the happiness of individuals?'[4]

[3] De Beauvoir, pp. 33, 241.
[4] Viola Klein, *The Feminine Character: History of an Ideology*, New York: International Universities Press, 1949, p. 102; the citation in my text is drawn from Chapter VI which resumes the theories of Helen B. Thompson, author of *The Mental Traits of Sex*, Chicago University Press, 1903.

The Californian divorce rate went up 40 per cent in the year in which the term *dissolution of marriage* was officially substituted for divorce. Just as tests of vasodilators in the skin tell us that women blush when society tells them to blush, at exposure of even an ankle a century ago, say, so calling abortion by supposedly softened terms, such as *office gynaecology* or *termination of intra-uterine wart*, has had a similar 'liberating' effect. The actress Helen Hayes was once involved in a famous case on her withdrawal, owing to advanced pregnancy, from a play called *Coquette*. The producer closed up, and Actors' Equity Association duly sued. Arbitration had to try to decide whether motherhood was an *act of God*.

So with woman. If language shapes our thought to any perceptible degree, as several eminent linguists have considered that it does, our classificatory habits carry a bias that is wellnigh ineradicable at this stage of language development. 'Everyone should decide for himself whether or not he should have an abortion' ran one notorious slogan of a New York abortion clinic. Similarly, one has seen in a textbook – 'Man is a mammal who breastfeeds his young.' In the year that a fifteen-*man* table tennis team, including several women, visited China, my wife had a one-*man* show of her paintings in a Manhattan gallery and I received an instruction from a university Dean about a fresh*man* girl.

Women's groups have tried to reverse some of this semantic, requiring Ms to be prefaced before a woman's name on an envelope rather than the invidious Mrs or Miss distinction. *Chairwoman* and *Spokesperson* have both been tried but neither seems to have had wide acceptance. And indeed these timid replacements and circumlocutions would seem to miss the point. As Margaret Mead has put it, 'What in thunder is gained in reversing "God is He" into "God is She" except irritating people? It gets us nowhere. All you get with a reversal is the opposite again.' Trying to alter gender terms (*mistresspiece?*) seems fairly fruitless now: Turkish is devoid of grammatical gender, yet no one would claim especial liberation of Turkish women as a result.

The substance of the approach taken in this book is what woman feels herself to be in a given society. It is for this very reason that the study of several literary heroines proves such a helpful task in cultural identification. As Balzac repeatedly reminded his contemporaries (supposedly calling for one of his fictional doctors on his deathbed), there is a solidity of experience in the given universe of a firmly created novel. We are, or should be, given all we need to know within the compass of the fiction. It is thus with a sort of paradoxical stability that we can therein see what it means to be a woman. De Beauvoir tells us that, in real life, 'woman is taught from adolescence to lie to men' (hence the cult of the enigma, the mystery, of woman); and we are at once mentally sent back to Baudeliare's brilliant essay on make-up – 'Eloge du Maquillage', the word *maquiller* meaning both to make up and deceive – in which he senses woman as an inveterate artist. Hence, too, de Beauvoir feels that, 'The times that have most sincerely treasured women are not the period of feudal chivalry nor yet the gallant nineteenth century. They are the times – like the eighteenth century – when men have regarded women as fellow creatures.'[5]

Over-generalization as this may be, it legitimizes my reading of *Les Liaisons dangereuses* first, a work presenting us with an almost hermetically sealed society within which women *exist* without mystery, without appanage, and without question. They simply are. For mystery is what we pour into the classification called woman – what we create of her, expect of her, ask her to live up to. *The Second Sex* is probably de Beauvoir's greatest book not because she is herself a woman, but because here the existential analysis operates at its best.

For man does define himself through woman (the Other). Even the confirmed bachelor is repudiating a world of significance, identifiably. We form abstractions from these polarities, and abide by them throughout whole civilizations. Woman is man's peer, partner, and sometimes his opponent. Our first task

[5] De Beauvoir, p. 245.

is to establish that she exists.[6] This is no sophistry. The existential concept of the Other (in this case, somewhat as a projection rather than as a person) makes it extremely difficult to say anything about something called 'woman'. Constantly likened, in our metaphoric vocabulary for her, to rivers, brooks, rippling streams, woman changes like water in our hands, she is shrewdly Protean.

Although de Beauvoir puts it in one passage, 'It is extremely difficult to give a generally valid definition of the female', she yet herself defines woman, or implies that woman defines herself, by antithetical existence. In an extremely suggestive passage, yet one marred by the jargon of the period, she writes:

> 'And if it is so difficult to say anything specific about her, that is because man seeks the whole of himself in her and because she is All. She is All, that is, on the plane of the inessential; she is all the Other. And, as the other, she is other than herself, other than what is expected of her. Being all, she is never quite *this* which she should be; she is everlastingly deception, the very deception of that existence which is never successfully attained nor fully reconciled with the totality of existence.'[7]

The passage is a little unworthy, since de Beauvoir does not need to be as obscure as this. For she is striking at real truth, and a truth that impels one to trust women in fiction rather than in fact (or even faction). In the present pages I hope not to get involved, and bogged down, in what might roughly be called the ontology of sexuality. After all, it could be said that the body itself is a generalization (the moment when life ceases, for instance, came under considerable debate during the first Barnard heart transplant).

And fictive literature declines the burden of these philosophical problems. It therefore can be said to reveal woman's nature in a

---

[6] The entity that made Tertullian rave can scarcely be said to do so: 'Woman, you are the devil's doorway. You have led astray one whom the devil would not dare attack directly. It is your fault that the Son of God had to die; you should always go in mourning and in rags.'

[7] De Beauvoir, p. 185.

peculiarly sensible way, since it is not primarily biological, psychoanalytic, nor economic, though it may partake of all three modes at the same time. Within a created society woman must define herself by a set of relationships, and these form the stuff of literature. Indeed, de Beauvoir would seem to admit as much herself by incorporating her chapter on woman as seen in certain writers into an otherwise densely historiographical work. Once more art gives loving form to life, and it is through art that we can see reality.

*   *   *

But what sort of art? And created by whom?

History has many heroines. Literature has paid tribute to them. A Sappho, a Vittoria Colonna, a Louise Labé were more or less exceptional, in their times. Hence literature is said to present us with a 'male reality'. This has been a strident feminist argument of late. It was presented by Simone de Beauvoir also: 'Representation of the world, like the world itself, is the work of men; they describe it from their own point of view, which they confuse with absolute truth.' Our literary records are therefore inauthentic since they are heavy with male bias. Woman has existed, then, as so much subject matter for men to go to work on.

Even for the feminist standpoint – perhaps principally for the feminist standpoint – this argument deserves closer inspection than it seems to have had. Literature has many houses and the one drawn on for this book – fiction – was considerably created for women, directly influenced feminine development, and has probably numbered more practitioners from the 'fair' if not the second sex than any other art form. Today it is said that in America 96 per cent of all readers of novels are college-educated housewives. Publishers have responded by placing women editresses in their fiction departments (juvenile publishing is almost wholly staffed by women in America, with 60% of literary agents being female).

This may not invalidate the argument. Such women, it could be said, are merely participating in a male supremacist culture, to be judged by its standards – so many Auntie Toms, in fact. We shall examine below an example of the epistolary novel, a genre which grew up to express the female experience in the eighteenth century and which was extremely popular with women. Still, the argument stands – or can be made to do so. Laclos and Richardson were men, and the new feminine readership of the time was fascinated by a bedroom-eye view of the male's idea of the female (as in painting). Fanny Burney was thus simply aping a male mode, sharpening her intellectual tools to win in a male game. She was, in any case, a friend of Dr Johnson who Boswell tells us said, 'Public practice of any art . . . is very indelicate in a female.'

In other words, we are saying that our culture was created by males and that therefore all its models are male. For its 'absolute truth' is male. Jane Austen hid herself to write. The theory can be almost limitlessly extrapolated, like early Marxism. (Indeed, anything so open-ended can scarcely be called a theory.) Male apologists for women, writers who have furnished the sharpest tools for feminine emancipation, like Mill, Ibsen, Shaw, may have contributed sympathetic examples of chauvinist guilt, but they are excluded *per se* from being able to present the female experience, not only because they are not women – not one of them ever had a baby – but because they still write within an exclusively male culture. In fact (it is suggested) such male concessions may seriously distort, mystify and injure the female reality, thus reinforcing the male view. Tokenism. Should a scholar discover tomorrow that the Wife of Bath's Tale was actually written by an Abbess of the time, rather than by Chaucer, it would make no more difference than if it were learnt that the colour of Harriet Beecher Stowe's skin was really black. Both would be conceived to have crossed artificial borders, yet the prevailing bias stands.

It has been said that we are here dealing with a hopelessly open-ended 'argument', a reaction rather than an action. Perhaps any beginnings in culture must always be such. Yet the feminist cannot invariably have her cake and eat it; she will indeed only damage her cause if she tries to do so. I have emerged, somewhat shakily, from recent women's activist meetings impressed by the 'fact' that when men are rude to and abuse women, they are characteristic chauvinist pigs, yet when they are gallant to them (as in the matrist period) they are equally typically extending their dominance in a more crafty way – putting women on a pedestal is really a Machiavellian blinkering of them to their true condition. The whole of the courtly love convention may be written off on this score.

Such is the dialectic of desperation, and really has little to do with literature at all (the recent flood of Fem Lib books in America is, in the main, a remarkably monotonous phenomenon wherein genuinely useful biological background material is made to back up later polemic). Of course, it could be said that such women are being forced into unwanted roles, as polemicists, by a warrior society, but the mirror image in the utopian communism of the thirties is striking. 'When true communism is established' is changed to 'when true feminism takes over.' No one yet knows which either is or even, as Helen Thompson asks, if an asexual human society could exist. Thus debate on the subject must be so hamstrung as to fail to be worthy of the name. We are left with a lot of intellectual pyrotechnics of the kind which Claude Lévi-Strauss diagnoses as the real disease of Western culture, what Thomas Mann might have called the Settembrini instinct.

The culture is a male one, to be sure, for all women may do in a male supremacist society is to borrow or steal weapons until their own cultural tradition can be established. One of the most radical and strident of recent feminists, Shulamith Firestone, has conceded the chicken-and-egg nature of this controversy, acknowledging that there is no room in the male tradition for a woman's view, 'even if she *could* discover what it was'[8] (italics

[8] Shulamith Firestone, *The Dialectic of Sex*, New York: Bantam Books, 1971, p. 159: cp. 'women have no means of coming to an understanding of what their experience *is*, or even that it is different from male experience. The tool for representing, for objectifying one's experience in order to deal with it, culture, is so saturated with male bias that women almost never have a chance to see themselves culturally through their own eyes' (p. 157). So where do we begin? Presumably Mrs Firestone's book is similarly tainted by having been written in a male culture.

hers, and surely somewhat insulting). If women cannot by definition discover their own view, feminism seems fairly point-less: perhaps, then, in a final turn of the screw, women might profitably examine their own images as given in a male society – by writers of fiction. Here we at least find a feeling-out for permanent values, and much less polemical fist-swinging.

For since a female 'point of view' has never truly existed, and may not *ipso facto* exist, in our male-dominated societies – matriarchies being written off in the same manner as the courtly love tradition as so much guilty tokenism – it is surely permis-sible, and valuable, to inspect those fictional heroines who had the courage to take a hard look at what women are actually faced with in life, and to confront the male reality head on. Those selected here were largely created by men, for in this debate it remains dubious as to what a 'point of view' truly constitutes.

The term is terribly sloppy. It is so in many senses. Were we to take it, or its equivalent, on the face value given it by some polemicists the sex of a creative person would play a wholly determining role. Yet it is not allowed to do so in the Wife of Bath argument. Nor when such agitators discuss art (painting and sculpture). The sex of an artist is no guarantor of excellence in a work of art, one way or the other, any more than is skin colour, with which it is often so glibly confused. Sex and race are simply not equipollent. They may be used as such as political levers, but they cannot be trusted to perform the same function as philosophical concepts, without all loss of intellectual respect. Least of all may they do so in the service they are often set to, as hatred tools. Thus Mrs Firestone will write a sentence like the following: 'Perhaps this explains the peculiar contempt women so universally feel for men.'[9] Do women – all women – *univer-sally* feel contempt for men? Is the human race really founded on rape?

If the male 'point of view' is a determinant, we are alleging that imagination can never rise above sex, while charging that it does so:

[9] Firestone, p. 127.

'That women were intrinsic to the very content of culture is borne out by an example from the history of art: Men are erotically stimulated by the opposite sex; painting was male; the nude became a *female* nude. Where the art of the male nude reached high levels, either in the work of an individual artist, e.g. Michelangelo, or in a whole artistic period, such as that of classical Greece, men were homosexual.'[10]

This is all so hypergeneralized as to be almost worthless in the fight for women's rights (indeed, Mrs Firestone, in her sound and fury, completely misses a whole lot of weaponry available in the laboratories, notably established feminine superiority in memory and association). Were men homosexual in classical Greece? Which men? When? An Athenian slave of the fifth century B C?

Then, the 'very content of culture' is also form. The above reduction is by no means true, and does gross distortion to the relationship between concept and form. Sir Kenneth Clark has devoted a considerable part of a magnificent book to charting the movement from male to female nude in art, remarking parenthetically:

'Since the earliest times the obsessive, unreasonable nature of physical desire has sought refuge in images, and to give these images a form by which Venus may cease to be vulgar and become celestial has been one of the recurring aims of European art. . . . Since the seventeenth century we have come to think of the female nude as a more normal and appealing subject than the male. But this was not so originally. In Greece no sculpture of nude women dates from the sixth century, and it is still extremely rare in the fifth.'[11]

This is important to mention. If we are to read literature with any pleasure, let alone understanding, we have to admit that content can produce its own form, that if men and women have grown up for a long time in families, that form is likely to be

[10] Firestone, pp. 156–7.
[11] Sir Kenneth Clark, *The Nude in Art*, New York: Pantheon Books, 1956, pp. 71–2, London: Murray, 1967.

intrinsic to our literary records. The Christian cross (as Sir Kenneth again shows) was a sustaining symbol through a long period of painting partly thanks to its satisfactory aesthetic shape (the Holy Ghost, for instance, never had the same iconic reverberation, nor was this only on account of doctrinal prohibitions). A woman's body, as developed at a certain period, satisfied certain aesthetic ambitions. Art simply cannot be seen as a matter of political roles.

To make the charge that no one in a 'male culture' can objectify enough to project true womanhood is really to re-iterate the old Platonic attack on the imagination. Shakespeare never murdered anyone, so is disqualified from imagining what it is to be a murderer. This sort of thinking must be recognized at once for what it is, the ultimate philistinism and, indeed, covert ally of oppression. Only if we acknowledge this may we proceed.

For the whole point of the fictive experience is that it allows a vicarious participation which frees us from just such thinking, from the straitjackets of the natural kingdom (sex, race, age). Shakespeare probably knew few Jews and less Blacks, but in *The Merchant of Venice* and *Othello* he told us a great deal about the experiences of both races in a white Christian majority, and to say that such is a 'male' culture scarcely invalidates the imaginative act. Shakespeare's imagination was seemingly unhandicapped by sex for in the corpus of his work he phrased practically every possibility for women in a man's world, from extreme oppression to extreme revolution and even what is now called unisex (there are hints of 'cybernetic socialism'!). In *Three Sisters* Chekhov worked through many similar attitudes and situations. If he is invalidated on account of having had a penis, women are going to find the same tools used against them, when their innings comes. Surely they should hope to show a deeper maturity than that of the large mass of males who saw the early novel as a dangerous distraction, one to be put under censorship as far as women and children were concerned.

Thus in a passage in *Tom Jones* Mrs Western comes across Sophia reading a romance and, representative as the older woman is of the male squireachy, snatches it instantly from her:

'Sophia was in her chamber, reading, when her aunt came in. The moment she saw Mrs Western, she shut the book with so much eagerness, that the good lady could not forbear asking her, What book that was which she seemed so much afraid of showing? "Upon my word, madam", answered Sophia, "it is a book which I am neither ashamed nor afraid to own I have read. It is the production of a young lady of fashion, whose good understanding, I think, doth honour to her sex, and whose good heart is an honour to human nature." Mrs Western then took up the book, and immediately after threw it down, saying – "Yes, the author is of a very good family; but she is not much among people one knows. I have never read it; for the best judges say, there is not much in it."'

In Ibsen's *Ghosts* Pastor Manders performs the same male pre-censorship – what French publishing knows under the oblique governmental fiat of *dépôt préalable* – on a married woman, Mrs Alving. The following exchange takes place:

MANDERS. Do you read this sort of thing?

MRS ALVING. Certainly I do.

MANDERS. Do you feel any the better or the happier for reading books of this kind?

MRS ALVING. I think it makes me, as it were, more self-reliant.

MANDERS. That is remarkable. But why?

MRS ALVING. Well, they give me an explanation or a confirmation of lots of different ideas that have come into my own mind. . . . But what is the particular objection that you have to these books?

MANDERS. What objection? You surely don't suppose that I take any particular interest in such productions?

MRS ALVING. In fact, you don't know anything about what you are denouncing?

MANDERS. I have read quite enough about these books to disapprove of them.

We notice by this point in the nineteenth century a far more confident defence of 'books of this kind' than Sophia could find it in herself to make. Mrs Alving is made 'more self-reliant' by them and she gets a 'confirmation' of shared ideas. Such takes away feelings of loneliness and of course increases feminine solidarity; fiction is doing its work.

For the novel made a large departure in literary perspective, and had it been allowed to become so might have been even more of a vehicle of feminine aspiration than it has been. Certainly in England the novel made a strong break with previous literary forms not simply in matter (chiefly, the accent on individualism lauded in *Crusoe*) but in manner. As the Sophias of the day knew, novels could be read alone as they had been written alone, in private. Their rate of ingestion could be controlled, by no means true of a performed play. A heroine's boudoir letters could be sampled slowly, alone, like pornography today. The resources of the form decreased the element of control in the response – relaxed the ego, as analysts like to put it:

> 'The indispensable condition of such an experience, and the first stage of the experience itself, is a relaxation of the vigilance usually exercised by the ego. A willing suspension of disbelief, a receptive attitude, is essential not only to the enjoyment but even to the understanding of fiction.'[12]

We relax at the theatre, but hardly as much as in our own bed-rooms. The change in perspective was indeed one of psychology – libido, if you will – and made for that intimacy which prefigured the interior monologue. Emma Bovary was only the classic case of the novel's power over inner experience, one duplicated by that of other media today. There have been many others. We first meet Jane Eyre reading. Tony Buddenbrook is a German Bovary, a very prim and proper one, too. Pregnant by her lover, Tess Durbeyfield cries out to her mother, 'Why didn't you tell me there was danger in men-folk? Why didn't you warn me? Ladies know what to fend hands against, because they read

[12] Simon O. Lesser, *Fiction and the Unconscious*, Boston, Mass.: Beacon Press, 1957, p. 192.

novels that tell them of these tricks; but I never had the chance o' learning in that way, and you did not help me!'

Ironically enough, Mrs Western's position implies a semantic ratio to a work of art oddly akin to that taken by some feminist blue-stockings today. Certainly language is a kind of lie, for it is not life itself. Hazlitt, following the Wordsworth of Preface to *Lyrical Ballads*,[13] thought prose should be for fact, real life. Radicals, including Jean-Paul Sartre at one point, have given odd echoes to this dictum – prose fiction should provide a response to social, rather than psychological, demands.

The Lockean view of language, that metaphor is a natural lie, seems curiously congenial to the new feminism, some of whose proponents would seem to agree with John Dennis's summary of the situation: 'No sort of imagery can ever be the language of grief. If a man complains in simile, I either laugh or sleep.' Or reach for my hatpin. Scholars have observed that French fiction contemporary with Defoe is still somewhat too metaphoric to be 'authentic' – i.e. as the vehicle of a nascent mercantile bourgeoisie. This retardation, if it be such, then seems to provoke an extremely powerful realist correction – for realism comes in as the restraining principle of fantasy and brings our anti-social energies to book; so when we think of realism in fiction, we tend to think of France.

All this is to suggest that the symbolic act must be respected first and foremost as such. It is not actual, it is not a political happening. Surely such is all it is necessary to say here about the absolute authenticity of the imagination. Shakespeare undoubtedly worked within male-oriented beliefs. He had not heard of either diaphragm or placenta. He inherited a kind of mediævalism which was persuaded that men and women would remain basically the same, that the wheel of time would rotate, and that in our ends lie our beginnings.

[13] The famous passage goes as follows: 'All that it is *necessary* to say, however, upon this subject, may be effected by affirming, what few persons will deny, that of two descriptions, either of passions, manners, or characters, each of them equally well executed, the one in prose and the other in verse, the verse will be read a hundred times where the prose is read once.'

Hence his Romans often come out as Elizabethans dressed up, and hence his celebrated lack of attention to chronology, sometimes seen as carelessness. Our world, on the other hand, is strongly subject to chronology. In an industrial civilization time is money, and we are anxious to waste neither. Time is that linear tyrant to which we are all subject, and the novel reflects this, almost invariably running over time in some manner and emphasizing causality en route. Fielding used an almanac, recording the phases of the moon during the 1745 rebellion correctly, while Sterne toyed with temporal equivalence in *Tristram Shandy*, a technique in which a work takes as long to read as the actions in it to enact, in the manner of *Ulysses* (or, in painting, Mathieu's battle canvases). Balzac did his best to banish the anachronism. Even in as literal an account as *Madame Bovary* we surely find the extent of exact computation with the usurer Lheureux a shade heavy (e.g. Part Two, XIV).

It was really not until the work of the Russian novelists had been absorbed, later in the nineteenth century, that space could be seen as a possible fictional correlative of time. In Turgenev, for instance, time seems often to take second place to space, and spatial values, and he is basically a rural writer.

Thus we must be careful when we indict something called 'culture' as the carrier of a supremacist virus. Society has been male-dominated in the West for a long time – forever, according to some feminists – but to deny that the imagination may be at its best free of sexual prejudice can be damaging to even the most radical woman's cause, as well as simply petty (and, as Margaret Mead says, annoying everyone all round). Nowhere in literature has there been a more vivid proportion of testimony to woman's potential than in prose fiction of the past two hundred years.

For fiction is art, and utility is the negative of art. Reproduction is not an especially aesthetic process, least of all in the human female, a painfully inefficient childbearer in comparison with rabbits, rats or cats. And by putting women into realistic aesthetic context, by distancing her in proportionate relationships, fictive literature questioned basic assumptions – did the removal of utility from procreation make for a higher form of love in the relationship?

The theory that sexual pleasure can only accompany procreation seems absurd to us today, but it has undeniably been one of the longest-lived myths women have had to contend with. Even a relatively recent and relatively intelligent work like *Modern Woman* by Ferdinand Lundberg and Marynia Farnham openly perpetuates it as follows:

'For the woman, however, the pleasurable and procreative aspects of sexuality cannot, particularly psychologically, be so rigorously separated. There is in nature no dividing line between sex as pleasure and as procreation. Both are part of the same curve, invariably so in the case of the woman. As procreation is ruled out – for fear, distaste, prudence, ambition or what not – pleasure itself limps, sags, fails, disappears or converts into active displeasure.'[14]

Drs Lundberg and Farnham even bolster their sexual superstitions with some genuine injustice, worthy of St Ambrose, as that pregnancy is not nearly as painful as women claim – 'That it never became unbearable is shown in the fact that the pain never induced unconsciousness.' And anyway all reports of it come from mere women. The good doctors go so far as to claim that childbirth has deliberately been presented as 'the woman's Golgotha' since it was a feminist instrument which 'paid dividends'. It is noticeable today that it is usually the sexuality of the reproductive system – menstruation, childbirth, menopause – on which Fem Lib concentrates for ammunition in their arguments.

I do not observe this as an error, one automatically playing into the hands of those like Lundberg and Farnham. But I try to suggest in the pages which follow, particularly those on Hardy's Tess, that the instrument can be sharpened by contact with the aesthetic, which is not directly polemical. Of course,

[14] Ferdinand Lundberg and Marynia F. Farnham, *Modern Woman: The Lost Sex*, New York: Harper and Brothers, 1947, p. 295: the male-oriented metaphors at the end of this passage are not without interest.

the theory – if it can be dignified as such – presented above is roundly ridiculed and reduced to ashes by both de Beauvoir and Ruth Herschberger's wise and witty *Adam's Rib*. However, the very fact that our heroines here all, excepting Madame de Merteuil, look on love as a non-utilitarian mystery not only bathes it in hope, and often glory, but answers an entire cultural outlook. For the characters concerned it is sensed as such, a true creative task.

*　　*　　*

In *The Philosophy of Literary Form* Kenneth Burke wrote:

> 'A tragedy is not profound unless the poet *imagines* the crime – and in thus imagining it, he symbolically commits it. Similarly, in so far as the audience participates in the imaginings it also participates in the offense.'

By this time a lot of potent human experience has come to us in fictive form. We have learnt a lot about women from novels. The imagination simply cannot be written off as invariably a hidden male blackjack. For the way in which fiction works on us allows us to move through a sexual situation and liquidate some of our anxiety about it in the process – a process quite reversed when we are thumping tubs in a political cause. Indeed, such accounts for the sense of exhilaration any sensitive reader must feel when coming to the end of those paeans of praise to oppressed womanhood, Zola's *Germinal* or *L'Assommoir*.

Nor need this exhilaration necessarily be a sort of inoculation, what might be called a male chauvinist catharsis. It is true that by safely watching others knocked around our own feeling of escape augments. The inoculation idea, akin to watching a shipwreck from some cosy lighthouse, has had currency from Lucretius to A. E. Housman; it is resurrected every now and then to oppose the diet of violence being apportioned to our young by some new medium, the child watching slaughter on television from a warm armchair with a cup of cocoa handy. So we participate in the offence against women particularly since, as men, we can never be women; thus the symbolical expiation of guilt in the art work is especially factitious.

Obviously, in detective mysteries and westerns, literature of a fairly low order of psychological reference, we are reassured of our spectator rather than participant role. But here the characters are almost signs, rather than symbols (wearing black hat or white hat according to which side of the law they're on). In literature of high imagination we are not always calmed by the content – *Othello* is said to be almost unbearable for a really jealous husband – we are pacified by the form. Though a man may be raped (as in James Dickey's *Deliverance*, say), it is complained that a man will never become pregnant and have to bear children. Thus woman is ineluctably the Other, like the villain in detective stories, never you or me. Hence, in David Riesman's suggestion, safety-valve literature can be exceedingly spurious, since its effect is to make us more willing than ever to accept the harness of the dominant culture.

There may be something in this. Iconography, fiction, may liberate woman factitiously. It doesn't really happen. Society slaps on the manacles when the darkness of the motion picture house, or the calm solitude of the favourite reading chair, are relinquished. But we cannot deny the imagination its truly symbolic authenticity. It is a generalizing medium, operating as a whole. In *Brave New World* Huxley imagined certain 'liberations' for women – his Malthusian belts precisely predicted the pill – but he integrated such insights into cultural criticism, fearing, with Dostoevsky's *Notes From Underground*, that in an over-rational society man would be easily governable by satisfactions. After all, our experiments with clonic, parthogenetic, or placenta reproduction have certain implications for society; as a matter of fact, since they generally involve deposit of sperm within a neuter, or non-female, vesicle, they might enormously fortify male domination, since thereby the male alone would be responsible for continuation of the species. (This sexual self-genocide seems to be somewhat anticipated in the suicidal throat-slitting of each other by recent American feminists.) In short, by forming an artistic whole fiction has not only shown the depths of women's oppression, but has presented them in a cultural context.

When *Lolita* was first published in America, its patent parody of current sexual myths, including the idea that a woman's chief function was to be a housewife and mother, was largely missed – and missed by one furious feminist reviewer, or reviewer subsequently feminist, Elizabeth Janeway, author of *Man's World; Woman's Place*. Similarly, one has seen otherwise intelligent feminists attacking Flaubert (of all people), George Sand, Ibsen, George Eliot, and – repeatedly, of course – D. H. Lawrence (Kate Millett). Much of this hyperbolic rattling of the coffee cups – e.g. Betty Friedan's comparison of suburban American housewives with the inmates of Nazi concentration camps in *The Feminine Mystique* – does serious discredit to an honourable movement.

When *Lolita* first came out, Gilbert Highet, Anthon Professor of Latin Literature at Columbia University, called it 'a wicked book', adding, 'I am sorry it was ever written.' Supposed sin was shown in an alluring guise. There was no retribution for the sinner at the end, Humbert Humbert merely dying of a heart attack; and, though grandmothers in their thirties could be found in abundance in the American South, nevertheless love of very young girls was a vice – neanirosis. Presumably it was a vice in the Renaissance as in contemporary Buenos Aires, where a ten-year-old girl, Mirta Fontora ('Little Mom'), recently gave birth to a lusty baby boy.

Highet went on to suggest that we should hesitate to allow desirable portraits of undesirable tendencies (though Humbertism of course increased the species). It was the old anti-comic book argument all over again. Would we want a fiction showing arson as a delectable spree published? (And what of bigamy in *Jane Eyre*?) In his celebrated reply to Sir Walter Besant Henry James essentially retorted that we would and should: 'the province of art is all life, all feeling, all observation, all vision.' The imagination has to be whole to be ethical, it cannot be constrained by little astigmatic signposts saying It Is Forbidden to Walk on The Grass, or, by extension, It Is Forbidden to Write About Woman If Male:

'In the English novel (by which of course I mean the American as well), more than in any other, there is a traditional difference between that which people know and that which they agree to admit that they know, that which they see and that which they speak of, that which they feel to be a part of life and that which they allow to enter into literature. . . . The essence of moral energy is to survey the whole field.

Should Flaubert, for having surveyed 'the whole field' and for having said, as a male, '*Madame Bovary, c'est moi*', have been hauled into court for bad morals? He was – by a male society.

The end product of this misreading of symbolic art, which would require the didactic to be photographic, results in much nice Ninian low comedy as when, opening the hilarious House of Lords' debate on the publication of the unexpurgated *Lady Chatterley's Lover*, Lord Teviot rose to fulminate: 'Let us get down to the realities and the origin of this deplorable book. It emanates from the warped mind of the author. The story he tells is pure invention; it never actually happened.'[15] To suggest that no man can bear true testimony to the feminine experience, or no white record the Black experience, is pure politics, not literature.

Indeed, the tables can be turned. Is a woman writer disallowed from describing a male erection and subsequent male orgasm? The task of the creative imagination is not so much mere identification. Is Joyce's long unpunctuated apology for womanhood in the final soliloquy of Molly Bloom to be ignored since a man wrote it? What happens if it is suddenly learned that it was in fact penned by Nora, his wife, or his schizophrenic daughter? Is the answer that since all three were living in a male-dominated society they can be discounted to be regarded with any seriousness at all? As de Beauvoir herself suggested, acrimony in this field has become such that it is genuinely obscuring truth.

For some of the legerdemain of this sort has become so pat

[15] Hansard, vol. 227: no. 23, 14 December 1960, p. 529: James identified the same. Of Trollope, he wrote that 'He admits that the events he narrates have not really happened.'

31

that when one leading feminist looks at nineteenth century painting she lumps all nudes, all female subject matter, together as the biassed products of males (and can then surely not complain that, in Germaine Greer's sweeping statement in *The Female Eunuch*, 'women have very little idea of how much men hate them'). One can hear the ringing *Right On's* in response to such rhetoric. 'The tool for representing, for objectifying one's experience in order to deal with it, culture', writes Shulamith Firestone, 'is so saturated with male bias that women almost never have a chance to see themselves culturally through their own eyes'.[16]

Apart from riding roughshod over a single century of art – Ingres's nudes, marvellously ideal, are diametrically different from Degas's mundane, humdrum, rather plain women, inspired with pathos (what Sir Kenneth Clark calls 'the alternative convention') – someone like Mrs or Ms Firestone has then to draw short when women actually do see themselves pictorially through their own eyes, as in the work of Berthe Morisot or Mary Cassatt. These she then hurriedly squares up with her general thesis (an attack on 'the organization of culture itself') by some rapid rationalization. Such women painters merely ' "lifted" a set of traditions and a view of the world that was inauthentic for them. They worked within the limits of what has been defined as female by a *male* tradition: they saw women through male eyes, painted a male's idea of the female.'[17] The sympathetic liberal, scanning such sophistry in which you always win, must be pardoned for feeling there is a trace of cant in these incantations.

In the first place writing is not painting. Novels unfold in time, pictures in space. Partly that is what this book is about, or strongly sustains. It is very possible that women painters might take assigned values from men, since a painter is given a view of the world as a whole immediately in a finished work. Hence dominant forms persist. Berthe Morisot does seem singularly saccharine at times (but any more so than Sisley, Boudin?). A writer of fiction is in another boat. She writes alone in a lineal sequence, out of her own reveries. She becomes her own heroine,

[16] Firestone, p. 157.   [17] *Ibid.*, p. 159.

can exist on the margin of experience (like Ibsen's Hedvig, Hilde of *The Master Builder*). Does Jane Austen really give 'a view of the world that was inauthentic'? Who authenticates this inauthenticity? Austen is sharp, even caustic – and feminine in the best way, satisfying to most women to read. Did she really paint 'a male's idea of the female'? Young Léon tells Emma Bovary that he had come across an Italian print of one of the Muses – 'She is draped in a tunic, and she is looking at the moon, with forget-me-nots in her flowing hair. . . . She looked a little like you.'

The first stage in our approach to feminist fiction must therefore be a cautious one. We must beg a truce to the Auntie Toms, and indeed Aunt Sallies, of our argument. A man could, and did in fact, write, '*Madame Bovary, c'est moi*'. A man could, and did, in Kenneth Burke's terminology, participate in the offence. The imagination must be allowed the authenticity of de Beauvoir's 'absolute truth', else it is not imagination. It is a greater force in some, lesser in others – primary and secondary, in Coleridge's famous anatomy. The vision Flaubert achieved on behalf of womanhood at the end of *Bovary*, when Emma returns in desperation to her violator Rodolphe and confronts sexist supremacy at its most unashamed, could only be coarsened by a polemicist – of either sex. Here the very form of Flaubert's masterpiece holds its content at bay and informs reality with a pattern that is human, and whole.

'But for you, and you know it', Emma tells her seducer, 'I might have lived happily. What made you do it? Was it a bet? Yet you loved me . . . you said so.' A bet, indeed! As she leaves her male tormentor (Tess Durbeyfield's Alec), Emma feels 'as wounded men, dying, feel their life ebb from their bleeding wounds'. Then in a caustic comment Flaubert remarks of Rodolphe that 'With the natural cowardice that characterizes the stronger sex, he had carefully avoided her for the last three years'. I submit that this is all we need for the given issue. Pamphlets about test-tube babies, or how to garotte rapists, must remain the prerogative of those feminists who so readily fill bestseller charts, and who would doubtless put such passages down as so much dust-throwing, ingenious concessions by a male author to cover up his real desire for domination.

The imaginative act is what it is. People with large ears are no more likely to produce art of greater vision than those with small feet, though it is parenthetically possible that they might know more about the penalties attached to their idiosyncrasy in a given culture (cp. the artist-outsider as Jew). Tuberculosis appears to be one of the few afflictions with a correlation with the production of literature, though one would have to have far more statistics than are available before so concluding, and avoiding the celebrated mashed-potatoes syndrome (all murderers ate mashed potatoes). Quite a few nineteenth-century French writers died of syphilis, including Baudelaire and Flaubert. A large number of males wrote fiction.

So our final proviso, before approaching something of the genesis of fiction from the feminine angle, should insist on this point. It runs counter to de Beauvoir's 'absolute truth'. For how can you establish an 'absolute truth' intersexually without, as our most radical feminists would wish, changing the name of the game and trying to abolish sex altogether; this is currently called freeing women from the 'tyranny' of biology (breastlessness, placentae, and so on). In a universe in which most of us have to live our lives as given, such outcries must remain more like objections to the rules from the sidelines than anything. It is of course a natural injustice that no men have to endure their hymen being ruptured, as that no men have to bear babies (of which affliction Charlotte Brontë, among others, died),[18] but this really has little to do with equality, or even freedom.

Such a statement may be a hard pill for feminist politicians to swallow, but the heroines set out in array in this book looked facts in the face, and by 'facts' is meant the whole of human behaviour, in its largest sense. We can perhaps dismantle the family (though Margaret Mead doesn't think so), and we can say that in a significant way Ibsen's heroines did so long before Russian and Israeli social experiments to the same end. But we

[18] 'If men could get pregnant, abortion would be a sacrament' (Gloria Steinem).

can hardly reverse the human race, any more than we can unburn a match. All that can be done is to leap onto the nearest soap-box and shout out that some form of sexlessness is the next 'evolutionary jump'; after which, thanks to the shock value of the proposition, all you have to do is wait for *Life Magazine* to hammer on the door. As a matter of fact, such is the current state of 'debate' in this field that it is then possible to conceive of the next phase of radicals arguing that *not* to bear babies is itself a kind of penalty. The Preg Lib picket lines form up in one's imagination, heavy with hectoring placards – WE DEMAND THE RIGHT TO BE PREGNANT!

Again, none of this has too much to do with true self-deter-mination for women. It is surely in a sexual world, even in a male chauvinist world, that women have most heroically and most radically expressed their uniqueness. Those paraded in these pages were not 'imitating' male patterns. They stood in positions of sexual inferiority, of emotional vulnerability, from which they tried, not always successfully, to make an imaginative escape.

Men may have endeavoured to make such women think they were incomplete men, but they did not think so themselves. They knew what it was to be a woman and so they were true rebels, in their individual ways, paving patterns of revolt against other exploitative systems a long way from our own world in which several Presidents and Premiers are women and where, in America at least, 43 per cent of women are in the labour force, 75 per cent of these working full time (40% of New York City's jobs being held by them).

Deprived of examples of women in leading roles, our heroines acted, rather than reacted. Several fell victims to their temerity. Some would have concurred with Margaret Mead's summary of the man's world women have to enter – 'When I grow up I'm going to be a doctor, that's if I don't get married.' Not all of them would, for there is an answer to this argument, too: women *can* achieve, but they still don't have to. Men are given a directive by our culture to succeed, or else. And as de Beauvoir well puts it, in this field 'Each argument at once suggests its opposite, and both are often fallacious. If we are to gain understanding, we must get out of these ruts; we must discard the vague notions of superiority, inferiority, equality which have hitherto corrupted every discussion of the subject and start afresh.'[19] In passing, one can only say, perhaps, that the Aristotelian idea of woman as a defective being, taken on into the imperfect man of St Thomas, and even our own nineteenth century,[20] meets what might be called its philosophical comeuppance in the concept of clonal reproduction.

So there can be no question here of illustrating the more outrageous, and specifically American, of proposals for eliminating sexual inequality, notably by abolishing biology altogether (e.g. by 'cybernetic socialism' and/or 'polymorphous perversity'). Quite obviously we cannot ask Emma Bovary or Jane Eyre, nor even Ibsen's enlightened Nora Helmer, to preach any total destruction of the family – without their seeming somewhat unreal in the contexts in which they find themselves set, without disturbing the whole fabric of their art work, as it were. (Madame de Merteuil in fact got close to such a position at one point, yet did so by her *actions*). Jane Eyre, Cathy Earnshaw, Anna Karenina, even Tony Buddenbrook – none had heard of babies produced in laboratories. Goethe seems to have anticipated something of 'cybernetic socialism' in the bizarrely parodistic form of his Homunculus.

There is an extended and important conversation in Chapter XXIII of *Anna Karenina* between Anna and her sister-in-law Dolly, the naïve housewife overburdened by children. 'What wife, what slave could be such a slave as I am in my position?'[21] Anna asks her, flatly supporting her decision not to have any more children (in the history of contraceptive methods a far

---

[19] De Beauvoir, p. xxvi.

[20] In Henry James's *Washington Square* the female is, for the rational Doctor Sloper, the 'imperfect sex'. The fine William Wyler movie of this novel, *The Heiress*, starring Olivia de Havilland and Ralph Richardson, was interesting in that it tried, for better or worse, to intensify James and make an even more pro-feminist statement, having Catherine Sloper explicitly revenge herself on both her father and her suitor.

[21] Of this text I use the well-known Maude translation, first published in 1918.

more declarative opposition than any such might be today). The idea fairly bowls Dolly over – 'It was the very thing she had dreamt of, but now on learning that it was possible, she was horrified. She felt that it was too simple a solution of too complex a question.'

Dolly, who had come to this meeting 'not feeling happy' (in other words, yearning for familial freedom), suddenly finds its spectre a sort of Medusa head before her actions, and retreats hurriedly into the family as protective nest against the forces of chaos potentially unleashed by Anna, her intellectual superior (we note Anna's ideas on architecture, building, etc.). So Anna really poses the Fem Lib question in full here: 'Don't forget the chief thing: that I am not in the same position as you! The question for you is, whether you desire not to have any more children; for me it is, whether I desire to have them. And that is a great difference.'

It is, indeed. A part of Tolstoy may well have sided with Dolly here. But his aesthetic vision pulls Anna into the foreground, as a genuinely superior person. And throughout this book we are going to have to trust the tale not the teller, in Lawrence's famous formulation. When the Fem Lib position is integrally put in *Anna Karenina*, we hear the muted voice of the Russian master gravely answering, Yes, yes, this is an interesting point of view; I am fully familiar with its ramifications and rhetoric, but I am also quite convinced that it will not work at this stage of history. We shall return to this text below. It tells another story.

The point is not merely whether we can at this stage annul nature. Nor is it even whether the stridency of the current revolt may or may not be a conditioned reflex to male culture, one of those ideas 'devised by minds diseased by the system', in the words of Germaine Greer (including, by definition therefore, her own). In one sense, all feminism may be said to be contaminated by conditioning.

The point is deeper; it involves language itself. Are we or are we not symbol-handling individuals? Are we to run from a screen because warlike savages are advancing on us from it? Are we to disallow a novel about a happy arsonist because we cannot distinguish between extensional reality and symbolic information? When we are reading a fiction we are not using a how-to-do-it manual (how many Humbert Humberts were made by the reading of *Lolita*?). For this very reason the fount of feminist ideology is often most gripping and convincing when presented in fantasy rather than in fact, in fiction rather than sociology.

* * *

The crossroads between the two has admittedly become a bloody one, by now. All fiction is to an extent sociological since it tends to deal with human beings in groups. Even an isolate by Beckett is so by defection from the human contract. But the old charge that the novel was meretricious, and novel-reading a sort of vice, one strong in capitalist civilizations where busy-ness achieved high value, persists in America; given a novel, an American businessman will still reply, 'Thanks, my wife will enjoy reading this'.

We know that both English Victorians and American Puritans saw novel-reading as a form of moral debility. Unlike the operations of the male business world it seemed to require little effort, and was doubtless a suspect form of self-indulgence – the 'Skim and Skip', or 'Rapid Reading', ads still reflect this attitude, one through which the male has extended hegemony by turning repression into a kind of spiritual ideal. But the attitude, involving a view of femininity as passivity, has had to concede a lot of ground, if not collapse altogether, in a century when novel-reading – in Joyce, Proust, the later James – is often more difficult and taxing than non-novel-reading.

In England it was a woman who refuted once and for all the lying-account conception of fiction – that a novel was simply a romance for young maidens, so much literary candy to be taken on the level of fashion. In *Northanger Abbey*, for the most part an early work though not published until 1818, we find the young Catherine Morland and Isabella Thorpe meeting in the inevitable Pump-room at Bath to discuss novels . . . and fashion:

"'My dearest creature, what can have made you so late? I have been waiting for you at least this age!'"

"Have you, indeed! – I am very sorry for it; but really I thought I was in very good time. It is but just one. I hope you have not been here long?"

"Oh! these ten ages at least . . . Do you know, I saw the prettiest hat you can imagine, in a shop window in Milsom-street just now – very like yours, only with coquelicot ribbons instead of green; I quite longed for it. But, my dearest Catherine, what have you been doing with yourself all this morning? – Have you gone on with Udolpho?"

"Yes, I have been reading it ever since I woke; and I am got to the black veil."

"Are you, indeed? How delightful! Oh! I would not tell you what is behind the black veil for the world! Are not you wild to know?"

"Oh! yes, quite; but what can it be? – But do not tell me – I would not be told upon any account. I know it must be a skeleton, I am sure it is Laurentina's skeleton. Oh! I am delighted with the book! I should like to spend my whole life in reading it. I assure you, if it had not been to meet you, I would not have come away from it for all the world."

"Dear creature! how much I am obliged to you; and when you have finished Udolpho, we will read the Italian together; and I have made out a list of ten or twelve more of the same kind for you."

"Have you, indeed! How glad I am! – What are they all?"

"I will read you their names directly; here they are, in my pocket-book. Castle of Wolfenbach, Clermont, Mysterious Warnings, Necromancer of the Black Forest, Midnight Bell, Orphan of the Rhine, and Horrid Mysteries. Those will last us some time."

"Yes, pretty well; but are they all horrid, are you sure they are all horrid?"

"Yes, quite sure; for a particular friend of mine, a Miss Andrews, a sweet girl, one of the sweetest creatures in the

39

world, has read every one of them. I wish you knew Miss Andrews, you would be delighted with her. She is netting herself the sweetest cloak you can conceive. . . .'''

Prior to this ridicule, however, and in a passage which may actually have been written later, Jane Austen struck a scolding note:

'there seems almost a general wish of decrying the capacity and undervaluing the labour of the novelist, and of slighting the performances which have only genius, wit, and taste to recommend them. "I am no novel reader – I seldom look into novels – Do not imagine that *I* often read novels – It is really very well for a novel." – Such is the common cant. – "And what are you reading, Miss —?" "Oh! it is only a novel!" replies the young lady; while she lays down her book with affected indifference, or momentary shame. – "It is only Cecilia, or Camilla, or Belinda;" or, in short, only some work in which the greatest powers of the mind are displayed, in which the most thorough knowledge of human nature, the happiest delineation of its varieties, the liveliest effusions of wit and humour are conveyed to the world in the best chosen language.'

Here Jane Austen is certainly defending a new tool for her sex. And this complete responsibility of fiction was what Balzac meant to emphasize when he would reportedly end a conversation, 'Now let's get back to serious matters' – meaning fiction. It is often said that Balzac claimed primarily to be giving testimony to the period of Louis-Philippe, who accepted the Lieutenant-Generalship of the kingdom in 1830. He did not go as far as this in the celebrated 'Avant-Propos' to *The Human Comedy*, but he became aware of women's rights through his imaginative writings and – while proclaiming himself a Catholic Royalist – ran his great *roman-fleuve* alongside libertarian ideals. It has even been said that the novel became a sort of extension of the franchise itself, while *Madame Bovary* was repeatedly seen on publication as an act of political subversion – 'the pathological glorification of the senses and of the imagination in a disappointed democracy', A. de Pontmartin called it bluntly, and fairly correctly.

The trouble for women here – not always seen, or at least stressed – was that they were trespassing on the male world by writing imaginative prose at all. Everyone knows that Charlotte Brontë published as 'Currer Bell'. But the matter is more complex. Both *Uncle Tom's Cabin* and *Wuthering Heights* were written by women and while the latter strikes deeper into our consciousness, and has two copies read today for every one of the former, Harriet Beecher Stowe made public challenge of the male's prerogative in politics (a similar, weaker, parallel might just hold up between *Jane Eyre* and Amye Reade's *Ruby*). Her work was more immediately recognizable as such than that 'most thorough knowledge of human nature' shown by Jane Austen, more identifiable than, say, *Pride and Prejudice*, a document thoroughly subversive of male culture in which the heroine, slighted by the chauvinist aristocrat, refuses his first proposal and, like Jane Eyre with Rochester, only takes him back on her own terms, shriven.

So fiction was a primal heresy in women's hands since it was written in what was also the language of daily discourse, which meant that of the business note and political tract. Let women stick to poetry or, at worst, drama; there is no major play by a woman in the nineteenth century, and perhaps not even in the twentieth. (Mrs Aphra Behn seems to have been an exception *par excellence*.) In fiction woman came forward, both as author and character, in a new way; as the former she challenged male society on its own terms, by exposure, ridicule, and correction, while as the latter she acquired a new sexual resonance since her inmost thoughts and yearnings could be stretched over page after page, and were.

Austen herself in a way made the Gothic 'persecuted maiden' into a social being, and living criticism of the male world; her heroines may not be physically tortured but we are shown that mental suffering, brought on by male social norms, can be as bad. Her female characters have repeatedly to repress their emotions and impulses due to social codes not of their own making. Humiliated, mortified by male rebuffs, they may not answer, but burst into tears or remain 'in Coventry' or run to their bedrooms to hide their sorrow. There is a fine sample of such in Chapter One of Volume Three of *Mansfield Park*, where Fanny sits up in the old schoolroom, just like a schoolgirl about to be chastised, awaiting the remorseless footsteps of her just, but stern uncle who cannot understand why she is turning down a perfect suitor, just as she cannot, thanks to social inhibitions, reveal her true desires; the language of the passage speaks for itself:

> 'She sat some time in a good deal of agitation, listening, trembling, and fearing to be sent for every moment; but as no footsteps approached the east room, she grew gradually composed, could sit down, and be able to employ herself. . . . Nearly half an hour had passed, and she was growing very comfortable, when suddenly the sound of a step in regular approach was heard . . . it was her uncle's; she knew it as well as his voice; she had trembled at it often, and began to tremble again. . . . The terror of his former occasional visits to that room seemed all renewed, and she felt as if he were going to examine her again in French and English. . . . Sir Thomas came towards the table where she sat in trembling wretchedness, and with a good deal of cold sternness, said, "It is of no use, I perceive, to talk to you. . . . I had thought you peculiarly free from wilfulness of temper, self-conceit, and every tendency to that independence of spirit, which prevails so much in modern days, even in young women, and which in young women is offensive and disgusting beyond all common offence. . . ."
>
> "I am very sorry," said she inarticulately through her tears, "I am very sorry indeed."
>
> "Sorry! yes, I hope you are sorry; and you will probably have reason to be long sorry for this day's transactions."'[22]

[22] The entire quotation is from Vol. III, Chap. 1 of the text; but Fanny's feelings of wretched inevitability occur throughout. The reference to sitting down, when she is already sitting, is an unusual error of continuity in Austen here. All through the book there is something deliberately submissive, even masochist in the best sense, about women sitting down, and waiting.

Indeed, the revelation of this kind of truth is worth many a political tract. The immediate prosaic relevance of a novel does not determine its greatness, nor factual accuracy its truth to life. *Uncle Tom's Cabin*, close as it is to the externals of slave existence, seems more 'romantic' than a poetic masterpiece of a more imaginative nature like *Wuthering Heights*. Cocteau's *The Impostor* may well be felt to tell us more about war than *Ben-Hur*. Feminist fiction had to fashion new concepts of the form itself, in order to lock horns with the male supremacy. Style as vision.

Art, as Jacques Barzun has put it, 'awakens knowledge of a kind no other means can reach'. You do not impose a pattern of unity on the universe – what Malraux has called 'stylistic rectification' – by presenting a photograph, or didactic case history. The aesthetic novel is predicated on the Faustian sin, that 'danger is in words' (as Marlowe's damned intellectual acknowledges), a sense shared by oppressed classes through history, including heretics, artists, and women. The analogy between women and Blacks may be tenuous at best, if suggestive, but that between woman and artist is surely a more solid tie for our time, as well as incidentally taking revenge on the sex that made the muse female.

Nabokov's implicit defence of the aesthetic or poetic novel is singularly pertinent at the moment since a century ago poetry was still read, whereas today prose is called on to carry the affects of its sister medium (Galsworthy is ridiculed in *Lolita* and G. H. Orwell – *sic* – in the Foreword to *Invitation to a Beheading*). In the condemned cell of the latter work the protagonist reflects on his 'gnostical turpitude' – his crime of 'Not knowing how to write, but sensing with my criminal intuition how words are combined'. When T. S. Eliot remarked that 'creative advance in our age is in prose fiction', he did so in the context of Virginia Woolf.

The old charge that prose should shun poetry and knuckle down to the real business of life is perhaps summarized in a recent essay by William Cooper, attacking experimental French fiction: 'If we have to fight against having Belsens and Dachaus, how much help are we going to get from people who have already settled for existence itself being absurdity, nausea, or nothingness?' The shadow of Mr Zhdanov, Stalin's cultural commissar par excellence, stalks this position. Indeed, Cooper's friend and firm supporter, C. P. Snow (beside whom Zola seems sheer poetry), seems to feel strongly that the aesthetic novel has reached by now a cul-de-sac. Yet he himself writes in a style so laboured, so insensitive to words and rhythms, that it soon begins to seem self-parodistic. A self-parody that may eventually be set down as itself a form of experiment within the novel!

We cannot turn our back on literary refinements, and their implications. Today the paradox is that the non-fiction novel, or 'faction', cannot be as critical of society as a piece of pure sociological research, compiled by a scholar on whom it is not incumbent to criticize. (Novels have been written by teams in America.) The tool that Zola perfected as a social lever, as an instrument of criticism, has now come to be used in almost wholly conservative hands (Marquand, O'Hara, Snow, Cozzens), as consent. Fact cannot be substituted for insight, nor information for meaning. The Newspeak of most current sociological novelists is, then, the prose of a utilitarian culture. So in Russia we have tractor fiction, while in France where religion makes concessions to the imagination the poetic novel can still flourish (the conflict with God in Ibsen's *The Master Builder* is precisely descriptive of this.)

This is not to say that religion helped on feminism. The reverse would be closer to the truth. But the intuitional values in novels written by women seem always to have been high. Even if we turn from Austen and the Brontës to the pot-boiling Mrs Radcliffe, we find paradigms of feminine persecution that must surely have struck home unconsciously to the Catherine Morlands of the day, as well as providing the simple escapist sop. We have one critic in fact demonstrating that even the most 'Gothic' novelist stimulated the idea of woman as a general victim, and showed the disabilities under which women labour in society: that, unreal as were the dripping dungeons, chains, and mouldering castles of the Radcliffean repertoire, they did turn attention to prison conditions . . . and reminded of other chains.[23] Of course there are, on the sidelines, as it were, a host of lady novelists today who are still performing the function assigned fantasy by a male capitalist culture, and are domesticating the female rather than freeing her. They are encouraged by commerce. No one lost money on *Gone With the Wind*. The remarkable thing is to re-read Zola carefully and realize how much of his research he kept out of his novels, how symbolic these are in values, and how easily he wore his social insights (e.g. that sexual failure is a spur to political power). American libertarian realism – Norris, Dreiser, Farrell – seems a dead mode today. Wright Morris looks back on Sherwood Anderson as his fictional father, and the change is characterized in the adoption. Women have always been able to participate in the fictive act when this is fully symbolic since it has always been their 'secret life' to be other than they are. What woman, in a male world, has not been forced into some self-protective dissimulation and that cunning which is the analogy of art?

To recapitulate: it is, as Kierkegaard observed, a misfortune to be a woman, yet a greater one not to know the nature of this lot. This knowledge, woman's weapon as a sex, cannot be given entirely by polemic. A sociology can represent a given condition to us, and urge us to correct it. But a fiction which involves fantasy can help us 'know' it, psychologically, and thus learn the real roots of the oppression. Poe might be a far better guide to understanding women than C. P. Snow.

Indeed, it is for this reason that popular fiction was for long considered so much escapist opiate by the ruling male establishment. The latter thought they could allow the Gothic romance which, like the comic-book or television soap opera today, invariably ended with some genuflection to the status quo, punishing adulterers and blasphemers the while it paid court to its readership. Titillative literature is usually a literature of assent.

We all die. And are involved at some time in the anguish of this knowledge. Tolstoy brings this home to us in *The Death of*

[23] See: J. M. S. Tompkins, *The Popular Novel in England* 1770–1800, London: Constable, 1932.

45

Ivan Ilyich. So at present are we all sexually determined at birth – with one or two bizarre exceptions. Fiction helps us to get out of these straitjackets for a moment, to overcome our biological limitations. In fiction we can make life stand still, and we can make it run. For a while we are forgiven, and can forgive.

Like so many children at play we can, for a time, shorten the hours or lengthen them, live in other skins, at other ages – we can even be an infant experiencing its own conception (Joyce's experiment to this end having recently been taken to brilliant conclusion by the children's writer, Maurice Sendak). And we can live as another sex. This is intensely important since such fiction asks us to change our attitudes, rather than automatically confirm them. The five heroines studied here are chosen partly for this vicarious existence they give us, not only as differing feminine spirits but as aspects of femininity itself. And for this reason the nineteenth century, during which women, both oppressed and emancipated by nascent industrialism, began to see the dawn of a new freedom, has been heavily drawn on here.

It might be asked why no American heroine was chosen. This was not especially deliberate, but one reason was probably the author's own clumsy lack of confidence in the existence of an American fiction *per se* . . . at least at this time. Melville, Hawthorne and others are often held up by Americanists as creating a truly indigenous novel, one which could only express and carry shades of the new reality they confronted. This may be so in most general terms, though it has surely yet to be proved; but as regards woman's role in the family of such fiction, it is hard to identify especially American quandaries. Except in one area.

This area introduces another uncertainty, which is even more impressionist. The author of this book was born and raised in England, and so finds it extremely hard to relate to certain assumptions, and even mythic patterns, that are sometimes taken as axiomatic by Americans. The fear of male impotence in novel after American novel (Mailer, Jones, particularly all the 'tough' writers) surely finds scant parallel in Europe, where typically (as in *Lady Chatterley's Lover* or Toller's *Hinkemann* play) impotence is a direct result of a war, society, rather than being self-inflicted.

If anything, race is even more perplexing in its claims in America than sex; thus Shulamith Firestone, referring to Calvin Hernton's *Sex and Racism in America*, claims that the book 'merely described the obvious: that white men have a thing for black women'.[24]

I find this statement quite astonishingly arrogant. They may in America. They almost certainly do not in England, France, Germany, Italy, Sweden, Russia, etc. In two schools and one university in England, where the male sex exchanged the frankest confessions imaginable, I never once met this notion, let alone heard it as an axiom. And when Mrs Firestone goes on breezily to claim 'that black men have a thing for white women', one longs to ask her if she has had permission of black men to make this sweeping assumption. Again, 'white women have a secret sympathy and curiosity about black men' is a fiat remark I have tested on English women friends to be met with complete bafflement. I grew up in a family of numerous sisters, none of whom showed any signs of this particular 'sympathy and curiosity'. The complacence of our American feminists is really extraordinary. 'Why are the fears of the common man so sexual in nature when it comes to the Negro?' Are they? In short, this predilection to talk about the whole of the human race on the basis of a part of it seemed to make it wisest to leave American exempla to one side.

This is not to say that America has produced no great fictional heroines. The work of Henry James is replete with them, as of repressed femininity generally. In Doctor Sloper of *Washington Square*, for instance, James presents us with no less than a text-book case of sexism and in Catherine, his daughter, one of its most touching victims. Catherine is confronted with the two

[24] Firestone, p. 105. In *Madame Bovary* the young clerk Léon listens to a little ethnographic homily on women. When he interposes, 'And negresses?' Homais replies, 'They are for artistic tastes.' Flaubert may have been thinking of Baudelaire's Jeanne Duval here, but the statement is left undisputed. One loses interest when debate in this area turns into so much terministic policy. On the one hand, it is said that white Americans have created the myth of the Black stud, or supersexual Negro male, but on the other he is also impotent, when argument so desires (cp. 'The Myth of the Impotent Black Male', by Robert Staples, in a 1971 issue of *The Black Scholar*).

men almost all women have to come to terms with sooner or later, father and suitor; both think almost wholly in terms of the cash nexus.

Catherine starts life, we notice, as the 'inadequate substitute' for the first-born but prematurely dead son. The 'geometrical proposition' that is her father, a man who 'had never been dazzled, indeed, by any feminine characteristics whatever' (a Jamesian litotes for informing us that he despised womanhood), crushes all feeling out of the girl, extending his dominance over her after his death. The suitor, meanwhile, 'had made himself comfortable, and he had never been caught'. He appears at the end, when she realizes 'this person was nothing'.

As Catherine then takes up her fancy-work in the parlour – 'for life, as it were' – the suitor has the gall to ask her aunt, 'But why the deuce, then, would she never marry?' In plain little Catherine Sloper, as in other martyrs to woman's lot in life, we read the true nature of male tyranny. Hers had been 'the desire of a rather inarticulate nature to manifest itself', but by the end of the book she has had all affection, let alone love, stamped out of it.

No sociology can codify the abundant depths of woman's love. Fiction may help us to do so. In the pages that follow we shall see woman as lover, mother, victim – above all, as heroine. And to put this variegated figure that is modern womanhood in some fictional perspective it would be best to pass very briefly over the growth of the form. For fiction rises side by side with feminism.

* * *

The literal library of treatises that now exists on the genesis of the novel insists that our last literary form, fiction, starts its own tradition. What is this? Why? How does fiction differ from other written forms, from poetry or drama? Why did it become such a thoroughly congenial medium that Wordsworth's dictum today seems reversed and that an authority like the perceptive American critic Irving Howe can write, 'the majority of readers in the last two hundred years have found in the novel the literary form which most clearly satisfies their wishes for a close correspondence between life and art'? There have been varied answers given to these vexed questions and woman's role in the development of this new vehicle of culture has all too often been seen as ancillary.

It was not so. Women sensed from the start that the novel displayed and investigated human character more fully than ever before in literature, and with less limits. It is of course readily conceded that a large – and largely idle – female readership, of the type excoriated at the start of *Northanger Abbey*, guzzled up the prose romance. We know the place, later on, of the evening reading hour and what it meant for a public without movies and television. Here the warm darkness of the cinema in which fantasy could be allowed full rein was anticipated, as the attentive group sat around papa reading by the fireside. Disbelief could be suspended, the ego could relax, while a spurious ideal of moral improvement might justify the wildest actions in any story.[25] But if the reading was invariably by the paterfamilias, it still must deeply have stirred the surplus of daughters gathered around, and surely gave an engrossing, vicarious view of womanhood to the sons and heirs of the dominant society. It seems rather that feminine influence on fiction was primary, not parenthetical.

Before any case can be made for this, however, we have first to assure ourselves what is meant by a novel. This is not easy. In *The Birth of Tragedy* Nietzsche pointed to the Socratic dialogue – 'Plato has furnished for all posterity the pattern of a new art form, the novel, viewed as the Aesopian fable raised to its highest power.' Problems of definition abound here because, as Ian Watt has shown in *The Rise of the Novel*, narrative fiction came to assume the terms of all previous written forms, including essays, travelogues, and eventually the poem itself. We have seen Hardy's Tess talking about novels as etiquette books. André Gide finally put the form as form well into question by stepping

---

[25] For a record of the 'conversion' element even in the penny press of the time, see: Margaret Dalziel, *Popular Fiction 100 Years Ago*, London: Cohen and West, 1957.

out of *The Counterfeiters* and, in so many words, asking quite what the point was in going on. It is all too easy to confound confusion here, but unless we chalk out some guidelines before embarking on our journey we shall leave our feminist apologies over-open to attrition at the edges.

For the origin of the novel will no doubt always remain a Gordian knot of definition. Cautious scholars are becoming increasingly wary of classifying specimens of seventeenth and eighteenth century prose as fiction, in measure as more and more other scholars show such to contain large chunks of fact. If fact was fabricated in narrative prose of this time, source studies are now abundantly documenting a feedback in the operation, as the austerity of American scholarship surpasses that of France and pedants carry off, antlike in their jaws, prize morsels of fact from the fiction (A. W. Secord and J. R. Moore from Defoe, for instance).

Of this early period the many voyages, travel diaries, pirate romances, whore biographies can scarcely be grist to this modest mill, until it is wholly proved that such were fabrications of the fantasy. The early slander and scandal narratives, too, seem to have been extreme examples of *romans à clef*.

What can be ventured here, however, in order to try to help, is twofold: (1) what preceded Defoe and Richardson in England – and it was heavily feminine, and indeed erotic – made their popularity possible; (2) we tend to look on the novel, as all else, teleologically, in a kind of constant race of ahead-of-ness, asking the novel always to improve in a given direction (in its case, realism) like a motor car. The great studies of the genre tend to see the novel as a technological artefact, in consonance with the civilization it assisted into being, constantly 'advancing'.

This attitude, as John F. Richetti has well demonstrated,[26] reduces still further the worth of hugely popular novelists antecedent to those we think excellent today. Yet the narratives of the famous Mary de la Rivière Manley, arrested for writing *New Atalantis* (1709) which fascinated even Lady Mary Wortley

[26] John J. Richetti, *Popular Fiction before Richardson: Narrative Patterns 1700–1739*, Oxford University Press, 1969.

Montagu and was immortalized by Pope in a line of 'The Rape of the Lock', rest on sexual archetypes that were culturally conditioned and which Richardson confidently exploited. It is important to admit this happening across the Channel, too, for Laclos wrote out of a tradition of libertine literature in all senses.

Mrs Manley and Eliza Haywood may have turned out a sort of semi-licentious trash, but they began a vogue. It was read. The former's fantastic *Secret History of Queen Zarah* of 1705 appears to have been a fairly full-blooded blast at the Duchess of Marlborough, but it was also a *catalogue raisonné* of feminine psychology of the time. The published preface to this work is, as Professor Richetti delightfully puts it, 'not so much literary criticism as market analysis'. In her 1725 *Memoirs of a Certain Island* Mrs Haywood tried to repeat her predecessor's trick, and to some extent succeeded in doing so. Both ladies, according to Bonamy Dobrée, 'may well remain unread'. They may, indeed. But in the first four decades of the eighteenth century they were pre-eminently popular, and pre-eminently feminine. Mrs Manley herself seems to have been a rather pathetic case, an aristocratic orphan seduced into a bigamous marriage who died in the office of a printer to whom she had been mistress; though finding her fat, Swift still underestimated her age, on acquaintance.

There is great erotic intensity in these early feminine, if not feminist, writers. Male sexuality is depicted as selfish and corrupt and, as Professor Richetti suggests, this erotic ideology serves the needs of the same reading public as was served by Defoe:

'It may well be that the moral and religious antitheses to be found in popular works like *Robinson Crusoe* and the *New Atalantis* derive ultimately from some sort of Protestant archetype of the individual theological condition; the parallel seems striking and the hypothesis attractive.'[27]

Laclos shows us that 'scandalous' revelations can also contain a deal of social history in them; they would not touch off the response that some inflame if they did not. Or, as Richetti puts it:

[27] Richetti, p. 22.

'Scandal novels owed a significant part of their popularity, that is, to their ability to evoke an essentially fictional world whose inhabitants were not so much real persons as they were embodiments of popular concepts, capable of provoking personal fantasy and projection precisely because they appealed to an immediately available and more or less communal mythology. . . . The popular scandal novel or "chronicle" is of great historical importance because it shows us this fable in the process of being widely disseminated in prose narrative form, being transmitted, in a sense, as an effective erotic-pathetic cliché to the audience for which Richardson is to write, creating an emotional convention as it were. . . . It is probably no accident that the most considerable writers of scandalous memoirs during the early eighteenth century were women, and it is certainly likely that their most eager readers were largely women as well.'[28]

In truth, what facts we have seem to bear out the primary significance of feminine influence on the new mode. First, the increase in fictions (not in size of editions) was slow, though impressive. An average of seven titles a year between 1700 and 1740 increases to forty by the end of the century, true. But it is only thereafter that the floodgates are truly opened. In other words, only after the vast pan-European upheavals and emancipations which, while they did not directly liberate women, certainly irrevocably shook male confidence and altered the male attitude towards womanhood.

Secondly, and even more pertinent to our proposal, there is the assumption about every fiction that it is presenting a version of human reality. We note that Gide did not give up; he let his characters continue, and indeed continued to contribute comments on them outside the novel concerned, in journals, diary entries, letters and the like. Throughout the history of fiction there has

[28] Richetti, pp. 125–6: he adds, 'It is important to say this without lapsing into that condescension with which the Augustans regarded female literature and scribbling women, for the changes which took place in prose narrative are partly the result of the changes in the market brought about by the needs of an expanding female audience.'

been this common allegiance on the part of its authors to respond to and redeem reality. The tools for achieving this – via participatory narrators, hearsay, interior monologues, novels written like plays (*Jean Barois*), with the objects they display actually stuck on their pages (Lionel Chouchoun), or novels like packs of cards, with pages to shuffle (Marc Saporta), even from the point of view of a dog (Jules Romains, Rudyard Kipling) – all have shown infinite subtlety but have primarily agreed in exploring what Camus called 'the human nature'.

To claim that heterosexual experience can only be depicted by one sex would be precisely Margaret Mead's reversal – akin to curtailing any discussion of the subject in the manner of those critics who would have us believe that most feminists are lesbians and so regard 'normal' sex as unsatisfactory, thereby disqualifying themselves for writing about it. No dogmatism can endure long in the novel. Flaubert thought he was giving witness. That he did so in his major work to a woman's psychology hardly invalidates his insights; in fact, this is what fiction is about.

Now the term *novel* can be said to insist on some form of news, and thus suggests itself as the style of a culture setting a high value on originality, less important in Chaucer's day. This connotation seems to have got established in England rather than in France, where it has even started to leave the short fictional form (as in the fifteenth century Boccaccian imitation *Les cent nouvelles Nouvelles*). Even in England the term *novel* only acquires the article in the middle of the eighteenth century, whereas in the sense of a generic catch-all *fiction* establishes itself even later, having subsequently meant a feigning, deceit or dissimulation. In France *fiction* has never really stuck. It is only quite recently that the *franglais* publishing term 'science-fiction' had, for the purposes of classification, to replace the more limiting *anticipation*. England was the first great technology, in short, where it paid off, as in modern America, to be new. Balzac was derided for his contemporaneity.

A new search for reality, then, coeval with a neo-Cartesian emphasis on particulars, obviously made for an upset of universals. In the novel it quickly made for realistic particularity of the kind that is the hallmark of Balzac, Dickens, and Zola – philosophically, socially, economically. Aesthetically, it was impelled into being as a rude correction to romance. Socially, it was hustled into the political arena, largely by Zola, in order fully to face our problems and formulate answers to them (*Germinal* was used as a tract on how to organize labour in coal mines and *l'Argent* how to avoid another financial crash like that of the Union Générale). Economically, the impulse to realism was undoubtedly accelerated by social breakdowns and a new bourgeoisie shoving the outgoing feudal class off the stage, a middle class who required to see their dominant philosophy in print: Crusoe, with his needless contracts and computations, is the classic case in point. Science was to add another spur.

Clearly the close objectification of the family that these pressures were to entail meant presenting woman's role in a new way. 'Realism is indefinite enumeration', wrote Albert Camus. So Zola, an ardent early photographer on the side, shows us woman as slave in *Germinal* as never before – living in worker barracks comparable to concentration camps, breeding like a rabbit, and reduced finally, in the form of Catherine in the depths of the mine, to a naked, perspiring, exhausted pit pony tethered to a truck of slag. The 1850 English Commission's *Report* on mines and colleries had revealed exactly the same, but Zola's was a far bloodier and more brutal accusation. It was as if he shone a sudden spotlight on all the factual investigations and exposures that had preceded him, and so reduced to human unity, and immediate corrective action, something like (in England) Henry Mayhew's immense, ponderous, four-volume *London Labour and the London Poor* of 1862. Indeed, Zola's very names, before his characters act, are suggestive in themselves, of course: when a man's surname inflects, and the wife of a miner called Maheu becomes simply *la Maheude*, we see the wife as principally a property extension of her husband. So if the novel was news, it was above all new news of women.

And as long as it presented the new, its form could fluctuate, be what it liked. Formal fictional conventions were notoriously small, and early aroused the principal curiosity of women writers

(Austen, Charlotte Brontë, George Eliot, George Sand). We have longish letters by George Eliot and the famous Chapter XVII ('In Which The Story Pauses A Little') of *Adam Bede* where she expresses 'delicious sympathy' for Dutch paintings showing 'faithful pictures of a monotonous homely existence' and regards as the novelist's duty 'to give a faithful account of men and things as they have mirrored themselves in my mind'. There are the letters exchanged between Flaubert and Sand on the shape of the novel during 1875 and 1876. We have some parenthetical comment by G. H. Lewes, some equally parenthetical but infinitely more perceptive comment by the Goncourts between 1851 and 1870, two disappointing books on the novel by Zola, the prefaces of Conrad and James and others, but no body of theoretic and normative discussion of novel composition until late in its career. In England fiction scarcely had an aesthetic until the 1920s, when Percy Lubbock systematized James in his *The Craft of Fiction*, to which E. M. Forster responded with his suggestive *Aspects of the Novel* of 1927, with Edwin Muir and others following up.

At their inception our novels were accorded expository reviews rather than criticism; unlike America, we still retained the term *notice* of a novel. In *The Monthly Review* (1749–1845) or Smollett's *Critical Review* (1756–1817), these may have been extended but they were not in the proper sense normative, any more than were Scott's *Lives of the Novelists* (1821–24), while only one of Arnold's *Essays in Criticism* is about a novelist (Tolstoy). Arnold criticized by ignoring, a peculiarly British habit, and he ignored both Dickens and Thackeray. Likewise, Jane Austen had been largely lacking in 'notice' by the big reviews. England long lacked its Sainte-Beuve – or even a Cuvillier-Fleury, Sainte-Beuve's intelligent rival.

Lack of legislative criticism in England was probably symptomatic; it had a psychological as well as purely literary source. In England the male-dominated society remained singularly stable and, in a phrase, only the dumbest calves select their butchers. The country, and century, of The Great Family was hardly likely to welcome Hardy. Tolstoy found Ibsen repellent.

55

At the same time, the high degree of particularization, called for by the need to control a large amount of social material, cut both ways. On one hand, it acted as an ego-protective, delimiting the world and relieving tensions. As in the detective mystery the readership saw enemies punished, virtues of the given society rewarded, desires secured. Not, however, in Flaubert or Zola. Nor in the best of Dickens or Hardy.

For, on the other hand, the realist inspection unleashed too many devils. The theory that we create protection from social guilts by giving repressed elements rein in an art work, only to put them back in a sort of Pandora's box of hidden emotions later, like a child, is swamped by the best realism, as was evinced not only by the prosecutions of Baudelaire, Flaubert, and Zola, but also by the demonstrations against the *théâtre libre* of Antoine (from Jean Jullien's *Sérénade*, through Ibsen's frenchified *Les Revenants*, to Brieux, Porto-Riche, and even Curel). Even a dramatist of the *théâtre social* as mild as Paul Hervieu aroused initial opposition astonishing to us today.

The literary psychoanalyst Simon Lesser may well write, '*in reading fiction we do not have to be afraid*', but in fact (as Baudelaire's short poem *Héautontimorouménos* suggested) only the mighty may contain within them both victim and executioner. When faced directly with a realistic work of art that touches on our most intimate experience it is hard to contain all elements aroused by it; it was men who walked out of the early Ibsen.

So it was for this reason that in the prosecutions of *Bovary* and *Ulysses* charges were often made that these fictions were not merely obscene, they were disorderly, unkempt. To us today both works seem models of the most scrupulous construction. But the complaint was that of Highet against *Lolita*. The imaginative form behind the created story was simply not seen, nor sensed, by obtuse readers. The adulteress was not literally punished, there was no reassuring pattern of retribution imposed to keep the world at bay. These were sensational heroines and the sensation was simply exploited – Flaubert was frequently called 'romantic' as though that were a crime. In sum, the author, on this end of the realistic effect, does not seem a social enough ringmaster of his creations.

All this must have been extremely reverberative for women. It is often observed that it was not the rapacious *tricoteuses* who first sat around the guillotines of the French Revolution, it was a solid *Bürgher* class which had been denied outlets for their libido and were on their way to power. In this sense the novel is securely anchored in the culture of cities, or burgs. For it is also firmly planted on the psychology of its readership – women, another revolutionary class. Of the two genres of fiction discerned as predominant by Clara Reeve's *Progress of Romance* of 1785 – realism and romance – women knew which side their own bread was buttered.

For women, like children, knew that they did not satisfy their ideals in life; and the point about the kinship (missed by Mrs Firestone who fusses over it) is that women are *not* children any more. Romantic fiction imposed a pollyanna patchwork on society's injustices and, especially, on male behaviour. At the most elementary level women knew that the heroine did not in real life marry the handsomest and richest man, nor was virtue invariably vindicated, the villain punished, and religion triumphant. Life was not happy. They were undeceived. So they read about someone called Madame Bovary and kept their eyes open. The book became a very subversive document, indeed. Women knew the world for what it was. The reading Mrs Alving is questioned about by Pastor Manders is clearly the new realism. Throughout the play the allusion of contagion – by the new ideas as by syphilis – is present.

Women must have read this way. Obviously, Emma Bovary's story is not simply that of a provincial wife who takes lovers on the side – such could be found in the penny press, the equivalent of any issue of *True Confessions*. Moreover, Gothic fiction had always presented a conveniently vague heroine, easy of empathy. So they saw something else in the reciprocal interaction of character and environment presented by the new realism as a living criticism of the times. Our sexual, like our social, hopes are doomed to deception. Like Emma's face, or that of Zola's

Nana modelled on it, purity is 'determined' to decay, in a world rapidly becoming Darwinized. 'Chastity', Harry Levin has written, 'is liable to corruption, even as prostitution is compatible with holiness.' Both Emma and Nana (who bestrode and rode her male fool of a lover around her bedroom) presented images of social revolt in their sexual histories.

The fount of fiction was feminist in its deepest appeals. It had to be. Natural scenery, interiors of rooms, all were mobilized to correlate with inner feelings. Of Hardy's *Tess*, for instance, Ian Gregor goes so far as to claim that 'At every stage of the tale interior states are visualized in terms of landscape.' Fiction was speaking in a new code to women.

Furthermore, Defoe and Fielding, and then the sentimental novel in both England and France, turned from plot to follow the psychology of characters – and these had to include women. *Moll Flanders* drew pertinent pro-feminist comment from Virginia Woolf:

> 'The advocates of women's rights would hardly care, perhaps, to claim Moll Flanders and Roxana among their patron saints; and yet it is clear that Defoe not only intended them to speak some very modern doctrines upon the subject, but placed them in circumstances where their peculiar hardships are displayed in such a way as to elicit our sympathy. Courage, said Moll Flanders, was what women needed, and the power to "stand their ground"; and at once gave practical demonstration of the benefits that would result.'

Both Defoe, who wrote a sympathetic tract on women's education, and Fielding, who theorized about the 'comic epic in prose' in the three Prefaces to *Joseph Andrews* and the eighteen to *Tom Jones*, interested themselves in social rejects or outcasts. Women were such. Moll was one of them, and the very stuff of fiction. The vagabond or, as it is sometimes called with modifications, picaresque novel has a long antecedence and Defoe was right to insert a woman into it. Rabelais's Panurge, Shakespeare's Falstaff, Nashe's Jack Wilton, Grimmelshausen's Melchior Sternfels von Fuchshaim – what we immediately notice about such characters is their strong and secular questioning of what today might be called 'establishment' values. Values of transcendence. Falstaff mocked something called honour. Women had to produce babies.

The life of the rogue-picaro was whimsical, subject to chance, and the laws of this world. Existential woman, as predicated by de Beauvoir, had to share this view. Recommended by Rousseau, *Robinson Crusoe* presents us with a literal outcast who has to form his own pattern of life, declare his own mastery of the world's 'material'. We recall that Flaubert felt himself to be completing Cervantes in a mercantile era. Moll Flanders remarks, 'the Market is against our Sex just now'.[29] In a word, the great fictional hero or heroine was allowed to scorn allegiances of all kinds – to gods, kings, societal abstractions like honour and, by implication, to male dominance itself.

It is true that the Victorian period re-imposes this later. But the damage has been done. The Sophias of the parsonages and rectories had felt the illicit liberty. In the novel they saw themselves externalized in a new way. As aristocratic patronage ceded to commercial publishing, a transition usually marked by Johnson's famous letter to Lord Chesterfield, women could and did subscribe to the new romances, and within this glossy apple the worm of realism was already writhing. Psychological truth was gnawing at the social. For who was this new readership?

It is said to have been insatiable in England. The theatre was not widely spread enough to satisfy the nascent bourgeoisie and, in any case, there were circumscriptions surrounding this form of entertainment for women. Decreasingly so with the novel. Women could, as Sophia evidently did, read in private and turn back to check reflective passages, as they might not at the theatre. The large sales of *Pilgrim's Progress* in the seventeenth century (for a hundred years the biggest seller after the Bible, in England)

---

[29] In the Crowell 'Critical Library' edition of *Moll Flanders* this celebrated comment is glossed by the editor, J. Paul Hunter, as follows: 'i.e. woman's matrimonial bargaining power is poor in the present social situation.' The transliteration makes an absurd *reductio*. Moll's is a general lamentation, against woman's lot in a man's world altogether.

is hardly at issue here, for Bunyan's masterpiece really got read as so much secondary scripture. The new novel secularized. What's more we must bear in mind that its shock value was far more intense then than now. As Albert J. Guerard puts it at the start of his fine book on Hardy, 'The fictional heroine or villainess who in 1870 permitted a premarital kiss must in 1915 commit adultery if she wishes to provoke the same horror in her readers; by 1945 she must be a pervert or a murderess.' By 1972 the term *pervert* is too mild. In the year in which the celebrated St Louis sex researchers, Dr William Masters and Mrs Virginia Johnson, got a US Public Health Service grant to test almost every aspect of sexual behaviour, sodomy was performed on the New York stage remarkably realistically, a Swedish movie showed a woman copulating with a dog, and an "artist" exhibited sculptured excrement in a Manhattan gallery to yawns from the *New York Times* ('These aggregations of colonic calligraphy contain many formal excellencies . . .'). It is hard to purify our minds of these impurities and realize what the giving of her body must have meant to Emma, Tess, or meek Jane Eyre.

By the end of the eighteenth century England's population was of the order of six millions, with a novel readership estimated at 80,000. Not large, but by present standards discriminating – and largely female. In 1765 the library of a shoemaker's hand (perhaps an exceptional man) included *Paradise Lost*, Gay's *Fables*, translations of Epictetus, Pomfret's poems. Lackington's autobiography, or *Confessions*, tells us that he started bookselling with five pounds and was soon selling 100,000 volumes annually. And he complained of illiteracy!

Nor were these books cheap. Watt cites careful income statistics. Most novels were coming out at this time in two volumes duodecimo, for the readership there was had leisure and time on their hands. The daughters and wives of the richer farmers, shopkeepers, tradesmen, parsons, were not spending their days bent over the sink; the new novel, prior to the growth of public libraries and to cheap journals which ran serializations, was fairly costly.

All the more reason, then, to sense that for women it meant

a great deal. There may have been an obvious emotional enthu-
siasm for *Pamela, Clarissa, Evelina,* but the theory of escapist
distraction cannot be made to cap entirely their huge popularity.
Women were seeing a sexual servant class transforming their
environment, changing, acting, As Virginia Woolf put it, 'we
admire Moll Flanders far more than we blame her'. The woman
was active. And while we shall never know the exact interpretation
put on the new heroines of fiction in the boudoirs and bedrooms
of country houses, we would be insensitive not to acknowledge
that the accent on secular individualism struck a strong chord
in women's breasts.

In the emphasis put on the *kind* of reading Emma Bovary
indulges in (a parody, of course, of the novel as romance and
manners-book), it is sometimes forgotten that she is introduced
to the clandestine literature in her convent school by a woman,' an
old maid who came for a week each month to mend the linen . . .
and on the sly lent the big girls some of the novels, that she always
carried in the pockets of her apron'. The new novels were – to
borrow Marianne Moore's delightful phrase – '*imaginary gardens
with real toads in them*'.

Wish-fulfilment literature presupposes that there are wishes
to fulfil. In the pages that follow we will share some of these,
in a series of representative women who were also active individuals. They may not be radicals in our political sense of the
term – if they had been, their stories would have been put on
the Index Expurgatorius of the circulating libraries alongside
Moore's *A Mummer's Wife* – but they are perhaps all the more
interesting, and lovable, for that. *Dangerous Liaisons,* which
went through fifty editions in Laclos's own lifetime, was said
to have been owned by Marie Antoinette but to have been kept
by her under plain wrapper. Yet, as André Maurois has pointed
out, *La Nouvelle Héloïse* tells a contemporary story of feminine
innocence that seems to have been equally popular. Laclos in fact
chose his epigraph from it.

Women wanted to learn about women. And the point is
that feminine psychology, and therefore oppression, was advanced by almost any truly sensitive novel about them. Not all

women are, as some men seem tacitly to assume, harlots; but harlots and artists, as Baudelaire suggested, were both outsiders, on the fringes of society. When the established order is clearly criminal and repressive, crime itself becomes a social good. Moore than one 'lady critic' – from Virginia Woolf to Dorothy Van Ghent – has seen the ingenuities of Moll Flanders, constrained by the circumstances of being a destitute woman, as truly creative as well as socially inventive. In the five heroines who follow we shall hope to identify something of this liberating universality and see that women who give form to unfair lives are informing the world, and us, with love.

2

MADAME DE MERTEUIL
Woman as Sexual Object
With A Coda On *Cousine Bette*

'One is not born, but rather becomes, a woman. No biological,
psychological, or economic fate determines the figure that the
human female presents in society; it is civilization as a whole that
produces this creature, intermediate between male and eunuch, which
is described as feminine.'
Simone de Beauvoir

In Choderlos de Laclos's sole work of fiction, *Les Liaisons
dangereuses* of 1782, we find one of the most spectacular cases of
sexual revenge by a woman in the whole of literature, including
that of the Renaissance. For any serious reader soon has to see
that the book documents far more than a vendetta against a
single, unfortunate individual, the Comte de Gercourt, it quickly
passes into an attack on the male sex itself. The recent Vadim
movie from the text wholly vulgarized this objective.

In any case, the revenge against Gercourt, who exists principally as a kind of absence – he is apparently an officer cam-
paigning in Corsica, presumably in the Comte de Vaux's anti-
Paolist army there – is superbly excessive, and a creative act in
itself. The character is so shadowy that one is surprised to
find him referred to in the most monumental (nearly eight-
hundred-page) work on Laclos to date as '*le sot Gercourt*'. But
this estimate of what is virtually an inexistence would seem to
owe somewhat to the scholar concerned's ability to locate comparison with Gercourt in libertine literature prior to Laclos,
in the theatre of seduction in France, and in particular in an

evidently deservedly little-known work *Lettres du chevalier de Sainte-Alme et de Mademoiselle de Melcourt* by Mlle de Saint-Léger.[1]

An early footnote in Laclos's work informs us that poor Gercourt had had the temerity to abandon his beloved of the time, the Marquise de Merteuil, for a lady who had reciprocally betrayed the Vicomte de Valmont for his own favours,[2] and 'that it was then that the Marquise and Vicomte became attached to each other'.[3]

This is what the French call *exact*. The Spintrian web of adulterous incest unites the anti-lovers who abolish love, and use sex to subvert the family. But let us resume something of the story itself, before examining its background and psychology.

The luckless, shadowy, and unheard-from '*sot*' Comte de Gercourt has been then, directly and indirectly, the source of sexual insult to both Madame de Merteuil and Valmont. 'You can see that love has not blinded me', says the former, and the reader is invited to see that indeed it has not.

For by the end, and before Laclos afflicts her with smallpox in a highly factitious retribution, she has manoeuvred the following: her new lover and accomplice Valmont has very violently seduced Gercourt's intended, the witless Cécile. He has caused her to have a painful miscarriage ('the physician has given her illness a name'), an 'accident' which drives her sentimental lover Danceny nearly insane, but over which the pair positively exult (Letters 138, 140, 144). About it Madame de Merteuil herself merely remarks, to Valmont, 'let me offer you my condolences on the loss of your posterity'.

But Valmont has persisted further in their joint task. The final turn of the screw requires that the ninny's son, to be born after she is married to Gercourt, will be in fact a Valmont. As Madame de Merteuil puts it to the latter:

---

[1] Laurent Versini, *Laclos et la Tradition*, Paris: Librairie Klincksieck, 1968, pp. 142–3, 315.

[2] 'It is rare for women to leave men.' (Shulamith Firestone.)

[3] I use the admirable Lowell Bair translation throughout; in some present editions of this Letters 62 and 63 have unfortunately been transposed.

'Of little Cécile's health, for example. You will give me precise details of it when I return, will you not? I shall be glad to have them. After that, it will be for you to judge whether it will be better for you to give her back to Danceny, or to try to become a second time the founder of a new branch of the Valmonts, under the name of Gercourt.' (Letter 145).

Worse yet. Valmont has not only violently raped the girl, caused her to have a miscarriage which he calls 'amusing', and has in all probability made her pregnant, he has taken pains to debauch her vocabulary, he has poisoned her sexual semantic.[4] Thus when the chivalric warrior Gercourt returns from his (anti-liberal) wars, he will find his pure rose not only thoroughly sullied but sexually foul-tongued, a simple slut in bed. Thus Valmont:

'I spend my leisure in thinking of ways to regain the advantage I have lost over my ungrateful prude, and also in composing a kind of catechism of debauchery for the use of my pupil. I amuse myself by calling everything by its technical name, and I laugh in advance at the interesting conversation this will produce between her and Gercourt on their wedding night.' (Letter 110.)

So in every way the twin avengers go far beyond the literal requirements of their task – to the very destruction, or 'overkill', of sexuality itself. Gercourt gets justifiably forgotten. One finishes by feeling his absence as weakness. The attack becomes one not merely on a male, nor even on conventional morality as such, as the more percipient critics have seen, but rather on the whole biassed rigging of biology itself. The young girl Cécile is a perfect example of de Beauvoir's 'erotic transcendence' and what one might call the politicizing of puberty: 'For the

---

[4] A whole section of Professor Versini's book (Chapter 4) demonstrates a virtual pedagogy of erotic parody, pastiche and pun by Laclos, akin to but far more brilliant that that of Cleland; the English reader has to be warned of insuperable problems of translation here—words like *decent* and *veneration* simply do not bring over their lexical equivalents in Laclos.

E

young girl, erotic transcendence consists in becoming prey in order to gain her ends.'[5]

It is highly unsatisfactory to read *Dangerous Liaisons* as no more than an amusing coda to the virago or Marfisa tradition in literature. There is no doubt but that it is such, and that this 'female Tartuffe' (as la Merteuil has been called) falls into line with Lady MacBeth. But why did Faguet, in his great conspectus of eighteenth-century French writers, so neglect Laclos?

The *mariage raisonné* for which France has been famous, and which persists into the present in its provinces, certainly comes under scathing ridicule in this book. Gercourt is thirty-six, Cécile only fifteen; the disparity is not all that improbable given the era, but Laclos somehow, without saying much, seems to put it into a context that makes it disgusting. In the background the girl's mother bleats vain protests – 'I shall not have her marry one man and love another' – though she is in fact 'disposing' of her daughter like so much portable property. She has made a 'commitment' to Gercourt without Cécile's sanction or perhaps even original knowledge, and Laclos succeeds in making this sexual bartering of souls extremely filthy. He does so largely, I think, by juxtaposing it harshly against a highly refined civilization with the most subtle scruples in other matters, the world we call 'French' with all its rarified ratiocination, aesthetic skills, and social graces. It is in this world that Cécile's naiveté is a living social anachronism:

> 'I do not see why I should be the only one to prevent myself from loving; or is it wrong only for unmarried girls? I once heard my mother say that Madame D—— loved Monsieur M—— and she did not sound as though she thought it was very bad; and yet I am sure she would be angry with me if she even suspected my friendship for Monsieur Danceny.' (Letter 27.)

In a nutshell, Laclos's novel presents the sexual power struggle as a fundamental social antagonism, or antinomy. If woman really wants to, she can win this war with ease and thus unlock

[5] De Beauvoir, p. 316.

the doors of politics itself.[6] In fact, she did. Laclos's work was the prognosis of a class on its way to the guillotine, around the dripping heads of which women were eventually to sit knitting. In his notes on *Dangerous Liaisons* Baudelaire observed, 'The revolution was made by voluptuous men. Licentious books therefore comment on and explain the Revolution.'

This again seems exact. It was not simply that we had a long record of male power standing in for sexual power (extending now from Machiavelli's *Mandragola* to the admissions of Léon Blum), nor was it merely that the libertine was interested in, among other things, liberty; as we know from other writings of his, Baudelaire senses behind him a virtual tradition of licentious or gallant writings, often by aristocrats, in which revolutionary ideas were embedded. Professor Versini is thus able to say, without trying to be clever, '*Le roman d'un révolutionnaire est le dernier roman aristocratique.*'[7]

Surely this was pre-eminently exemplified in de Sade, writing scabrous literature and leaning out of his cell window in the Bastille, before he was removed therefrom, shouting revolutionary instructions to the crowds beneath. The evidence of how totally de Sade has been misunderstood, and distorted by social fears, is shown in the horror and terror of him of many contemporary feminists. Most of what de Sade said has been obscured by social prejudice (his work has, in any case, come down to us in a more disheveled state than that of any recent writer). In fact, he shares much with Laclos, though inclining far more to the mechanical philosophers like Holbach and La Mettrie. Man is still a part of nature. That being the case, we must unfortunately evolve some laws by which to protect the weaker among us. '*Il faut toujours en revenir à de Sade*', wrote Baudelaire, '*çest'-à-dire à l'homme naturel, pour expliquer le mal.*' Christian mortality was inadequate to this task since it did not recognize natural man.

In the second volume of *Aline et Valcour* de Sade's anti-

---

[6] 'Oh, you men and your heroics! Do I always have to earn my Canadian Club the hard way?'

'Yes.' (Advertisement for Canadian Club whisky)

[7] Versini, p. 207.

Utopia turns out to be absolute monarchy dominated by male chauvinist pigs (lecherous cannibals) with women as subdued sex objects. A priesthood is in charge of education. Exactly everything de Sade saw around him and most feared. His hero Sainville then founders on an island for a fortnight where he discovers the reverse, a society without prisons or death penalty, with men and women equals, children brought up outside the family, total freedom of the press, incest harmless and sodomy looked on with indifference. Like rape, murder is considered more in the context of an undesirable and eventually eliminable sickness – 'it should never be punished by murder' (i.e. capital punishment). There are no property laws. In a word, 'if you make them realize the necessity of virtue, because their own happiness depends upon it, they will be honest people by egoism'.

Laclos participates in this realism, for he too was a true heir of the Enlightenment. Both Laclos and de Sade proposed that we should take a new look at women, for it was the humbug of bourgeois mortality, grounded on a male-dominated religion, that had kept women in subservience for so long. One wonders, indeed, how many of the termagants of Fem Lib, enveighing against something called sadism, know that in de Sade's ideal state there is *complete sexual equality in every department of life*. In fact, Apollinaire advanced the notion that this was the motive of de Sade's work and precisely why he wrote *Justine* and *Juliette*.

Enlightening sidelights get thrown on this from time to time. In common with Laclos, de Sade predicated a greater intensity of sexual drive in women than in men. At present writing a lot of feminist ink is being spilled about trying to stop prostitution – as degrading to women, insulting, and suchlike. De Sade approached the problem from the other end. We cannot negate our sexual drives, and those in women are immensely powerful. Some men are always going to want immediate sexual enjoyment; this did not imply possession ('I have no right to the possession of the stream that I come to on my road, but I have to its enjoyment'). So rather than proposing that men should not have access to prostitutes, de Sade said that women should have similar access, at any time, to desirable males – who would not be allowed to refuse their slightest sexual whims. There is, as de Beauvoir suggestively induces (and she wrote her great essay on de Sade alongside her feminist study), a strange co-fraternity between sadism and stoicism.

We should not let the matter be muddled by a clinical cathec-tion called 'sadism', to which almost everything is attributed which society most fears, from the Moors murders to the latest inebriate who runs over a child with his new car. Feminists are wrong not to read de Sade. When he wrote that the marriage contract was based on power, he did not say that it should be so, merely that it was so, and that if women wanted power they had better seek out an equality of contract:

'The necessity mutually to render one another happy cannot legitimately exist save between two persons equally furnished with the capacity to do one another hurt and, consequently, between two persons of commensurate strength: such an association can never come into being unless a contract is immediately formed between these two persons, which obligates each to employ against the other no kind of force but what will not be injurious to either; but this ridiculous convention assuredly can never obtain between two persons one of whom is strong and the other weak . . . everywhere, to be brief, everywhere, I repeat, I see women humiliated, molested, everywhere sacrificed to the superstition of priests, to the savagery of husbands, to the playfulness of libertines.' (*Justine*).

It is surely this element of psychosexual political prediction which the basic boudoir-battleground metaphor of Laclos's book serves so well, the same that made the pederast André Gide (who admired Blum who, in turn, wrote a feminist review of *Mansfield Park* in 1899) exclaim that 'Laclos was hand in hand with Satan'. For Baudelaire God was maternal and birth a fall, an expulsion from Eden, and his terror and his delight are in this fall.[8]

[8] Pierre Emmanuel, *Baudelaire: The Paradox of Redemptive Satanism*, translated by Robert T. Cargo, University of Alabama Press, 1967, p. 83.

Here, too, lies Laclos's chief break with the English epistolary writers; we know that he admired Richardson. *Clarissa* is mentioned in his pages and Miss Howe helped him with Madame de Merteuil. But Laclos is 'French' and sees woman as more creative than man. She is a finer human instrument and can play havoc with the male whenever she chooses.

Hence the celebrated 'cynicism' about something called love. Rid yourself of this absurd male fetter, Laclos proposes (and la Merteuil opines), it is woman's only Achilles's heel – and you will be free. If men are vulgar enough to become enslaved to your body, calling the end-product love, stand aside and let them make fools of themselves. You will thus always be one step ahead. Virtue (as proposed in the British epistolary novel) can be no real panacea. It is a male concept and a male harness to a male culture. Virtue has never liberated any woman from anything.

Our 'philosopher in chains' said the same from prison and, contrary to popular cliché, there are pages of de Sade that could have been written by Betty Friedan. Who asked that laws be 'flexible', 'mild', and 'few' or that we must 'get rid forever of the atrocity of capital punishment'? De Sade gave up his post as magistrate partly on account of this objection, asked for property to be properly distributed, and lamented, of women, 'Must the diviner half of humankind be laden with irons by the other? Ah, break those irons, Nature wills it.' But de Sade seems too set in the nosology of Fem Lib by now for there to be any true understanding of his position, let alone pardon for it. This is a pity. But the same spirit of the Enlightenment shines in Laclos, where we may without danger admire it.

So Laclos could recommend his work as a sort of *livre de chevet* for unmarried maidens of the day, citing without too much of a tongue in his cheek a mother who said to him, after reading the manuscript of *Dangerous Liaisons*, 'I think I would be doing my daughter a real service if I gave her this book on her wedding day.' If Laclos had wished to repudiate the philosophy of Madame de Merteuil, he would have ended his work on a note of miraculous conversion; but this is precisely where he strays from his tradition (e.g. Chevrier, Madame de Saint-Aubin). André Malraux has pointed out that there is no letter from la Merteuil after her defeat, we are only told, extremely parenthetically, about her. Laclos would have been completely faithless to the immanent values of his fictional society if he had shown us his Megaera repenting.

*   *   *

It is hard for us today to judge the true appeal of fiction in the form of letters. With us such have become matters of business, annually decreasing beside the telephone, tape-recorder and the like. As anyone who has tried to teach elementary English there knows, it is getting harder and harder in America to find any young person who can write a really witty, civilized letter.

In England even of our own not-so-distant youth, however, letter writing was habitual. Girls wrote long, involved and often emotional letters to each other. Boys at school often communicated scripturally with others in other houses at the same establishment, although it would have been simpler and speedier to have called on them. American speech standards have been mainly regional. In England, however, a good deal of anachronistic redundancy had to go on in order to effect true courtesy. Also a degree of obsolescence. 'How d'you do?' is met with the structural question 'How d'you do?' Lengthy, time-wasting salutations (as in, notoriously, Spanish letters) proclaim formal politeness, a putting-out. The number of letters passed between characters living in the same house in *King Lear* troubled early critics far less than the sexist ending. Their unlikelihood has only relatively recently been ridiculed. Early on in Laclos's work there is a significant opening to one letter from Cécile Volanges to Madame de Merteuil, confessing that it is easier for a young girl in her position to write letters about her sentiments than to utter them – 'How well you understood that it would be easier for me to write to you than to speak to you!' (Letter 27.)

The reason for this is hardly far to seek. In a society that represses woman such outpourings are a secular confessional, a surrogate *journal intime*, and in fact, after Pamela's arrival in Lincolnshire, her letters shadow into her Journal (which then becomes reciprocally rich in letters).

This not only excuses any 'artificiality' in the mode, it strongly liberates a psychological vein which can be deployed on behalf of women, and was. Not only did Richardson and Burney use the letter novel, but so did (in an age beginning to grapple for the first time with problems of literary censorship) Smollett and Galt, the latter one of the first to interpenetrate his narrative and reflective passages with a fairly full canon of the vernacular – in his case, Braid Scots or the Doric – which is to say the way his characters' thoughts were thought.[9] Spirits as disparate as Restif de la Bretonne and Anne Brontë (*The Tenant of Wildfell Hall*), as Frederick II of Prussia and Swinburne (*Love's Cross-Currents*),[10] were to employ the new form, one spoofed pleasantly enough in the 'Venosta' letters of Thomas Mann's last fiction, *The Confessions of Felix Krull*.

So in many ways the letter novel was a genuine act of feminine liberation, and accordingly popular at once as such in the fiction-reading countries, England and France. We shall come to inquire why below. In the mediaeval household, to say nothing of the family grouping that preceded it, the silence and intimacy predicated by novel reading were apparently impossible, or highly unusual. The letters of the fourth-century Symmachus were largely factual and, as every Latin-weary British schoolboy knows (or knew) to his cost, even those of Cicero and Pliny are largely informative, being records of daily life. No doubt the best of these had considerable stylistic grace, but many might surely have been written in other forms, as tracts perhaps;

[9] Professor Versini's voluminous study of Laclos contains an Appendix II devoted to 'Romans Epistolaires Parus de 1700 à 1800', in which I counted 288 entries. These were almost exclusively French and English. Scottish fiction is oddly ignored, for a Frenchman. Galt would have been late for inclusion, yet not Smollett.

[10] It may be that parts of this work rework Swinburne's incomplete, botched masterpiece *Lesbia Brandon;* the point here is that he was evidently tempted into the method under scrutiny as a potential for relieving his (largely sado-masochistic) hangups.

and to claim some sort of hyperbolic stylistic purity for them may be the prerogative of university dons, but it is also to lead into a linguistic cul-de-sac, for who is the arbiter of such qualities in a 'dead' language like Anglo-Saxon? Are we really ready to conclude that all Italians are in truth speaking corrupt Latin?

Next, as a functional method of passing a message, the letter began to acquire a grammar and to become, indeed, a formal event (as still it is, indeed, in some of the smaller ex-British West Indian islands today). Instruction in such formalities then grew up, so that by the eighteenth century what seems to have happened is that two epistolary streams coalesced and joined the general flow of the novel, lending it a sudden infusion of emotion, and resultant impetus. Defoe himself sensed this in his *Continuation of Letters Written by a Turkish Spy in Paris* of 1718 (another work that should have appeared in Professor Versini's epistolary bibliography, but doesn't, though *Moll* is mentioned *passim*). Richardson, commissioned to compose a letter writer, created in Pamela a heroine of the rising merchant class – and the letter novel was suddenly secure. It remained for Laclos to adapt this fully, and serve the true ends of its means – feminine emancipation.

We must of course first concede the new form's principal convention, that its letters are not really letters at all. They are what Cécile says they are, dramatic soliloquies, intimate revelations of herself, which she can only really recognize when they are written out. A kind of emotional diary, or couch confession to oneself, if you will (cp., in this regard, Scott's *Redgauntlet*). We are far from the first to observe, for instance, that quite a few of Pamela's letters are penned in the knowledge that they will never reach their destination (will fall into the hands of Mrs Jewkes, etc.). The same holds true, to an extent, of those written by Cécile. For it seems that her mother is vigilant enough to be able to spot a minute difference in a key, yet the girl goes on writing highly self-incriminating letters! The case is even more extreme with Madame de Tourvel, a circumspect person who might be expected to know better. But no, she falls prey to 'love' (unreason) and is seen at the end begging Valmont for 'the return of those letters which ought never to have existed'. (Letter 136). Why did she ever let them do so in the first place?

We can now address ourselves to the question of the tremendous appeal, the strong vogue, feminine in all senses, which the epistolary novel exerted in fiction-reading Europe of this time. Clearly, the reader became a new sort of confidant. To overhear another's intimate confession must always produce a certain *frisson*. But in this case we are overhearing, in the early English letter novelists and the French libertine tradition, the confessions of a thoroughly 'alliciant' heroine, her mind tortured by apprehensions and doubts, when her body is not being physically threatened. It is, in fact, what is generally known as the textbook sadistical set-up, as our heroine wrings her hands, blushes, bursts into tears, implores for mercy, God, heaven and so on, in a thoroughgoing enactment of some penitent schoolgirl, all dimity and bent bonnet, awaiting the briny birch. An unleashing of forbidden demons, to be sure.

But Laclos lets more out of the bag. He here perfects the English novel of the genre, and is confidently more concise. As is well-known, Richardson repeatedly embroidered – and one critic has it that this sort of letter-writing took the place of tapestry-weaving! – on a Perils-of-Pauline situation, an eristhistic anticipation of the moment when the heroine would lose her virginity. It could be spun out indefinitely. The bells of England tolled when Clarissa Harlowe 'died'.

An intelligent, impoverished army officer snubbed by the nobility of Grenoble, Laclos went further. He realized that to give woman a voice and then make her into a type of masochistic martyr might be good aphrodisia, and even partake of art, but it was fundamentally ducking the issue. Indeed, if he were merely writing for money (and commercial reward was certainly an ingredient of Richardson's attitude), why did not Laclos write another novel, a sequel to his considerable success, instead of returning to desolatingly provincial soldiering and an increasingly large wife – as he himself put it, 'The more there is of you, the better'?

Parenthetically, one could point out that those we consider

today as the leering pornographers, pandering to depraved tastes for money, were in fact nothing of the kind. The debt-ridden Cleland wrote his masterpiece for a paltry sixty pounds (though five years after *The Woman of Pleasure* was published he was offered a government pension if he wrote nothing more of the kind), while the penniless exile Nerciat, proscribed by the Republic, perhaps reduced to espionage, edited by Apollinaire and well represented in Professor Versini's bibliography, received almost nothing for his Arcadian aphrodisia and knew with all such writers that they would be pirated instanter. Nerciat explicitly asked: 'See, these things were made for your delight as well as mine: are they not beautiful in their fashion? Do they not establish a bond between us, are they not an immortal testimony and record of the greatest pleasure accessible to our senses, do they not perpetually nurture and encourage it, release the tensions and gild the tedium of your lives, offer you the beatific vision of actions subsisting in an ideal climate? Do they not offer you, even, a glimpse of Paradise?'

Laclos daringly accepted Richardson's and Nerciat's challenge. If you let woman have her say, then you must do so honestly, you must expose the whole dynamics of a repellently male-dominated society which may have developed high mental refinements, but is still selling off its daughters like cattle. So Laclos did not need eight or ten volumes for his sex war. His philosophy is presented with telling Gallic clarity in la Merteuil's extended confession in Letter 81. He was depicting a new woman, one who not merely rejected society, like Tolstoy's Anna, but tore it to shreds, until she was able proudly to claim, 'I can say that I am my own work.' Feminism can go no further.

* * *

This is not a book in which we wish to wrestle with the minutiae of literary criticism. There is death in that dictionary, indeed. All we need to bear in mind here is that Laclos wrote out of a French tradition of *galanterie* as well as through the English epistolarists. His two closest antecedents seem to have been

Diderot's *La Religieuse* of 1760 and Pierre Henri Treysac (or Treyssat) de Vergy's sentimental series *Henriette, Comtesse d'Osseran* of a decade later. In both amorous conquest implies an activity of the mind, not simply a sensual spinning-out of erotic possibilities as so often in Richardson. In this respect it could be said that Laclos gives us our first feminine Don Juan.

The birth of this legend in Spain presented it with a setting of duennas, cloistered ladies, and balconies needing climbing. The seventeenth-century Don Juan, as derived from Gabriel Téllez, is more of a model of masculine prowess in general, than specifically of a seducer. The stratagems needed to overcome the barriers on the way to women involved literal physical strength and could be looked upon as quasi-military; when the Spanish redactions spread to Italy, and then to France, where Molière's famous hero sets an inconstancy pattern rationalized as a love of plural beauty, these arts of conquest are domesticated to the drawing-room. Byron then boldly and amusingly reverses the trend, the principal concern of his Don Juan being at times the avoidance of being seduced.

I do think Laclos can be brought into this tradition. His military vocabulary has been frequently commented upon. In *De l'Amour* Stendhal wrote, 'Love in Don Juan's manner is a feeling somewhat like a fondness for hunting. It is a need for activity which must be aroused by different objects and which places our talent incessantly in doubt.' Nor does this escape the sharp eye of Simone de Beauvoir:

> 'The erotic vocabulary of males is drawn from military terminology; the lover has the mettle of a soldier, his organ is tense like a bow, to ejaculate is to "go off"; he speaks of attack, assault, victory. In his sex excitement there is a certain flavour of heroism ... when referring to their love relations, the most civilized speak of conquest, attack, assault, siege, and of defense, defeat, surrender, clearly shaping the idea of love upon that of war.'[11]

Precisely the metaphors of Laclos, in fact, who thereby

[11] De Beauvoir, p. 351.

parodies the whole male semantic of 'having' a woman. By the time one has finished *Dangerous Liaisons* one realizes that no one 'has' Madame de Merteuil, she 'has' them; in short, the idea of sheer expenditure of sexual energy implying accentuated masculinity is reversed, or corrected. It must be said that the tradition asks for this. Madame de Merteuil is not merely a *femme fatale;* she has the political alertness of the male and shares more in the image of titanic womanhood, disregarding all bounds, which so seduced the *Sturm und Drang* poets in Germany (as more moderately reflected in Schiller, Goethe's *Stella*, and of course the fuss over Friedrich Schlegel's *Lucinde*). Eventually the titaness desexes man; Crébillon fils' *Le Sopha*, with its implication of an impotent Juan character, leads logically to a homosexual in the role, as suggested in H.-R. Lenormand's *l'Homme et ses fantômes* of 1924. Madame de Merteuil turns without too much trouble, it seems, to tribadism. These metamorphoses of Don Juan have a definite psycho-sexual application; many women will attest that having 'conquered' her, a man may feel relieved not to have to perform the sexual act. In many a rapist there is a Julien Sorel longing to get out.

Thus Laclos came at exactly the right time. He gathered all these fictional strands together and pushed the epistolary novel on about as far as it could go – without falling over into farce (as a matter of fact, Letter 101 from Valmont to his valet, and enclosed in another, does seem fairly preposterous). Hence the form perfectly replies to its content, the basic sexual minuet mocking society at its most vulnerable points.

For some modern readers, in truth, he does go too far. One critic, Godfrey Singer, feels that the fact that people living in the same 'castle' correspond with each other 'deprives the book of verisimilitude' and ends by making it absurd. This is to misread fiction. In any case, most of the characters do *not* live in the same house and, incidentally, a *château* is not a castle any more than an *hôtel* in Balzac is necessarily an hotel. Madame de Merteuil seems to be living in a compact little eighteenth-century *nid*. The message-passing in such a milieu mocks the incestuous politics of Versailles and, before tub-thumping about women not being allowed into politics there, we should remember that a lot of men weren't, either. Poor army officers, to boot.

So when Laclos has Valmont write to his valet Azolan at some length, a man whom he could presumably go to see and speak to directly at any time, the author is surely not asking us to take this literally. He is slipping us a wink. Letter 101 concludes, poker-faced, with the advice, 'Be careful not to lose this letter. Reread it every day. . . .' To your own valet?

With such warnings in mind we find that, rather than lapsing into artificialities of the mode, Laclos is cleverly parodying his content through his form, striking at his society through its conventions. Hence his technique is perfectly satirical. The coming combat between classes is prefigured in a merciless duel between the sexes. Let us glance briefly at the twists and tricks to which Laclos subjects his model, the letter novel, for his leger-demain is not merely that of a great literary virtuoso, it says a lot about woman's role in the love relationship.

To start with, there are of course a number of letters within letters (e.g. Letter 141) and/or enclosed within them. One is anonymous. Then there is a delightful comment on the absurdities of woman's subservience in Letter 82, from Cécile to Danceny; for here she tells her admirer (with her intended safely in the Corsican maquis) that thanks to a tacit agreement or pact she cannot talk to Valmont 'in front of other people', just before Valmont himself is to rape her. In other words, you communicate best in such a society, or mis-society, by the sexual organs!

Not only do we find the many letters deviously delivered by hand and stuffed into pockets or bodices (v. Letter 76), there is the celebrated epistle written by Valmont, who must have had a steady hand, on a whore's back or belly – the slut Emilie serves as his desk in Letters 47 and 48, and is so referred to later in Letter 138. After this, it would surely be the most obtuse reader who did not take la Merteuil's comment, in Letter 74, that it was a *letter* which made her see some sincerity in Valmont, vis-à-vis his new rival Prévan, as sarcastic ('It took nothing less than your letter to make me pay attention to him').

It is an exquisite sadism ('I enjoyed her agitation') which

Valmont indulges when he has his own letter to Madame de Tourvel delivered to, and read by, that virtuous lady in his own presence. A rape of the mind, indeed. Other letters from Valmont to the '*intendante*' Tourvel travel back and forth, as she refuses them, like so many epistolary yo-yos – 'it has always been the same letter going back and forth; I only change the envelope' (Letter 110). Valmont even dictates one letter from Cécile to Danceny, turning his gull of a girl friend into a Galatea of erotic revenge.

If the letter habit is supposed to be feminine, Laclos appears to be saying here, then let us take it to the end of the line, exhaust all its possibilities and deride male supremacy through the accusation itself. Laclos's whole technique is a sort of sexual minuet married to the political forms of his decadent male society; one event is recounted to and seen through the eyes of a number of varying characters, particularly as in the ninny Cécile's rape by Valmont, of which her own description appears significantly second, after Laclos has let Valmont give his 'cynical' account of it. The technique, that of making the event the catalyst by means of which you characterize, is to be utilized again and again in 'experimental' fiction (and in symptomatically anti-masculine novels, too, like Ford's fine *The Good Soldier*).

The technique has one flaw. It requires extreme characters and, as in Balzac's 'continuation' of such sexual revenge in *La Cousine Bette*, which we will consider below, only the excessive beings tend to come into focus. (Madame de Tourvel remains shadowy and weak.) Nor would Laclos surely have contended the contrary. There is an anguish in his vision. He was writing a sexual anagram of power politics. Valmont and la Merteuil are liberated and 'enlightened' because amoral. Danceny and Madame de Tourvel belong to the kingdom of heaven, and will have no effect on things here on earth. In truth, young Cécile almost calls for her rape. It is hard not to feel that this trembly little tease, out of the pages of some eighteenth-century equivalent of *Playboy*, fully deserves her fate. The feeling is summarized by Valmont in Letter 140:

'Never before, perhaps, had a girl ever kept so much innocence while doing everything necessary to get rid of it! Ah, there is one girl who wastes no time on reflection!'

The form, then, is delightfully excessive, in harmony with what we have resumed as the plot. For its time its theme is fully feminist. In a male society a certain amount of loaned power may rub off on privileged women, but in fact they remain a relatively helpless sub-class which has to fight for its freedom at every point – daughter, lover, mother. Laclos faces the realities and replies that to be completely free a woman must eliminate her emotions – or what man sees as her emotions ('love') – equip herself for the bedroom-boudoir battle, and so acquire influence if not power.

Valmont sounds this theme in the fascinating Letter 40 to Madame de Merteuil, one which should be read aloud at every Fem Lib meeting where it might temper the claims to belligerence and originality of some of the shriller dragons present. 'I did not think I ought to lose the opportunity of allowing her to give me an order', Valmont writes here, 'for I am convinced that the illusory authority which we appear to let women take is one of the most difficult traps for them to avoid.' Our male author then allows his creation to go on to exemplify that freedom from scruple which, in love at least, is usually referred to as cynicism – 'But you may be sure I did not surrender without conditions. I was even careful to make one which was impossible to grant, so that that I shall remain free to keep my word or break it.'

Exact, again. What men have calmly called 'principles' must be shown up for what they are, power hypocrisies; once she liberates herself from these, woman will become free. In the process she may have to learn to hate men as they hate her: cp. 'women have very little idea of how much men hate them' (Germaine Greer – who else? – in *The Female Eunuch*). Similarly, in *Sexual Politics*, Kate Millett writes of the 'envy' she observed in various men when Richard Speck murdered eight nurses. Doubtless exaggerated for the sake of extremism, the sense may still be felt in the Biltmore bar around the time when male commuters are preparing to rejoin their respective battleaxes (military metaphor intended).

In the famous Delilah letter (81), already mentioned as the centre of Laclos's text, Madame de Merteuil tells Valmont in so many words that women have been oppressed so long their hate is far harder and sharper than that of men ('How I pity you for your fears! How clearly they show my superiority over you!'). She continues:

'I was born to avenge my sex and dominate yours. . . . Tremble above all for those women, active in their idleness, whom you call "sensitive", and of whom love takes possession so easily and so powerfully. . . . How many modern Samsons there are whose hair I keep between the blades of my scissors! I have ceased to fear them; they are the only men I have some-times allowed myself to humiliate.'

This is the very image of the dominatrix; the small ads in the schlock magazines spring to mind ('Docile young man seeks woman experienced in discipline . . .'). A civilization based on authority, and submission, is not unlike the army, requiring an enemy, crime, the Other. Laclos saw that blind Law was going to be torn down, and civilization of contract installed. Thus the Merteuil/Valmont philosophy is at all points a debunking realism, one consonant with the spirit of the rising bourgeoisie and to inform the novel with greatness in the century to come.

Thus 'love' must be revealed for what it is, the ultimate absurdity. La Merteuil writes to Valmont that 'You can see that love has not blinded me' (Letter 2), and with a sacrcastic jeer Valmont later responds in kind, 'Ah, do not profane love thus!' (Letter 137). Elsewhere he had confessed, 'I must have this woman to save myself from the ridiculousness of being in love with her' (Letter 4). All this is crucial. It raises the question as to why Baudelaire thought Laclos's novel – '*Livre essentiellement fran-çais*'.

A comment of this nature is scarcely amenable to empirical testing. However, poets have repeatedly associated places with women – one thinks of Archibald MacLeish apostrophizing

America as a girl lying on her left side, her flank golden – and France is popularly received as Marianne. Anyone familiar with the great French flesh-pot resort towns must be tempted to concur that Laclos's book is 'French' to its voluptuous, sharp-clawed core, and beyond.

Nor is this merely a matter of sexual frankness, with which, until recent American permissiveness, we Anglo-Saxons long associated the French, and for which we once envied them. It is often forgotten today how extremely frank even quite young girls could be in society prior to Victorian Puritanism. This was in Shakespeare's day, of course, a commonplace, but even Jane Austen shows us woman using in polite society language of a far more 'liberated' nature than she could employ a century later. This is all the more impressive when you take into account that neither Austen nor the Brontës had in mind naturalistic ideals of dialogue in fiction. They were primarily concerned with reveal-ing the psychology of the speaker. Thus at the start of *Mansfield Park* the sophisticated Mary Crawford remarks to the 'stick' Edmund: 'Certainly, my home at my uncle's brought me acquainted with a circle of admirals. Of *Rears* and *Vices*, I saw enough. Now, do not be suspecting me of a pun, I entreat.' This from a girl in her early twenties. In 1908 we meet the following passage in Arnold Bennett's *The Old Wives' Tale:*

> ' "You are fond of dogs?" asked Mr Povey . . .
> "I have a fox-terrier bitch," said Mr Scales, "that took a first at Knutsford; but she's getting old now."
> The sexual epithet fell queerly on the room. Mr Povey, being a man of the world, behaved as if nothing had happened; but Mrs Baines's curls protested against this unnecessary coarseness. Constance pretended not to hear. Sophia did not understandingly hear. Mr Scales had no suspicion that he was transgressing a convention by virtue of which dogs have no sex.'

Not long after this passage was written, Lawrence was getting hauled over the coals for the use of the word *stallion* in his first fiction.

Laclos strongly emphasizes and reiterates that in sex women

want pleasure. He also makes quite sure that this must be understood and exploited by the male if he wants to retain his power. 'You surely know better than I, Monsieur', says Valmont's valet at one point, 'that going to bed with a girl is only making her do what she likes; making her do what you want her to is often a very different matter' (Letter 44).[12] Unlikely profundity in a valet, perhaps, but one that touches Valmont closely and sends him into an ecstatic quote from Alexis Piron's *la Métromanie*. Madame de Merteuil reinforces this to Cécile after her corruption by Valmont – 'He has taught you what you were dying to know!' (Letter 105.)

Yet one longs to risk saying that the whole work is 'French' in deeper senses. Late eighteenth-century France was an Apollonian civilization, its aristocracy refining itself out of existence (and meeting its final fate with considerable courage). In this context the intellect is a double tool, one destructive on both edges of its blade. Baudelaire saw Madame de Tourvel as representative of the solid middle-class values broken up by intellect.

In modeling her own personality, the surrogate sculptress Madame de Merteuil did not suppose she could be physically other than a woman. She was not familiar with the forthcoming American 19th Amendment. Yet, as has already been suggested, the acquisition of rights does not automatically guarantee increased influence. France is the country of the Salic Law. Women could not succeed to the throne. But even de Beauvoir concedes the unusual influence of women in France – almost as a consequence of this exclusion: she cites St Clotilda, St Radegonde, and Blanche of Castile. Elsewhere she touches on this unverifiable matter of feminine 'influence' in France:

> 'the Norman peasant woman presides at meals, whereas the Corsican woman does not sit at table with the men; but everywhere, playing a most important part in the domestic economy, she shares the man's responsibilities, interests, and property; she is respected and often is in effective control.'[13]

[12] Surely this is an echo of Rousseau's belief that a woman 'should reign in the home ... by contriving to be ordered to do what she wants.'

[13] De Beauvoir, p. 124.

To one, like the author of this book, who lived on and off in a country house in Corsica for over a decade, this is interesting enough; in fact, it is probably an exaggeration, inapplicable even in the dourly pro-Corsican south, in villages like Sartène, where even in the 1940s there was almost certainly not the sexual segregation mentioned (moreover, most Corsican women today would still be insulted to be considered French!). But de Beauvoir hits the heart of the agricultural situation; women may not have had rights, but were extraordinarily important. I know that my own wife was particularly respected in those many years in Corsica for her abilities, in a way she is not always in a city culture. Loath as we may be, with our one-man-one-vote democratic shibboleths, to acknowledge this, we should do so before dismissing Baudelaire's comment about Laclos's book as an airy generalization.

One could perhaps dramatize the point this way. In 1969 a small, thin, frail *lycée* teacher in Marseilles, a thirty-year-old woman divorced from her husband, had a brief love affair with a pupil, a big, bearded youth of sixteen. As a result, she was hounded with the tenacity of the Inquisition – by the boy's (Communist) parents, by her colleagues, and – with astonishing fanaticism – by the public at large, when the press revealed the enormity. She was accused of '*détournement de mineur*' – roughly, deviation of a minor. The Napoleonic code does not mention corruption of minors as such. As a result, she was thrown into the grim Baumettes prison, where she remained six months awaiting trial. Half an hour after she was given a suspended sentence ('*sursis*'), the government prosecutor appealed for retrial and a harsher penalty, principally one that would make it impossible for the woman ever to teach again. Gabrielle Russier, the teacher, terrified and alone, killed herself.

During her trial it was pointed out that a Dean of a university faculty had just seduced one of his students, a girl of seventeen. The disparity in age was far greater than that between Gabrielle and her lover. The Dean was fifty. He was not prosecuted for deviation of a minor. The difference in age between Gabrielle and her Christian was only fifteen years, of no consequence were the sexes reversed. In the same area, Aix-en-Provence, in the year following Gabrielle Russier's suicide, a woman was sentenced to twelve years' imprisonment on the suspicion that she had egged on a man to commit murder, the actual murderer only receiving eight years. During the same year two brothers got into a fist fight near Paris over what to feed their dog. One killed the other. He got precisely two years.

The Gabrielle Russier affair rightly became a *cause célèbre*. Yet despite the fact that she was nine before women could vote, and twenty-eight before married women might have their own bank accounts in France, let alone obtain advice from a physician about contraception, the female author of the most moving memoir of her writes:

> 'All this is puzzling in a society where women on the whole have a better time of it than women in English-speaking countries. Frenchmen do not seem to resent women or be afraid of them, they are not bored by feminine company (all-male clubs or outings are rare and considered ridiculous), the war of the sexes scarcely exists. Equal pay for equal work is the law of the county, and women often hold more important jobs than do women in America.'[14]

Though a woman found guilty of adultery in France may get two years in prison (equivalent to a male murder), a man can escape with a fine; yet, paradoxically, in comparison with America, divorce is not difficult to obtain. Or, rather, should one say that it is regarded as on quite another plane? If you 'reduce' woman to a man, you will be inclined to consider her, if you are a man, as either an inefficient inferior (Nietzsche's office-boy) or a potentially dangerous competitor (the American female executive). On one level, the result will be what we have seen in the recent airline personnel disputes in America; here militant women's groups – stewardesses – simply created their

[14] Mavis Gallant, 'Things Overlooked Before', *The Affair of Gabrielle Russier*, with a Preface by Raymond Jean, New York: Alfred A. Knopf, 1971, p. 23 (I cite a passage not to be found in the many excitably feminist reviews of this book at the time in America).

reversal, militant men's groups who successfully demanded equal employment time for stewards on flights. In the event, women lost. Nietzsche put the dilemma as follows, in *Beyond Good and Evil*:

'This is what is happening today; let us not deceive ourselves! Wherever the industrial spirit has triumphed over the military and aristocratic spirit, women are now striving for the economic and legal independence of an office boy. "Woman as office boy" is imprinted over the portal of modern society as it is emerging. But while women are seizing these new rights, while they are seeking to become "master" and writing "woman's progress" on their flags and rags, the opposite is taking place with frightful obviousness: *Woman is retrogressing*. In Europe since the French Revolution, the influence of women has *waned* to the degree to which their rights and claims have increased. And the "emancipation of women", insofar as it is demanded and furthered by women themselves (not merely by shallow male minds) thus shows itself as a peculiar symptom of the increased weakening and dulling of the most feminine instincts. There is *stupidity* in this movement, an almost masculine stupidity, for which a well-made woman (who is always a clever woman) ought to be deeply ashamed.'

We have said that amorous conquest is for a writer like Laclos an activity of the mind. He is simply able to write such a fundamentally pro-feminine book because he is an artist almost before he is a male – his empathy is aesthetic. He sees erotic transcendence in women. As de Beauvoir puts it, 'Woman will not accept her status as the inessential unless she becomes again the essential in the very act of abdication. Being made object, lo, she becomes an idol in which she recognizes herself with pride.'[15] What Laclos says through his fiction is that though women want pleasure in sex, they are far more creative in his eyes than men. 'Animals love at close quarters', Gérard de Nerval was to say, 'souls love at a distance.' This *amor de lonh* is a fully feminine

[15] De Beauvoir, p. 328.

property. The female sex arouses passion, man merely accomplishes what has been set in train. Madame de Tourvel's guardian expresses it as follows: 'A man enjoys the happiness he feels, a woman the happiness she gives. This difference, so essential and yet so seldom noticed, has a marked influence on the whole of their respective behaviour. A man's pleasure is to satisfy desires, a woman's is chiefly to arouse them' (Letter 130).

For the most part, then, man is a sexual animal. Woman exists on another level – she 'becomes' prey, as de Beauvoir well puts it. Valmont admits as much when he tells la Merteuil, 'Oh women, women! And you complain if you are deceived! Yes, every treachery we employ is stolen from you' (Letter 100). In the long Letter 125, in which Valmont recounts how he finally broke down the stoically virtuous Madame de Tourvel, taking her with tears streaming down her cheeks, there is the suggestion, hard to transmit in translation that, as both attained orgasm, Valmont himself began to aestheticize sex – *L'ivresse fut complette et réciproque; et, pour la première fois, la mienne survécut au plaisir'*. Bair gives, 'my rapture outlasted my pleasure'. Which is fair enough, except that by eighteenth-century euphemism Laclos lets us know that Valmont wants to continue since 'for the first time' he had become a second Merteuil, using sex rather than being used by it, and thus truly liberated. His 'pleasure' was Dionysiac, his 'rapture' Apollonian and artistic, and thus for a moment, as he confesses in this letter, he really meant what he said.

At this point Valmont starts contemplating his own rights over la Merteuil. After all, he has served her faithfully and fully. So he has to learn his lesson the hard way. 'What have you done that I have not surpassed a thousand times?' Madame de Merteuil writes to him. Is Valmont jealous of Prévan (in whom she herself was totally uninterested until Valmont mentioned the man in the first place)? Well then, she will twist the knife in his side, or even, by implication, his genitals:

'Can you suppose that after having made so many efforts I shall not enjoy the fruits of them? That after having raised myself above other women I shall consent to crawl like them between rashness and timidity? That I could ever be so afraid of a man as to see safety only in flight? No, Vicomte, never. I must conquer or perish. As for Prévan, I want to have him and I shall have him; he wants to tell it and he will not tell it: that, in a few words, is our whole story.' (Letter 81).

Directly Valmont starts imagining he has rights over her, Madame de Merteuil takes off, seduces Danceny, shows him the letters and thus, as it were, sets him like her hound at Valmont's throat – and Danceny kills Valmont in a duel. (Laclos is unable to resist a final irony in having the guardian of Valmont's victim Madame de Tourvel, and Valmont's own aunt, lodge a complaint about the duel to the Public Prosecutor on behalf of the deceased!) Like *Hamlet*, the story ends when most of the leading males in it have been killed off.

We have mentioned above the case of another tragic 'victim of passion', Anna Karenina. Tolstoy undoubtedly saw her as such, and, indirectly therefore, of a society which had let itself become a calculating male hierarchy. But the attitude to the social grounding of the character is quite different from that of the French fictional critics. Both Anna and Emma Bovary are awoken to, and thirst for, true love, rather than 'love'. Both end in suicide. Both evince masculine traits and manners. As J. P. Stern reminds us of Anna: 'she rides in a man's habit, smokes, plays tennis, practices birth control, takes morphine against insomnia, keeps a disreputable English nurse, discusses Zola and Daudet.' Tolstoy disapproves – 'his judgments on all these iniquities are reflected in her moral disintegration.'

In conversation during 1883 Tolstoy highly praised M. S. Gromeka's article on the novel – 'He explained what I unconsciously put into the work' – which for us today reads like one of the reddest of the rednecks celebrating male chauvinism:[16]

---

[16] Looking at a 1971 photograph of four leaders of the National Women's Political Caucus in San Clemente, Secretary of State William Rogers scathingly likened the line of ladies to 'a burlesque'. President Nixon cut in with a grin, 'And what's wrong with that?'

'Marriage is still the only form of love in which calm, natural and unobstructed feeling builds firm links between people and society, preserving freedom for action, giving strength and stimulus, creating a pure world for children, and creating the soil, the source, and the tool for life. But this pure family principle can be built only on a firm basis of genuine feeling. It cannot be constructed on an external calculation. A subsequent infatuation with passion, like the natural consequence of an old lie, will destroy the passion, improving nothing, and bring about final destruction, because "Mine is the vengeance, and I shall repay." '

Gromeka is here citing the celebrated epigraph which has caused so much critical ink to be spilt. To most women readers it generally seems that whatever Tolstoy's attitude to Anna, and however it may have changed during the writing of this book, the real vengeance will fall – on the battlefield, no less – on Vronsky, who brought on the whole tragedy by having sexual desire for Anna. What J. P. Stern is essentially observing is that Tolstoy's tale may here illumine such remarks as those made later, consciously, by Tolstoy the teller – 'at last his love meets her self-hate, his concern with the moral theme finds its echo in her matured conscience, and she comes as it were to understand his mind. The measure of Tolstoy's achievement is simple enough: he cannot save her, but he never abandons her.' Such a feeling is surely what tempted Arnold into an uneasy respect for Anna. For our purpose I should wish to stress that this 'matured conscience' is a *creation* by Anna of herself. To quote once more her all-important address to Dolly, 'Don't forget the chief thing: that I am not in the same position as you! The question for you is, whether you desire not to have any more children; for me it is whether I desire to have them.' The difference is a great breach, for a woman. It is truly a matter of kind, rather than degree.

I have risked labouring this point a little since it is really the clue to the long Delilah letter (81) in Laclos's work in which, as we have seen, Madame de Merteuil proudly claims, 'I can say that I am my own work.' Her control of her own character (which she describes in thoroughly aesthetic terms as 'a purity of method') is an artistic act, and thoroughly emancipatory. Though Valmont thinks he is free, she is completely in charge of him – 'As for prudence and shrewdness, I am not speaking of myself, but what woman would not have more than you?' He is a mere ancillary to her own *gloire* ('I needed you for my glory'), all his victories are really hers. She is a woman who has worked on herself with the care of a sort of psychoanalytical sculptor; she tells us once that she has even inflicted 'voluntary pain' on herself and made her face maintain an expression of pleasure throughout:

> 'I carefully noted both pleasure and pain, and I saw nothing in those various sensations except facts to be gathered and meditated upon.' (Letter 81.)

The rigorous training has paid off. She is finally free. Her end is purely spurious. She should have been seen sitting around the guillotine, for what she has done, and partly why she is *'essentiellement française'* (one notes the quotations from Voltaire) is to shatter male illusions to power. The pretty pastoral background has been ripped apart like so much tawdry tinsel, the set decoration behind which a male supremacy held rule, and which is now laid brilliantly bare by intellect. If 'intellect' can be amoral, so can sex. It is significant that Madame de Merteuil is a woman and Valmont 'the oracle of the younger men' (Letter 32). In fact, more than one critic has seen that Madame de Merteuil is beginning by the book's end to have homosexual inclinations for Cécile, a logical enough extension, after all, of her erotic role when the 'dominant' males are so despicable. In short, Madame de Merteuil has by the conclusion turned herself not into a superior sort of woman but into *another kind of being*. This is operative, and for which she has, on the realistic level, to die. Tolstoy may have seen certain aspects of society as corrupt but he suggests, in a sense, that we are stuck with society. With Laclos one is less sure. He is a genuine libertine, and a revolutionary *avant son jour*.

It is for this very reason that *Dangerous Liaisons* is a novel rather than a poem, or play. It shares in the whole cutting-down mentality which gave rise to fiction, and would eventually secularize society (Madame de Merteuil plays God with a vengeance). Religion is here fairly roundly ridiculed (Letters 4, 6, and especially 51 to which a footnote needlessly adds that la Merteuil despised the church). Early on Valmont aims his arrows explicitly at Madame de Tourvel's piety:

'I shall have that woman; I shall take her away from the husband who profanes her; I shall even dare to ravish her from the God she adores.'

Thus Madame de Merteuil is left darkly dying, amid 'sinister events', evidently unutterable, and hopefully so. Like Rodolphe's to Emma, the letters live on, and indeed create their own sort of anti-life. At the end of *Madame Bovary* Charles runs into Rodolphe who he now knows has cuckolded him; he sits opposite his sexual rival at a café, over an August glass of beer, and reflects – 'He would have liked to have been this man.' Then for a second a spasm of fury, vital life, takes hold of him, but he quickly relapses and 'soon the same look of mournful weariness returned to his face'. He tells his deceiver, 'I can't blame you for it.' A whole male world is contained in that quiet little confrontation.

*   *   *

Balzac's *La Cousine Bette* is often held up as the finest work of his latter period, roughly from the mid-eighteen-forties on. The central spider of action in it is another woman, Valérie Marneffe, who was – according to Balzac himself – intended to be a kind of successor to Madame de Merteuil. The comparison between the two is as interesting from the feminist point of view as that between Flaubert's Emma and the Portuguese Eça de Queiroz's Luiza, of 1878.

To press it home, however, involves one in having to make a number of self-protective provisos, on the purely literary plane. We have said that realism came in as the restraining tail to fantasy in fiction – the first definition in Johnson's *Dictionary* is as 'relating to things, not persons'. Hence the high degree of objectification already touched on. In his 1842 Preface Balzac does not in fact mention realism as such, and he really minimizes the social history side of his work. He does, however, insist on facts.[17] We know too well by now the degree of care he lavished on financial computations and the like in his 'comedy', paralleled only perhaps by England's *Crusoe* which was so much the outrider of an incoming way of life that Virginia Woolf described it as 'one of the anonymous productions of the race rather than the effort of a single mind'. Certainly, in his study of 'the causes of social effect' Balzac was in the same complete harmony with a nascent civilization.[18]

We know too that the astute Thibaudet described Balzac as one of the first great novelists to compete with God – 'The *Comédie humaine* is the *imitation* of God the Father.' The novelist who creates a closed universe, or perfect type, is likely to be secular in this sense, and Joyce indeed pays tribute to both Balzac and Flaubert when he has Stephen end his little disquisition on Lessing, 'The artist, like the God of the creation, remains within or behind or beyond or above his handiwork, invisible, refined out of existence, indifferent, paring his fingernails.'[19] Percy Lubbock must be given credit, in England at any rate, for stressing this new turn of definition in Balzac, where everything we touch, see, and feel takes on real value:

'He cannot think of his people without the homes they inhabit; with Balzac to imagine a human being is to imagine a province, a city, a corner of the city, a building at a turn of

[17] 'If the meaning of my composition be well understood, it will be acknowledged that I accord to indubitable facts of every-day life, whether secret or open, to the acts of individual existence, and to their origin and cause, the same importance that, up to this time, historians have attached to the public life of nations.'

[18] 'My book has its geography as well as its genealogy, and its families, its places and its things, its people and its facts.'

[19] I have always felt it to be a tip of the hat on Joyce's part to Flaubert that he has Bloom printed in the newspaper account as Boom, i.e. without the *l*; despite Wells's character of that name, this reminds the indoctrinated reader of the fact that *Bovary* first came out as by Faubert.

the street, certain furnished rooms, and finally the man or woman who lives in them. He cannot be satisfied that the tenor of this creature's existence is at all understood without a minute knowledge of the things and objects that surround it. . . . Balzac is so sure that every detail *must* be known, down to the vases on the mantelpiece or the pots and pans in the cupboard, that his reader cannot begin to question it. Everything is made to appear as important as the author feels it to be.'[20]

Realism is presumably the copying of reality. But Balzac is only as realist as he wants and needs to be. *La Cousine Bette*, for instance, covers nearly eight years, but one critic has spotted that the only passage calling any attention to the time of year is one mention of lilacs being in bloom.[21] It is highly understandable that neither Balzac nor Flaubert would want to ride under the so-called realist banner. It was not close enough to real reality, for one thing. Flaubert, in particular, dissociated himself from it, in tune with the Baudelaire who saw photography as the new spirit of mammon avenging itself on the masses. The term was scarcely considered critically necessary until it got abused. It later came to stand in for subversion, of course, or pornography. 'REALISTIC . . . FRANK . . .' shouted the mottoes on the marquees of the Hays Code movies.

Realismus was used by Schiller and the Schlegels, the former ascribing such to the Greeks (in *Über naïve und sentimentalische Dichtung*) and envisaging it as correcting romance, in common with Goethe's famous distinctions to Eckermann. The problem appears to have been enormously over-complicated by criticism, which has found it necessary to stake out boundaries between varieties and velleities of the practice, as in Zolaesque naturalism, Italian *verismo*, the Russian brand of Belinsky and Chernyshevsky (so strongly opposed by Dostoevsky), and so on. All this is the stuff of English Literature university courses, doubtless due to

[20] Percy Lubbock, *The Craft of Fiction*, New York: Viking Press, 1957, pp. 220–1.
[21] Samuel Rogers, *Balzac and the Novel*, University of Wisconsin Press, 1953, p. 48.

be regurgitated to the bug-hunting governesses (of both sexes, as all ages) presiding over doctoral orals.

Here it surely suffices to say that *réalisme* occurs as a literary term in France in 1826. Only later did it become a slogan and a catch-all. We have already suggested that by present-day standards Zola reads for the most part as a symbolist, while both Balzac and Stendhal, stigmatized as realists by the 1840s, could not possibly be considered so today, after Crane, Norris, Dreiser and the rote of brutal male realists in America.

We know that Courbet put his rejected paintings in the *Pavillon du réalisme* in 1855, and that a year later, as Baudelaire brought out his translations of Poe, Champfleury started his magazine *Le Réalisme* (edited by that Courbet of literature, Edouard Duranty). At this time the son of a young clerk, Jules Fleury (Husson), was writing novels which presumed to photograph reality with fidelity, one of which has an adulterous theme that somewhat anticipates *Bovary* and was highly successful – *Les Bourgeois de Molinehart*. We also know that Flaubert was accused of realism at the trial of *Bovary* and can well understand his dissociation of himself from all forms of literary programmes. Yet, as surely as Balzac, he required the author to vanish behind his creation, 'paring his fingernails'.

It is true that Zola's Preface to the second edition of *Thérèse Raquin*, put beside that of the Goncourts to *Germinie Lacerteux*, does declare a theory – of determinism. But if 'romanticism *is* realism', in the suggestive theme of a well-known book by Jacques Barzun, the reverse also applies and 'the esthetic principles of a Zola, or, more consciously, of a Thomas Hardy, are often nothing more than reaffirmations of romantic beliefs against a constricting convention'.[22] Medically dubious today, Zola's repetitions of heredity and environment (utilized by Ibsen in both *Ghosts* and *The Wild Duck*) are akin to certain psychological absolutes with us. Call such realism, naturalism, or '*actualisme*', all were methods of exposure. The very nudity of Nana in her overdressed era was a social criticism.

[22] Jacques Barzun, *Classic, Romantic and Modern*, New York: Doubleday Anchor Books, 1961, pp. 58, 220.

Hence such investigatory techniques were usually on the side of women, and increasing numbers of authentic heroines start to emerge. Of Jane Austen, the Brontë sisters, George Eliot, Simone de Beauvoir writes that 'We do not find in them, for example, the irony, the ease of a Stendhal, nor his calm sincerity. Nor have they had the richness of experience of a Dostoevsky, a Tolstoy: this explains why the splendid *Middlemarch* still is not the equal of *War and Peace; Wuthering Heights*, in spite of its grandeur, does not have the sweep of *The Brothers Kara-mazov.*'[23] This is extremely loaded since there are few male novelists who can compare with Tolstoy or Dostoevsky (besides, Jane Austen has immense 'irony 'and 'ease', at least in English). When the small numbers of women novelists are taken into account, their productions are extraordinary.

For, when poured into the novel, or *news*, Camus's 'indefinite enumeration' must mean an emphasis on new facts, unexplored areas of society – thus on women. When the emphasis is on simple things, too, which, as Lubbock suggests, play almost as important a role in Balzac's work as people, it is often decisively symbolic. Wenceslas's absurd but significantly entitled statue of Samson and Delilah has a strong effect on the action of *La Cousine Bette*, just as do Hulot's wife's diamonds; these are worth as much to the theme as the *Amor nel cor* seal or phrenological head in Flaubert's *Bovary*. Such emphasis has of course made Balzac congenial not only to the French '*chosistes*', or 'new' novelists like Robbe-Grillet, Butor, and Sarraute, but also to the Marxists. Engels wrote, 'even about economic details I have learnt more from them than from all the books of all the pro-fessional historians, economists, and statisticians of the time.' Money . . . cash . . . comes to be a virtual character in Balzac's drawing-rooms.

This new ratio between character and environment makes the melodrama more ours than his. We have created a male civilization based on money. Balzac is observing the monomanias proper to this state. Monetary-sexual greed, jealousy, ambition are with him like so many monstrous mediaeval 'humours',

[23] De Beauvoir, pp. 667–8.

95

obsessive imbalances that make their owners pop up all over, as if they can't be killed off, and this, to an extent, excuses some of the plot hokum and coincidences. Percy Lubbock has a persuasive comparison of how Balzac would have rendered Anna Karenina; he would have pressed home far more solid social detail and rooted the wonderful psychological sweep of her development more securely in a given milieu. As it is, 'her passion for this man, the grand event of her life, has to be assumed on the word of the author'. And in a lesser author it would not be.

The distinction is all-important when it comes to sexual relationships, of course. Balzacian exaggeration and monomania – Grandet's for money, Hulot's in *La Cousine Bette* for sex – are like so many social types, and types of a society which has fractured the human personality. It has well been said that Balzac's three chief fictional interests are money, lust, and magic. They in fact supply the 'romantic' strain for his work, money and lust acting as a sort of possession by devils. One only has to look at the fantastic farrago of sex-death at the end of *La Peau de Chagrin*, or the death by slow sexual frustration in *Lys dans la vallée*.

Frankly, after a few volumes of *The Human Comedy*, one is in a world in which women are being screwed, bought, sold and killed in a sort of ferocious rote, when the males aren't assassinating themselves by the very strength of their desires. Properly read, it adds up to a pro-feminist picture. We recall that Balzac, author of the *Physiologie du mariage*, believed himself to have sympathy for women's lot and was the author of that immortal comment, 'Never begin a marriage with a rape'.

Balzac's picture seems to me to spring from a wholly different view of 'love' than that held by Tolstoy. For the latter, in Barbara Hardy's words, 'This complexity of "love" is a part of his unified view of personality. No single emotion of pure love exists, no separation of sexual from non-sexual vitality.' After the declaration of her 'infidelity' to her husband Karenin, Anna is offered, in so many words, a little quiet sex on the side; but she declines to fall into this basically masculine cliché. Balzac bears witness to a far more fragmented world and gives us, in a way, a franker view of sex.

For instance, in Bette herself he shows us a little social tragedy of womanhood, that artificially enclosed order of the *vieille fille* in France of the time, the helplessness without sexual power of the great clan and class of unmarried women. Spinsterhood as slavery. And Flaubert will show us the same pathetic results in wizened old Catherine Leroux who, in *Bovary*, gets a medal at the agricultural show for fifty-four years of farm service (from a man with the significant name of Tuvache, into the bargain). He does the same in that touching little story he wrote at the end of his life for George Sand (who died during its composition) 'Un Coeur simple'. Here the old maid who dies imagining her parrot to be the Holy Ghost is called Félicité with fiercely Flaubertian irony. We note, too, that in *La Cousine Bette* Josépha (beside whom Adeline Hulot seems pitifully ignorant in the sex-war) maintains that the government ought to set up gymnastic classes to teach virtuous women how to handle men, in direct anticipation of such trends in New York today. As Balzac well put it in his Preface, 'When Buffon described a lion, he needed but few additional words to draw the picture of a lioness; whereas, in society, a woman is not always the female of the male.'

La Cousine Bette is a study of sexual obsessions in a male-dominated world, one that succeeds that of Laclos and the revolutions. The main women in it, Bette herself and Valérie Marneffe, are virtually demons. Bette's story, a revenge for child-hood slighting, soon cedes in intensity and purpose to that of the latter, a titaness with the tough vigour of a *poule de luxe* for whom a retired general and a retired scent merchant possess total sexual mania, by which they are ruled in the manner of one of Zola's 'temperament' characters.

The atmosphere is one of constant sexual frenzy with Valérie Marneffe, the Merteuil of the action, finally convincing four men each is the father of the child she is allegedly carrying – and finally smashing, too, the china-doll idyll between young Hortense and Wenceslas (who represent 'love'). Was this what made Baudelaire call Balzac 'a passionate visionary'?

Well, it is fairly easy to make a case against Balzac and, I think, against *La Cousine Bette* in particular. Martin Turnell makes an intelligent one, asking, 'what in fact does the *Comédie humaine* "prove" or, to put it in another way, what does it do to us? Does it alter us? Does it modify our experience? I think the answer must be that it doesn't.' Surely the screw has been turned too far. As fathers, lovers, husbands enter and exit at speed through various doors one seems to be watching some vaudeville stage set. There is a feeling of Feydeau-like burlesque, which reminds us in turn of Balzac's interest in the theatre (and his affection for *Vautrin* of 1840). The whole edifice teeters on the comic, yet at the same time we read that Hulot's obsessed pursuit of women causes the death of his brother and all but kills his wife. The scene in which he is found in bed (evidently still a sexual athlete at seventy) with Valérie by her husband and the police is the stuff of farce. Too, the deaths of both Valérie and Crevel (we now know) were intended to be broadly 'comic', in the same vein as our conclusive sight of convulsive old Hulot being caught by his wife fumbling the kitchen wench. The comic technique, in short, seems seriously to detract from any sense of social tragedy. One cannot really believe in this panting pack of buffoons. How is this author a 'visionary'?

It is very possible that it helps to be a woman to answer these objections. The sexual chase in which men so stertorously indulge does strike her at times as fatuously comic, and turns men into Bergsonian *'pantins'*, or little strutting puppets of humour. This is not only true of the mediaeval period, but of the present – 'I have known of schoolgirls going through the "lovers' lane" in the Luxembourg Gardens expressly to have a laugh', writes de Beauvoir.[24] The sense of melodrama is there, all right, even if fictionally it does make a rousing break with the polite tradition, in France, of the hermetically sealed domestic novel (and finds itself so repudiated by Gide). Maurice Blanchot writes of Balzac that 'The *idée fixe* takes possession of words and extracts from them a series of images which lead to a veritable hallucinatory dance.'

[24] De Beauvoir, p. 330.

98

In an urban civilization of male money values love becomes lust-barter, and it is as impossible to be sexually successful *and* honest as it is to be financially the same (Grandet remarked that to go bankrupt was the most dishonourable thing in life – and he stood for a class is saying so). In the final analysis *Bette* is more about Hulot than herself, and we come to believe in Hulot with an odd degree of consensus when one takes into account his lack of verisimilitude on the "realistic" plane. Indeed, it is quite remarkable how Balzac holds the reader throughout, despite the kitsch.

And despite, too, the backdrop of city life in which he was less at ease than he was with the provinces. A countryman like Flaubert, he could locate his excessive temperaments well enough in the rural scene; but here he is handicapped by the narrow teeming streets of pre-Haussmann Paris and the cluttered rooms of an over-furnished era. The grip he holds on us, then, must spring from deep social perceptions, from, in fact, precisely what he says he is out to study, a sort of zoology of the human ape: 'It is the principle of animal life that each creature should borrow its external form, or, to speak more exactly, the differences of its form, from the environment in which it is destined to become developed. The zoological species result from these differences.' Balzac wanted to know what made men and women tick. In particular, the latter. *205/88*

Balzac – of all people! – is not going to be held up here as a little father of feminism. But he did make some radical insights in the field. He attacked Scott for the falsity of his women characters and, in someone like Valérie Marneffe who he said was a successor to Madame de Merteuil, he shows us woman fighting man as sexual object, without rest and without mercy.

Balzac suggested, too, that married women who took lovers *with* the connivance of their husbands, like Valérie, were thereby the most powerful contenders in the lists of sexual politics, since they had doubly broken the constancy of 'love' as a cultural concept. We note that Valérie, a true virago figure, pretends repeatedly to be just a poor weak little woman, a nothing thing. What does this so-called constancy comprise?

Balzac defined it as the 'genius of love'. Again, woman was involved in a continual aesthetic task. And this task, one of achieving some sort of balance in the tensions and anxieties of daily (and nightly) life, was tremendously demanding – cripplingly so, as we see in Ibsen. Our society has placed immense psychological demands on woman – to be wife, mistress, companion in a matter of hours. One thinks of the famous good-bad syndrome imposed on the American wife, having to perch on her pedestal and lie on her back, and pressured into abnormal anxieties by her advertising in both poses. The resolution of such cruelly conflicting demands was thus analogous for Balzac to some artistic task:

'Love, which is both a great folly and the austere joy of great souls, and pleasure, which is sold in the market-place, are two different aspects of the same fact. The woman able to satisfy these two contrasted demands is as rare as a great general, writer, artist, or inventor.'

Elsewhere Balzac wrote:

'Many men want two editions of the same work, though it is an immense sign of a man's inferiority if he is unable to make a mistress of his wife. Variety is a mark of impotence. Constancy is always the genius of love, revealing the true power of a poet.'

So Balzac is not advocating the role of courtesan in Valérie Marneffe. He simply shows her case, on the road to female liberty. Edward James Oliver writes, 'there is more than one sort of morality in his work – and this is surely the reason why his comments are not more resented, for they are not a set of prejudices or principles imposed on life without reference to particular cases: they arise from those cases, and came from the same inspiration in his own mind.'[25]

There were many other insights Balzac developed on the side, in this respect. His interest in the early *roman policier*, doubtless

[25] E. J. Oliver, *Honoré de Balzac*, New York: Macmillan, 1964, p. 145; London: Weidenfeld and Nicholson, 1966.

partly responsible for much of his melodrama, led him to feel
that the vicious are more charming than the virtuous. Everyone
seems to like or implicitly pardon the despicably enslaved Hulot
in *Bette*. In common with a criminal, that is, a woman is often
forced to please more, put out more, than she really feels, thus
involving herself in constant dissimulation, or *maquillage*, of her
true feelings.

Then Balzac may have been unduly influenced by his religion,
as in his evidently serious theory that virgin natures somehow
conserve psychological energy and can therefore prove highly
vital. Bette plots and plans the ruin of the Hulots with a devotion
of hatred that is like a little obsessive religion in itself. But it
would be a coarse reaction to conclude that Balzac is merely
making a clarion call for feminine revenge in Bette. What he is
really showing is that in a balanced society all her vitality could
have been used for good.

But his society was not yet ready for their Hedda Gablers.
Though Tolstoy was repelled by Ibsen, Thomas Hardy (whom
the Russian master admired) went twice to *Hedda Gabler* in the
1890s, and the play's sympathy for woman even won over James.
'Self-realization', Ibsen wrote, 'is man's highest task and greatest
happiness.' In his new biography of Ibsen Michael Meyer adds,
'One of the greatest tragedies of women, he thought, was that
their will-power tended to remain undeveloped.'[26] But Ibsen put
beside his Hedda the passive, 'feminine' Thea and, in the words
of Maurice Valency, 'The difference between the two aspects of
womanhood could not be more emphatically demonstrated.
Hedda cannot help a man create, either biologically or intellec-
tually, because, with relation to the man, she desires to arrogate
the masculine role to herself.'[27]

This is neither self-realization nor equality in the truest sense.
Hedda's limited freedom as a woman is endangered by the Judge's
knowledge; he has initiated sexual power over her and she will

[26] Michael Meyer, *Ibsen: A Biography*, New York: Doubleday, 1971,
p. 665.
[27] Maurice Valency, *The Flower and the Castle*, New York: Macmillan,
1963, p. 201.

kill herself rather than submit. But with Anna, Emma, and the tragic list of those 'great abnormals' of the nineteenth century, women who would die rather than give in, Hedda commits suicide for a larger frustration than the simply sexual (the suburban charade Claire Bloom made of this play, under the direction of Patrick Garland, hurt Ibsen's message as much the fatal-woman interpretations of an earlier generation). All these women had great creative powers which in a man's world they could not express. So in a way Balzac was a 'visionary' in *Bette*, making his fiction serve Byron's words in *Don Juan*:

> Man's love is of man's life a thing apart,
>   'Tis woman's whole existence; man may range
> The court, camp, church, the vessel, and the mart;
>   Sword, gown, gain, glory, offer in exchange
> Pride, fame, ambition, to fill up his heart,
>   And few there are whom these cannot estrange;
> Men have all these resources, we but one,
> To love again, and be again undone (Canto I, 194).

> Alas! the love of women! it is known
>   To be a lovely and a fearful thing;
> For all of theirs upon that die is thrown,
>   And if 'tis lost, life hath no more to bring
> To them but mockeries of the past alone,
>   And their revenge is as the tiger's spring,
> Deadly, and quick, and crushing; yet, as real
> Torture is theirs, what they inflict they feel.
>   (Canto II, 199)

3

JANE EYRE

With A Commencement on Catherine Earnshaw:
Beyond Biology

'I would fain have the Conduct of my Sex a little Regulated in this
particular, which is the Thing in which of all the parts of Life,
I think at this Time we suffer most in: Tis nothing but lack of
Courage, the fear of not being Marry'd at all, and of that frightful
State of Life, call'd *an old Maid.*'
Defoe, *Moll Flanders*

The world of the Brontë sisters is often described as a male
universe. Both Emily and Charlotte felt driven to write fictions
which have to do with the engagement of feminine passion –
spiritual in one, sexual in another – with men. Both males were
similar, mysterious and morose Byronic heroes, brooding and
apart. Both sisters wrote fantasy juvenilia that could serve as
textbooks for contemporary analysts; both were brought up,
we know, in a Yorkshire parsonage where father and brother
alike seem to have been of the stuff of Grade 'Z' Hollywood
melodrama, the latter drinking and doping himself while the
former lectured his young on the sexual differences when he
wasn't burning his daughters' favourite shoes or writing poetry
upstairs. Both sisters explored the taboo.

This is essential to recognize from the start since taboo unites
the unspoken, the unspeakable, the holy and obscene. It is where,
in a phrase from Kenneth Burke, 'scatology and eschatology
overlap'. Much of Swift's ridicule was in this vein. Marx cited
the 'holy' excrement of the Dalai Lamas. Publishers know that
blasphemy and obscenity are twin offenders, or have often been
so considered, in the censorship courts.

A reminder of this relationship should take us closer to, rather than farther from, Charlotte Brontë's *Jane Eyre*. How else explain the extraordinary attacks on the irreligion of a book which seems, at first sight, to defer to Christian values at every point, with Charlotte herself remarking primly of her Gothic hero Rochester, 'He is taught the severe lessons of experience and has sense to learn wisdom from them'?[1]

Though Charlotte told George Henry Lewes (George Eliot's personal Rochester) that *Jane Eyre* 'finally found acceptance',[2] the atrabilious attack by Elizabeth Rigby (later Lady Eastlake) of the time was directed at the book's heathenish nature:

'This, to our view, is the great and crying mischief of the book. Jane Eyre is throughout the personification of an unregenerate and undisciplined spirit, the more dangerous to exhibit from that prestige of principle and self-control which is liable to dazzle the eye too much for it to observe the inefficient and unsound foundation on which it rests. It is true Jane does right, and exerts great moral strength, but it is the strength of a mere heathen mind which is a law unto itself.'

Jane Eyre a heathen? Why, in an early poem Charlotte actually pictured herself as a missionary to infidels and has Jane Eyre so tempted after flight from Rochester! There is much of an admirable book devoted to the discovery of religion as a theme throughout *Jane Eyre*.[3] The offence is other, and it is rank.

Charlotte – and, to an extent, Emily – offended against the male world ('a law unto itself'), and man ruled both sex and religion. Richard Chase caught this well in an article on mythic pattern in the novels of the Brontë sisters, for here Chase's

[1] Letter to W. S. Williams, 14 August 1848; in: *The Brontës: Life and Letters*, Edited by Clement Shorter, vol. I, London: Hodder and Stoughton, 1908.

[2] Letter to George Henry Lewes, 6 November 1847, *Ibid*.

[3] Robert Bernard Martin, *The Accents of Persuasion: Charlotte Brontë's Novels*, London: Faber & Faber, 1966.

particular critical approach, at times limited, proved a fine instrument for getting at meaning.[4] He takes Rebecca West's analysis of inferiority in Charlotte much further, claims that 'the Brontë novels are concerned with the neuroses of women in a man's society', and roundly affirms, 'obviously *Jane Eyre* is a feminist tract'. It is. Yet it is one of extraordinary psycho-sexual sophistication.

Chase points out, what is immediately evident, that 'the sisters came to admire and fear most: sexual and intellectual energy'. *Jane Eyre* and *Wuthering Heights* he sees as embodying this libidinal force. Of Helen Burns in the former, whose death was founded (according to Mrs Gaskell) on that of Charlotte's elder sister Maria, Chase points out that 'the impalpable principle of life and thought' that the fictional schoolgirl mentions is indeed sexual energy – and masculine sexual energy at that. A power struggle results in both books. Both writers symbolically geld their heroes.

As a matter of fact, in Charlotte's redaction of the myth, Rochester loses his hand which, at a crucial moment in the relationship, Jane surely feels, without too much equivocation, as a surrogate penis ('a hand of fiery iron grasped my vitals'). In another part she sees a hand coming through a cloud in the sky. So sex and religion can be said to cohabit in her fantasies clearly enough. In any event, the hand has to come off and, as Chase nicely puts it, 'The tempo and energy of the universe can be quelled, we see, by a patient, practical woman.'

If Emily was not quite so 'practical', she too can be enlisted on the side of the angels in the feminist debate. Before proceeding, therefore, to an analysis of her sister Charlotte's remarkable investigation of a woman's psyche, let us glance briefly at *Wuthering Heights*.

*　　*　　*

[4] See: Richard Chase, 'The Brontës, or Myth Domesticated', in *Forms of Modern Fiction*, Edited by William V. O'Connor, University of Minnesota Press, 1948.

Today, we are told, artificial reproduction, fertility control, cybernation are 'just around the corner'. Even parthenogenesis (virgin birth) then becomes a possibility. Test-tube babies, the artificial placenta, insemination and inovulation will soon alter the barbarisms of present human reproduction, and make for an altogether other balance between our sexes. The latest trend, at present writing, in this aspect of our brave new world appears to be thoroughly Huxleyian – 'clonal reproduction'. This form of asexual child manufacture seems well on the way, according to one of its (parthenogenetic?) foster parents, Nobel Laureate James D. Watson of Harvard, discoverer of the 'double helix'. Frogs can now be made to reproduce asexually, why not us? 'A human being – born of clonal reproduction – most likely will appear on the earth within the next twenty to fifty years.'[5] Doubtless, other scientific wonders of the kind will ensue.

Would Emily Brontë, who never bore a child and had her principal heroine die in childbirth (or 'two hours after'), still have written her one great fictional work, *Wuthering Heights*, in such knowledge? She would, indeed, since her superb prose poem is generally an investigation into being, probably the only ontological novel of consequence in the English language. Sir Herbert Read called it the closest thing in English to Baudelaire ... which is presumably to take Baudelaire as a great moral investigator, concerned with man's relationship to what we deem, in its widest sense, nature.

Emily Brontë demanded to know what human existence meant. Our freedom depends on certain recognitions of reality and our use of placentae, clitoral orgasms, test-tube and/or adopted babies and the like depends on cultural absolutes, which in turn reflect our view of the universe. Emily herself may have felt chiefly responsible to 'the God within her breast'. For our analysis that scarcely matters. Neither Christian nor Marxist sees anarchy or madness as freedom, and the tale told by *Wuthering*

[5] See: James D. Watson, 'The Future of Asexual Reproduction', *Intellectual Digest*, II: 2 October 1971, pp. 69–74 (originally presented as a paper at a meeting of the Panel on Science and Technology, Committee on Science and Astronautics, U.S. House of Representatives).

Heights is of that existence itself which is the locus for our freedoms. In this sense the book is not so much asexual as pre-sexual.

She was certainly a strange woman, this pale consumptive who could, according to her sister Charlotte, beat her pet bulldog to bits with her fists. The famous fantasy world of Gondal she created as a girl, and which helps explain much of her poetry, was dominated by a *femme fatale*, Augusta, who ruthlessly reduced husbands, lovers and male children, though such is true of many a girl's early fantasies (as witness the Sheena and Super-girl comic-books, to say nothing of Barbarella). Perhaps, in her day-dreams, Emily became a man because she could not be a man; this has been suggested. Mrs Gaskell thought her like a man, while the Belgian schoolmaster M. Heger was explicit – 'She should have been a man'. In a long analysis of her poems, published in *Notable Images of Virtue*, the poet C. Day Lewis claims that she evinced 'a boy's values, rather than a girl's'. He summarizes as follows:

'She wanted liberty. Well, didn't she have it? A reasonably satisfactory home-life, a most satisfactory dream-life – why, then, all this beating of wings? What was this cage, invisible to us, which she felt herself to be confined in? "In the midst of her life," wrote A. C. Benson, "which she loved in every smallest detail, she was haunted, it seems, by a sense of rebellion at her limitations." And of Heathcliff, into whom Emily Brontë, hardly knowing what she did, packed all the darker side of her nature, Miss Ratchford says, "Heathcliff's life went out, not of bodily illness, but of the constant beating of his spirit against the limitation of material existence."

My own belief is that the source of Emily Brontë's proud recalcitrance, her preoccupation with themes of captivity, exile and freedom, was her sex, the limitation of not being a man.'

It is all too easy to discern, in the current wave of feminist revolt, a considerable content of class jealousy at having been born, as it were, on the wrong side of the sexual tracks. Charlotte described Emily's nature as 'Stronger than a man, simpler than a child'.

But *Wuthering Heights* bears no mark of that limitation to which Day Lewis refers. It dares to deal with the whole of that social and psychological bed in which science was to plant its apple-tree of knowledge. It is surely correct to describe it, therefore, as about 'the impersonal essence of personal existence' (Clifford Collins). The same critic goes on to remark that 'The love of Catherine and Heathcliff may be described as a life-force relationship, a principle that is not conditioned by anything but itself.' Too much American feminist reform is recording itself as *What's in it for me?* Emily Brontë declined the vulgarity of some bitter diatribe against the received fact of being a woman. She probed more generously, and far deeper . . . into the persistence of being itself.

* * *

By saying that Emily asks the ultimate questions, we mean just that. Sex may be a polar antithesis, as skin colour has been forced to become in the United States of America (occasioning all sorts of difficulties of translation when the blushing or paling of someone defined as a Libyan in a French text has to be rendered in Americanese). Neither is as antithetical as life and death. People have changed their sexes. No one has been proved immortal. Nor is this to be frivolous. As Lord David Cecil simply puts it of Emily, 'She believes in the immortality of the soul.'

Before examining just what this means, we must further contextualize Emily Brontë's vision; to do so will also help us understand Jane Eyre. For Lord David this concern on Emily's part makes *Wuthering Heights* a different *kind* of novel from any written in the English language, and possibly even outside it (de Beauvoir's linking of the novel with Dostoevsky is itself significant) – 'Like Blake, Emily Brontë is concerned solely with those primary aspects of life which are unaffected by time and place.' Also, one might add, by sex. This may not add to her literary excellence, but it must make her interesting to a feminist. Each new film version of *Wuthering Heights* treats it as a great love story. Which it is not. In essence it has little to do with what the cinema-going public calls 'sex' at all.

In the perusal of nearly every extended criticism of consequence affected on this work I must at some point or another have come across citation of the famous 'I *am* Heathcliff' speech, or otherwise Heathcliff's own final apostrophe, almost equally ubiquitous, 'Last night, I was on the threshold of hell. To-day, I am within sight of my heaven.' In short, high attention has been paid to the hyperbolic passages of the book, those in which the writing attains great heights (it is forgotten how pedestrian some of the exposition on the Linton side of the ledger becomes).

Hence one can say that a consensus of scholars have felt what one might broadly call the 'poetic' part of the novel to contain the real core of the book. So much so that matters of verisimilitude get overlooked. After all, the social painting is extremely vague in comparison with *Bovary* or Balzac. The symmetry of the pedigree has been frequently remarked upon, and may indeed serve symbolically (as in the hint of incest), but it is artificial, and looks so when set out:

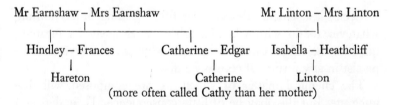

Similarly, the overhearing by Nelly Dean, also much commented on, is broadly 'conventional' – it has been estimated that only a tenth of the whole is direct narration by the supposed narrator, Lockwood!

Then the vampiric element, coarsely obvious today yet never really intelligently 'placed' in criticism to date, seems like a sop to contemporaneity, Gondal, and the now done-to-death 'Gothic' tradition. All these threads are important, and imaginatively functional, but unlike Richardson Emily did not write to sell (nor even, really, to please) and they are subordinate to the extra-ordinary driving force of the whole book's question, impelled as this well may have been by 'the limitation of not being a man'. What was this question?

In *Early Victorian Novelists* Lord David has answered it well. But his essay was written in the thirties and, though re-edited last in 1962, has been little advanced. Today, in the light of a new resurgence of radical feminism, he might have pushed it further. For Catherine Earnshaw is yearning for no less than an end to all human antinomies, one of the chief of which is sex. Cecil puts it thus:

'She believes in the immortality of the soul. If the individual life be the expression of a spiritual principle, it is clear that the mere dissolution of its fleshly integument will not destroy it. But she does more than believe in the immortality of the soul in the orthodox Christian sense. She believes in the immortality of the soul *in this world*. The spiritual principle of which the soul is a manifestation is active in this life: therefore, the disembodied soul continues to be active in this life. Its ruling preoccupations remain the same after death as before.'

Cecil's last sentence deserves careful re-reading. It has nothing whatever to do with Christian ghost stories, yet its meaning qualifies the effects of our behaviour while we are alive. Do we persist in any form? Of course we do.

The chemical matter of which we are composed will dis-integrate. But this may be of little consequence. To understand what Emily Brontë was saying in *Wuthering Heights* it can be helpful to have read some Japanese literature, even to have seen the better Japanese cinema wherein the dead remain decorously *present*. The more vital among us surely do persist as 'influences', and if we go through life on a persistent diet of hatred (even when such is rechristened 'revolution') we shall indeed 'remain the same after death as before'. Dead people pass through our minds with equal intensity to, and frequently greater wholeness than, their living simulacra.

In the case of Emily Brontë the supernatural is not the *after*-world. At least, it is misleading to equate it with such. It is, rather, the *with*world. Further existence of the species is a law under which we live. 'It is, in truth', Lord David writes, 'misleading to call it supernatural: it is a natural feature of the world as she sees it.' And it has considerable effect on our moral selves, here and now.

In this regard, one observes that throughout the book the Christian accounting for an afterlife (as such underlies the work of her sisters, Charlotte and Anne) is extremely unsatisfactory, to say the least. 'I shall not be at peace', moans the dying Catherine, her heart beating 'visibly and audibly' (for Nelly Dean). We note that in her famous dream she went to heaven but was forcibly flung out by the angels there. 'If I were in heaven, Nelly, I should be extremely miserable', she confesses, adding:

> 'I was only going to say that heaven did not seem to be my home; and that I broke my heart with weeping to come back to earth; and the angels were so angry that they flung me out, into the middle of the heath on the top of Wuthering Heights; where I woke sobbing for joy.'

Sobbing for *joy*. This, she maintains, is her 'secret', and if it has little to do with Christianity – it is, if anything, anti-Christian – it has even less consort with the presently fashionable interest in ESP (extra-sensory perception). Catherine Earnshaw simply believes that some vitality persists, and that a recognition of this could be the most successful revolution against social forms, and biological classes, imaginable. It would make us responsible for a full liberty of the race.

Heathcliff too comes to this recognition, 'that the dead are not annihilated' as he puts it just before he dies. It is even something of a pity that an appanage of the vampire merges into and thematically beclouds his end, since it distracts the reader from the joy and terror of his understanding:

> 'No minister need come; nor need anything be said over me. I tell you, I have nearly attained *my* heaven; and that of others is altogether unvalued and uncoveted by me!'

Joseph, the simpleton servant so done to death in fiction since, is a bumbling parody of North Country evangelism and, but for Catherine's bookish husband, the principal representative of received Christianity in the book. Heathcliff, of course, has no *Christian* name, Catherine is buried closer to the moor than the kirk, and so on. No, Emily Brontë's supernatural is hardly that of the plaster saints. Her 'hereafter' can scarcely be called such by characters of the order of Catherine and Heathcliff since both have seen the vision . . . that living includes persistence of being.

We have said that this vision is compounded of terror. It is. Catherine's husband Edgar Linton represents conventional sexual 'love' in so far as such raises its head at all in the book. A lot of store has been set by her comment that she loves 'the ground under his feet, and the air over his head, and everything he touches and every word he says'.[6] So she does, but Mary Visick who, in her *The Genesis of 'Wuthering Heights'*, opposes Cecil's view (or, at least, the primacy of its import for the author), lets slip a revealing phrase. She writes: 'Catherine loves her husband for the plain reason she gives Nelly; he is young and attractive, he is the first gentleman of the neighbourhood. . . .' Precisely. She marries him for the same reason that Toni Buddenbrook marries Grünlich, out of social duty and so that she can get a parental pat on the back. You can call this 'romantic sexual love', but if you do so, you are by implication saying quite a bit about the society which elevates this smoke-screen of emotion into 'romance', and a good deal more about woman's role in it.[7]

[6] Even here, we note, Catherine puts her feelings into the metaphors of persistent nature. Her own physiognomy is frequently described as such, e.g. 'Catherine's face was just like the landscape' (Chapter XXVII).

[7] To complete the critical picture fairly we should add that Miss Visick is representative of others who simply see conflicting forms of 'love' in Heathcliff and Edgar (as it might be in Rodolphe and Léon, for Emma Bovary). In this view Heathcliff degenerates into a slatternly bully and the best that can be said is that 'Neither world is victorious over the other'. We feel far more persuaded by the pre-moral, asexual presentation of Lord David Cecil, and that Catherine has another order of emotion altogether for Heathcliff. It is once more a matter of kind, rather than degree. The 1939 Wyler movie takes the Visick view to complete distortion: here Heathcliff kills Catherine.

But yet Catherine can speak of Heathcliff as the same constant in her being even after she is carrying Edgar's child. (Similarly, we shall find Toni Buddenbrook baffled by her father when he supposes she had ever been in something called 'love' with the execrable Grünlich, a pivotal scene in Mann's epic destruction of the bourgeois family). That Catherine knows the terror of her realization, how alien it is to what society calls love, is simply there in the 'I *am* Heathcliff' speech. At the risk of supererogation, let us quote it here again, for its language attains great heights: the tone is at first one of puzzled surprise, as though Catherine were talking to some dull-witted schoolchild who had been babbling something about her being separated from Heathcliff should she marry Edgar – 'Who is to separate us, pray?' Certainly not God. She goes on:

'I cannot express it; but surely you and everybody have a notion that there is, or should be, an existence of yours beyond you. What were the use of my creation if I were entirely contained here? My great miseries in this world have been Heathcliff's miseries, and I watched and felt each from the beginning; my great thought in living is himself. If all else perished, and *he* remained, I should still continue to be; and, if all else remained, and he were annihilated, the Universe would turn to a mighty stranger. I should not seem a part of it. My love for Linton is like the foliage in the woods. Time will change it, I'm well aware, as winter changes the trees. My love for Heathcliff resembles the eternal rocks beneath – a source of little visible delight, but necessary. Nelly, I *am* Heathcliff – he's always, always in my mind – not as a pleasure, any more than I am always a pleasure to myself – but as my own being – so, don't talk of our separation again – it is impracticable. . . .'

Spoken, or perhaps panted, of the young Laurence Olivier in the Wyler movie of the novel, these words sounded like the acme of romanticism. The irony is they are the reverse. The tone may be ecstatic but that is because deep truth often is a dreadful joy. Heathcliff is not a 'pleasure' to her . . . he *is* her. They together inhabit another level of existence, one in which there is no marrying nor giving in marriage. To resort once more to Lord David, here making unacknowledged equivalence with Wordsworth:

'Emily Brontë does not see animate man revealed against inanimate nature, as Mrs Gaskell does. She does not even see suffering, pitiful, individual man in conflict with unfeeling, impersonal, ruthless natural forces, like Hardy. Men and nature to her are equally living and in the same way. To her an angry man and an angry sky are not just metaphorically alike, they are actually alike in kind; different manifestations of a single spiritual reality.'

Unlike Jane Austen, Emily Brontë had no interest in constructing conduct in a viable, Christian society – and even Charlotte seems to have been lukewarm to Austen. In truth, there is really no sex in Emily's book at all, least of all between Catherine and Heathcliff who are brought up as brother and sister and who both marry siblings. In the one scene of passion in the book – the parting, conveniently witnessed by Nelly Dean – Heathcliff shows little male interest in Cathy at all. The important thing for him is that she is a force that is dying in the sense of disappearing from physical view. He is jealous of her essence being removed from the sensory world; and so when she is physically taken from him he is as much interested in her 'absence', at the end, as in her real self when living.

Sex, in sum, is a less divisive antithesis than that between life and death. Sir Herbert Read sees Emily as a sort of hermaphrodite.[8] But if we could grope, even dimly, towards some unity behind this our greatest human antinomy and conflict then we

[8] 'In the case of Emily the same causes produced a "masculine protest"' of a more complex kind, showing, indeed, the typical features of what I think we must, with the psycho-analyst, regard as some kind of psychical hermaphroditism. The outward expression of this state was evident enough. In her childhood the villagers thought her more like a boy than a girl.' Read's essay, 'Charlotte and Emily Brontë', was first published in *The Yale Review* for July 1925, and then reprinted in the same author's *Reason and Romanticism* of the following year.

might put ourselves in touch with elemental forces we seldom sense in our world of rigid right and wrong. We should partake of that 'infinite calm' which Nelly Dean sensed as she gazed at the dead Catherine. The vision is beyond biology, indeed.

In all the writings we have perused on this beautiful book no single case seems to have much remarked, let alone seen as primarily significant, that Catherine Earnshaw dies in childbirth. Sex kills her. And social custom. She marries, yes, 'the first gentleman of the neighbourhood', and directly she dies Nelly Dean reflects what hard luck it was on Edgar to have been left without an heir! 'The latter's distraction at his bereavement is a subject too painful to be dwelt on; its after effects showed how deep the sorrow sunk. A great addition, in my eyes, was his being left without an heir.' Too bad. The wife has died, the while.

Of Edgar we read explicitly, '*He* didn't pray for Catherine's soul to haunt him.' In the light of all this textual evidence it is thus extremely difficult to share Miss Visick's views. Heathcliff's is not simply another sort of 'love', the romantic kind, it is beyond love, asexual, pure of being . . . absolute. 'Every Linton on the face of the earth might melt into nothing, before I could consent to forsake Heathcliff', Catherine cries, and she does so 'with an accent of indignation'. She has had a vision of such total unity her mind has risen sheer above what the philosophers call classes, or sets.

* * *

We have ventured to suggest that the latter third of *Wuthering Heights* introduces vampiric elements which may weaken this vision of unity. Perhaps they need not do so. After all, one cannot prove or disprove vampires and the whole point is that one cannot. Yet there comes a point where concession to a tradition weakens art.

At the end Heathcliff recounts, again to the ubiquitous Nelly Dean, how he had dug up Catherine's coffin and tried to take her in his arms again. Once more the writing takes on intensity as he recounts how his spade scraped the coffin and he wrestled with its lid. All this is perfectly conventional. Heathcliff is the male vampire (or addict) demonstrating withdrawal symptoms and requiring his draught of blood (or fix) – we note that he is after her the night she is buried. Catherine is one of the 'undead', too, the vampire being traditionally the progenitor (by infection) of other vampires. 'If she be cold, I'll think it is this north wind that chills me; and if she be motionless, it is sleep.' And when he is confirmed in this belief, that she is neither dead nor alive yet continuing to exist, he stops:

> 'There was another sigh, close at my ear. I appeared to feel the warm breath of it displacing the sleet-laden wind. I knew no living thing in flesh and blood was by; but as certainly as you can perceive the approach to some substantial body in the dark, though it cannot be discerned, so certainly I felt that Cathy was there, not under me, but on the earth.'

Since both Emily and Charlotte give pronounced vampiric overtones to their major novels, we may pause at this point to touch on that delightfully dishonourable ancestry in European lore and legend the vampire has enjoyed, notably in Hungary, as epitomized in the case of Arnold Paul, or Pavlé, a *Heyduck*, who was finally killed in a road accident in 1727.[9] It is a considerable pity that, on one hand, popular prejudice associates vampirism with Bram Stoker's *Dracula* of 1897 and students of literature look to Montague Summers's *The Vampire*. We need a better study.[10]

Initially, the vampire was of course a man, an incubus before a succubus, and the superstition so obviously necrosadistic and haematomaniac as to be an archetype; it is indeed so considered in Ernest Jones's *On The Nightmare*. Summers himself scarcely has to suggest that 'It has been recognized by medico-psycho-

[9] 'About 1732, the affair of vampirism made a great noise in the Austrian states: and the report resounded through Europe. Report affirmed that this Hungarian had been, when living, sucked by a vampire; consequently he began to suck in his turn the inhabitants of the town.' From: 'On Vampires and Vampirism', *New Monthly Magazine and Universal Registrar* (London, 1820), vol. XII, p. 551.

[10] My student, Miss Diane Hecht, has to an extent repaired the omission in a Columbia University doctoral dissertation, but has not felt inclined to publish as yet.

logists that there exists a definite connection between fascination
for blood and sexual excitement . . . the impulse to bite is also
part of the tactile element that lies at the origins of kissing.'[11]
Continuing fascination with vampirism, especially in the American
technology (where some vampiric movie seems to be a perennial
of the cheaper circuit houses), lies deeper: today its sympto-
matology appears in almost every way an index of addiction – it
is hardly necessary to point out the attentions given to the
legend by Coleridge, Poe and Baudelaire – while its altered
tradition is a veritable retrospect of feminine emancipation.

Indeed, Professor Arthur Nethercot calls Southey's 'Thalaba',
whose vampiric passages fascinated Coleridge, 'the first introduction of a vampire into English literature',[12] correcting Summers
who would see John William Polidori's novella *The Vampyre*
as such. The latter tale, sensationally influential, was thought to
be by Byron when first published in the *New Monthly Magazine*
of April 1819, and so accepted by Goethe, whose *Die Braut von
Korinth*, of 1797, Mario Praz calls 'the first to give literary form
to the fearsome vampire legends which had arisen in Illyria in
the eighteenth century'.[13] The point for us here is that Polidori's
hero was a man, an east-European libertine with the name of
Lord Ruthven. Though he may have begun 'Christabel' in 1798
(after reading Goethe's poem), Coleridge undoubtedly responded
to the female, and indeed feminist, version shown by Southey
to create his Geraldine of 'Christabel', as well as, to some extent,
another addiction poem 'The Pains of Sleep'. He thus changes the
direction to be continued in Thomas Prescott Prest's immensely
popular, and perfectly preposterous, *Varney, the Vampire* of 1847.

Heathcliff is of course the male of the tradition, a true obsessed
alienate. As Northrop Frye has put it:

'Obsession takes the form of an unconditioned will that

[11] Montague Summers, *The Vampire*, New Hyde Park, New York:
University Books, 1960, pp. 184–5.

[12] Arthur H. Nethercot, *The Road to Tryermaine*, University of Chicago
Press, 1939, p. 71.

[13] Mario Praz, *The Romantic Agony*, Second Edition, translated by Angus
Davidson, Oxford University Press: 1951, p. 76.

drives its victims beyond the normal limits of humanity. One of the clearest examples is Heathcliff, who plunges through death into vampirism. . . .'[14]

Indeed, Heathcliff could stand in for some of the studies of haematomania given in Wilhelm Stekel's *Sadism and Masochism*. We note that his attractive pallor becomes a 'ghastly paleness' by the end, where we read further of his 'bloodless hue, and his teeth visible'. Nelly Dean muses, 'Is he a ghoul, or a vampire?' Finally, he is perfectly bloodless, and thus drained of all energy – 'I could not think him dead, but his face and throat were wreathed with rain; the bedclothes dripped, and he was perfectly still. The lattice, flapping to and fro, had grazed one hand that rested on the sill; no blood trickled from the broken skin. . . .' His eyes will not shut and Nelly notices in particular his 'sharp, white teeth', the fangs conventionally strong in order to sink well into the jugular, where the soul resided. Case 48 of Stekel's study features a young grave-digger who drank his own semen, plus his mother's urine, and began to dig up the corpses of women in order to suck any available fluids from them. Dr Stekel explains the case as having been caused by strongly incestuous wishes.

The classic compendium of vampirism, drawn on by nearly all writers interested in the subject, is probably that of a Benedictine Biblical scholar, possessed of a vast library in the field, Dom Augustin Calmet, who published his voluminous *Dissertations sur les Apparitions et sur les Revenans [sic] et Vampires* in 1747. It ran into several printings and was translated into English (though not too accurately). Put beside a 1910 study of Prosper Mérimée's 'La Guzla',[15] it suggests that what eventually

[14] Northrop Frye, *An Anatomy of Criticism: Four Essays*, Princeton University Press, 1957, p. 40.

[15] Vojislav Yovanovitch, '*La Guzla' de Prosper Mérimée; Les Origines du Livre – Ses Sources, sa Fortune – Etude d'Histoire Romantique*, Grenoble: Allier Frères, 1910. There are technical distinctions here: a *guzla* or *goule* is a revenant who feeds on the dead, a vampire on the living. But this distinction is blurred until quite late (see: Charles Nodier, *Contes fantastiques*, Paris: Charpentier, 1855, pp. 349 ff.).

happened to the vampiric tradition, as the nineteenth-century redactions let in women, notably in France, was that it turned back on itself and resurrected (in all senses) the succubus, the terror of the Church and against which the *Malleus Maleficarum* was largely directed.[16] The *vampira* molests sexually and closely threatens male supremacy (there has even been one analogy made to contemporary American wives sucking money out of males like semen). The meeting-place of all these elements can be seen in Alexandre Dumas *père*'s fantastic play, *Le Vampire*, which opened in Paris on 20 December 1851. Its title should have been plural for both vampire and vampira are let loose on a stage teeming with characters, scenes, and coincidences. A somewhat similar play appeared in London the next year. The female of the kind was firmly established.

As regards our analysis, can it be said that, while the male vampire is an analogue of the addict, the female vampire finds her kind in the feminist – in Catherine Earnshaw's longing to be a vampira, since Emily Brontë could not be a man? Look at the brilliantly Gothic opening. Lockwood is awoken by the tapping on his windowpane, breaks the glass and stretches his hand out to arrest what he supposes to be an 'importunate branch'. Instead – 'my fingers closed on the fingers of a little, ice-cold hand!' Bloodless and cold, Catherine is crying to get in to join her soul-mate. Secondly, after sneering at Edgar Linton's formal bourgeois qualities and background ('do you imagine I shall leave Catherine to his *duty* and *humanity*?'), Heathcliff rants – 'The moment her regard ceased, I would have torn his heart out, and drunk his blood!' There is more of the same.

The infection by Heathcliff is akin to that made by Rochester – scorn of convention, and what the world thinks. The material on which Emily Brontë here touches helps her advance her

---

[16] 'And what, then, is to be thought of those witches who, in this way, sometimes collect male organs in great numbers, as many as twenty or thirty members together, and put them in a bird's nest. . .?' From: *Malleus Maleficarum*, translated by the Reverend Montague Summers, London: John Rodker, 1928, p. 121.

myth on several levels. For the original vampire was undead – a thing. It had no sex. Even the witch-hunters of Holy Church could not imagine it as female – the succubus was a spirit, not a body – until the day when women could roam moors, and climb balconies, alone. Here again, then, Catherine and Heathcliff are asexual, bonded outcasts.

Charlotte's treatment was different, for her own purposes. Mrs Rochester is the vampira. Jane Eyre's first bedside vision of her causes her to think of 'the foul German spectre – the Vampyre', and when the latter bites her own brother Mason, the surgeon Carter remarks with surprise, 'This wound was not done with a knife: there have been teeth here?' Mason himself states explicitly, 'She sucked the blood: she said she'd drain my heart.' Later she goes for Rochester's throat, 'and laid her teeth to his cheek'.

Moreover, the vampiric elements could, in *Wuthering Heights*, be well accommodated in Christianity. In other words, Emily herself wanted to write about the so-called mystical. The second generation in her work are perfunctory and far less powerful. Yet one supposes she had Charlotte looking over her shoulder, and we know that Charlotte evidently thought Heathcliff a kind of devil figure, 'never once swerving in his arrow-straight course to perdition', and asked, 'Whether it is right or advisable to create beings like Heathcliff' (Editor's Preface to the New Edition), while she read the mild *The Tenant of Wildfell Hall*, by Anne or 'Acton', to be written 'as a warning to others' (Biographical Notice of Ellis and Acton Bell).

So the Christian devil identity is that foisted off on Heathcliff, the 'imp of Satan', by Nelly Dean. When Heathcliff is first brought back by Catherine's father from Liverpool, the latter remarks, 'it's as dark almost as if it came from the devil'. In common with Mrs Rochester in *Jane Eyre* Heathcliff is referred to in the neuter, an equivalent of 'the thing' – 'They entirely refused to have it in bed with them . . . so I put it on the landing of the stairs.' Heathcliff seems to be one of those 'black fiends', 'devil's spies', 'possessed of something diabolical', whose happiness lies 'in inflicting misery'. Nor should we let pass the detail that Heathcliff arrived instead of a whip (in truth, there is a whip-losing incident paralleled in *Bovary*). Asked what present she wanted her father to bring back from his visit to Liverpool, the young Cathy 'chose a whip'. And Cathy, 'when she learnt the master had lost her whip in attending on the stranger, showed her humour by grinning and spitting at the stupid little thing, earning for her pains a sound blow from her father to teach her cleaner manners.'

The devil identity – 'Is Mr Heathcliff a man? And if not, is he a devil?' – seems to be a control activity from the conscious side of Emily Brontë,[17] giving a nod to Christianity and thereby allowing generations of girls to misread her text, as a 'tempest in the soul' (the actual title of a critical essay of 1949), a story of 'perverted passion' (Charlotte again) and 'romantic' love which will always attract women in a male supremacy since it shows them as possessing a mysterious power over men of which they are presumed barely conscious themselves.

A rather natural temptation for woman, this notion in fact lays her open to masculine exploitation. For she is always the exception (she must feel), the Catherine Earnshaw or Jane Eyre who can rise above her class as a woman and make some gloriously eventuated exchange of herself with a man. We are far from deriding the feeling here. Something of it is there in Emily's story. But it is still not her story. Catherine is really not emotionally vulnerable at all. Consider her actions, her marriage to Edgar in the face of all she feels, and so forth.

The interested reader can best test it this way. The Edgar Linton-Nelly Dean axis of the story represents the rational, 'healthy' side. Or does it? Most critics find the Linton ledger awfully feeble. Surely a reader with any emotions at all finds them enlisted on the side of Heathcliff and Cathy, despite what the teller may tell. After all, who, among all the many critics, has strongly objected to the suggestion made by Joseph that Heathcliff may have murdered Hindley Earnshaw – 'un he

[17] The network of devil references and comment is well identified and interpreted in Philip Drew's 'Charlotte Brontë as a Critic of *Wuthering Heights*' *Nineteenth-Century Fiction*, XVIII, no. 4 (1964), pp. 365–81.

warn't deead when Aw left, nowt uh t'soart'? John K. Mathison puts our feeling fully, in an extended discussion of Nelly Dean's role in the story:

'In spite of all her fine qualities, nevertheless, she fails to understand the other characters and, more important, fails in her behavior in important crises of the action. From the emphasis on her admirable qualities, and from her final inadequacy, the reader is led to see that the insight of the normal, wholesome person cannot penetrate into all feelings justly.'

Quite so. The consequence of the tone, of the metaphorical organization, is to put us on the side of the vision rather than the actuality. The bloody expulsion of Isabella from the Heights – having been sent sprawling in Hindley's blood, she passes Hareton on her way out hanging puppies off a chair – scarcely seems to repel anyone, in our experience, as the facts (the beating of a defenceless woman) rightly should.

Heathcliff is a character who thrives on pain, *'der Geist der stets verneint'* ('I grind with greater energy, in proportion to the increase of pain'). But he is the effect of a cause: given at least three thrashings a week by Hindley as a boy (till his arm is 'black to the shoulder'), struck with iron weights and the like, the boy is persuaded not to reveal this persecution to old Earnshaw 'through a policy of expediency' (Mathison). And Nelly Dean herself is considerably responsible for this.

In other words, Heathcliff is brutalized by the supposedly refined or civilized class in the book, and when he takes his revenge upon it we applaud. He is attacking a hypocritical social code. By the end of the book he has parodied 'polite' society, the Heights eventually housing a tyrannical Dracula (in himself), a slut-like 'maid' (Zillah), a half-crazed religious clod (Joseph), an idiot boy (Hareton), and a drooling alcoholic (Hindley). The kailyaird school of fiction never improved the picture.

Thus Emily Brontë's contribution to feminism was subtle and indirect. It was not polemical. Her sister Charlotte was to deal with the immediate social injustices (*Jane Eyre* is rooted in the early realistic school scenes). The errand of Emily's work was to help us understand love, particularly that part of it which is extra-sexual reciprocity, mutual giving. Even Nelly Dean saw a 'selfishness' in Edgar Linton's 'love' for his new-won bride.

A good place to check this out is the catechism Nelly subjects Catherine to after the latter has revealed Edgar's proposal (Chapter IX) – note the many uses and misuses of the word *love*:

> ' "Why do you love him, Miss Cathy?"
> "Nonsense, I do – that's sufficient."
> "By no means; you must say why."
> "Well, because he is handsome, and pleasant to be with."
> "Bad," was my commentary.
> "And because he is young and cheerful."
> "Bad, still."
> "And because he loves me."
> "Indifferent, coming there."
> "And he will be rich, and I shall like to be the greatest woman of the neighbourhood, and I shall be proud of having a husband."
> "Worst of all! And now, say how you love him."
> "As everybody loves – You're silly, Nelly."
> "Not at all – Answer."
> "I love the ground under his feet, and the air over his head, and everything he touches, and every word he says – I love all his looks, and all his actions, and him entirely, and altogether. There now!"
> "And why?" '

Catherine is parroting received male social values. The girl of the manor marries someone who is 'handsome, and pleasant to be with' and 'young and cheerful' too. What a mockery of a woman's heart, sealed with the 'greatest woman of the neighbourhood' reference. And we perceive that, coming where it does, the passage about loving the ground under Edgar's feet, on which Miss Visick sets much store, is so much social babble to stop Nelly's questioning, and probing of something that lies almost too deep.

'In truth', writes Miss Visick, 'when Catherine chooses Edgar rather than Heathcliff she is choosing the ordinary satisfactions of life.' Indeed. And 'the ordinary satisfactions of life', as dictated by *Kinder-Kirche-Küche* requirements, have absolutely nothing to do with that life of the imagination Catherine Earnshaw, and generations of similar women, hunger for. How many girls since have had to drink to the dregs the bitter lees of marrying to gratify parental wishes? Catherine doesn't choose Edgar. Her society does.

Alongside Tony Buddenbrook to come, Catherine Earnshaw knows that such a 'choice' has nothing in common with that activity of the being in which all antinomies are resolved. The very shock she caused on publication of the book should be convincing enough evidence of the frontal nature of her assault on male strongholds, the *Quarterly Review* proclaiming that, if indeed the author were a woman, then it was one who had 'long forfeited the society of her own sex'. So Catherine looks forward to that final freedom the best of our contemporary feminists are requiring, when life can be created independently of sex, and be 'boundless in its duration, and love in its sympathy, and joy in its fulness'.

*　　*　　*

Having said as much, it is incumbent on us to 'reify' Emily's message somewhat, and we can do so to an extent by returning to *Jane Eyre*. The problem boils down to the fact that we do not know if we can consider ourselves Catherines and Heathcliffs, destined some day to live asexually, like rocks and moors together, in a blissfully better abode. Faced with life on earth here, we need to organize a viable female-male relationship now. What is our programme to be? Are we, in fact, to post time charts of housework in our kitchens and, as one recent American exhortation would have us do, rejoice every time hubby scrubs the tub or swishes dishes ('He is feeling it more than you. He's losing some leisure and you're gaining it. The measure of your oppression is his resistance').[18] This is scarcely what the French call serious. And it was to such questions as these that Charlotte Brontë, as if stimulated by her sister's brilliance (and, from her own confessions, deeply in awe of it), addressed herself.

Of course both sisters attacked sexism, in their diverse ways, one philosophical, one social. In both *Wuthering Heights* and *Jane Eyre* 'a relatively mild and ordinary marriage is made after the spirit of the masculine universe is controlled or extinguished' (Richard Chase). This is very nice. For the Victorian or pre-Victorian universe in England (the reference to *Marmion* sets the action of the latter fiction as prior to Queen Victoria) corresponds comfortably enough with Freud's final postulate of the Father-God, or Man-God, society, doubtless partially derived from it. The primaeval social order is here seen as duplicated in fact, with ruling males (all the more reinforced by a male-supporting Queen) and inferior men plus, on the lowest rung of the hierarchy, useless, dependent, and/or frivolous women. To back up this point, we should note the suggestion of incest in both Brontë books, the prime taboo in savage societies; in *Jane Eyre* the father-daughter relationship haunts that of Rochester to Jane until he becomes a cripple.

It is simply that the major Brontë sisters were too intelligent to accept this male-imposed universe without question and went out to challenge it, on two planes. Both Heathcliff and Rochester, therefore, have to be – for their fictional, and theoretic, purposes – godlike yet satanic. The tyrannical father (like the Reverend Patrick Brontë) traditionally represses while he stimulates desire. But according to Chase the Brontë sisters slightly chicken out. Their audacity is almost too great for them to handle. Both maim or subdue their heroes – an action particularly evident, as

[18] From 'The Politics of Housework' by Pat Mainardi (Know, Inc., P.O. Box 10197, Pittsburgh, Pa. 15132). Ms Mainardi is typically paradoxical in her standards. In this same pamphlet she writes, 'Most men are not accustomed to doing monotonous, repetitive work which never issues in any lasting let alone important achievement.' Some executive males may not be; most working-class males definitely are. De Beauvoir was far milder about the housework problem, and indeed admired American emancipations in this direction.

mentioned, in *Jane Eyre* – yet to 'extinguish' the male universe (as contemporary feminism is finding) is hardly the answer. It is little use living with a dummy, and so Charlotte indeed gives Rochester back some of his sight at the very end (she can hardly realistically restore his hand). 'If the devil is overcome', Chase points out, 'a higher state of society will have been achieved'. One beyond biology.

For, if you overcome the devil, you have no need (or little) of the God-figure when the latter is seen principally in terms of repression. Freed of such, the devil (as here, of sexual passion) can go to work. We venture to feel that contemporary feminists still have scant idea of the seriousness of the challenge made by the major Brontë books. They are an education in themselves. All the current huffing and puffing of the 'consciousness-raising' sessions miss the point, presenting the problem between the sexes as a quasi-athletic contest of 'domination'. With one part of herself Charlotte certainly spurned this vulgarized version as subsidiary. It is true that by the end of the book Jane is proposing marriage rather than the maimed Rochester, but this is beside the point, and anyway Rochester rightly tells her she had herself proposed in the first place. It is a matter of proper union, balance, between sex and intelligence. As Chase well puts it, when we understand these heroines, 'they acquire a new significance: it had not occurred to us that the stakes were so great'.

If Emily approached her 'love' story from a different level, Charlotte still allows her sister's language to have its say in *Jane Eyre* in the form of Helen Burns, a character studied too little. When we resume the varieties of religious experience represented in the book we arrive at interesting parallels pointing this up. In the almost coarsely caricatural Brocklehurst, cutting off schoolgirls' 'top-knots', we see Victorian Puritanism at its most repressive. In St John, who is intelligent (he reads a lot, studies 'Hindostanee'), we have a spiritualized Calvinism – the original for Brocklehurst, William Carus Wilson, may have lent to both portraits.

St John, a singularly repellent character for most women readers, puts strong pressure to bear on Jane to get her to marry him; the reason she nearly capitulates ('I was tempted to cease struggling with him – to rush down the torrent of his will and into the gulf of his existence, and there lose my own') is that as an intellectual he is a potential equal and, further, he has suffered similar miseries of the heart. 'I was with an equal', she reflects with him on the proposal to go to India as his 'weapon'. She adds, 'one with whom I might argue'. A moment later he tells her, 'you have a man's vigorous brain'. The temptation for Jane is to turn her back on 'biology'. But in a single ringing passage she tells us that 'I was sure St John Rivers – pure-lived, con-scientious, zealous as he was – had not yet found that peace of God which passeth all understanding.' Helen Burns had, and she dies in Jane Eyre's young arms, in love.

The structural parallel with Helen Burns's death is, of course, Mrs Reed's – in hate. But the structural parallel in spiritual orientation and development is Eliza Reed's conversion to Catholicism and donning of the veil. Jane repudiates this. She sees it as simply another act in the service of repression, accept-tance of a church that had historically found women inferior. Looking through the window during her visit to Gateshead, and reflecting on Mrs Reed's death, Jane 'thought of Helen Burns: recalled her dying words – her faith – her doctrine of the equality of disembodied souls.'

Equality is the operative of the second sentence. When we go back to Helen herself, we find a virtual summary of what Emily had been saying in *Wuthering Heights*, notably in Helen's long speech which concludes Chapter VI, one where the writing takes on a Biblical or liturgical intensity:[19]

'We are, and must be, one and all, burdened with faults in this world: but the time will soon come when, I trust, we shall put them off in putting off our corruptible bodies; when debasement and sin will fall from us with this cumbrous frame of flesh, and only the spark of the spirit will remain, – the impalpable principle of life and thought, pure as when it left the Creator to inspire the creature: whence it came it will

[19] Helen, in fact, has just before this speech made an unacknowledged quotation of Matthew 5: 44.

return; perhaps again to be communicated to some being higher than man – perhaps to pass through gradations of glory, from the pale human soul to brighten to the seraph! Surely it will never, on the contrary, be suffered to degenerate from man to fiend? No; I cannot believe that: I hold another creed; which no one ever taught me, and which I seldom mention; but in which I delight, and to which I cling: for it extends hope to all: it makes Eternity a rest – a mighty home, not a terror and an abyss.'

Strange speech in a schoolroom, one worthy, rather, of the pulpit. But once more the religion, the vital 'principle', is sex. Jane admires Helen Burns – 'it was the effluence of fine intellect, of true courage, it lit up her marked lineaments, her thin face, her sunken grey eye, like a reflection from the aspect of an angel' – but this is not her way. Charlotte was writing a companion portrait of love as the full life of the heart here on earth. It is true, as Chase says, that she maims Rochester ('castrates' him, if you will), but such is symbolic suffering for the 'master' race – a term we will return to below – and by the end Jane can claim, 'I am my husband's life as fully as he is mine'.

Setting the symbolic maiming, then, to one side, we see that Charlotte has her heroine doff her 'Quakerish' bonnet to the Helen Burnses of this world, with respect, but pass determinedly on to the task of organizing 'perfect concord' between a man and a woman now. Jane Eyre only marries Rochester when she can eventuate her full selfhood, in a relationship of complete mutual respect.

It has been well seen by one critic,[20] indeed it is quite evident, that it is precisely Rochester's anti-social tendencies – his rudeness, general breaches of convention – that stimulate Jane's own selfhood. He has recognized her inner life and is drawing it out to test it, as it were, against his: the references to *equality* on Jane's part begin to increase with this skilful probing and they do so

[20] Mark Kinkead-Weekes, 'The Place of Love in *Jane Eyre* and *Wuthering Heights*,' *The Brontës: A Collection of Critical Essays*, edited by Ian Gregor, Englewood Cliffs, N.J.: Prentice-Hall, 1970, pp. 76–95.

much to Rochester's delight, until he stings her into saying in the garden, 'Do you think, because I am poor, obscure, plain, and little, I am soulless and heartless? You think wrong! – I have as much soul as you – and full as much heart ... it is my spirit that addresses your spirit; just as if both had passed through the grave, and we stood at God's feet, equal – as we are!'

Rochester happily echoes 'As we are', takes her in his arms and proposes in these terms, i.e. hers:

> '"My bride is here," he said, again drawing me to him, "because my equal is here, and my likeness. Jane, will you marry me?"'

Shortly afterwards, when Jane says to him, 'I like rudeness a great deal better than flattery', Rochester underscores the *equality* references: 'You glowed in the cool moonlight last night, when you mutinied against fate, and claimed your rank as my equal. Janet, by-the-by, it was you who made me the offer.' She at once admits as much – 'Of course, I did.'

So it is social convention, repression, which really maims Rochester. In refusing to live as his paramour Jane Eyre is saying that their relationship must be sanctified by religion, and society; yet her inner self knows better – 'I had but to go in and say – "Mr Rochester, I will love you and live with you through life till death", and a fount of rapture would spring to my lips. I thought of this.' She *thought* of it – 'I longed to be his; I panted to return' – but rejected it and effectively blinded her husband-to-be. For if she had gone south to the Mediterranean with Rochester he would have been saved the maiming, even if Thornfield were burnt down.[21]

Here Charlotte Brontë makes Jane Eyre express those pious heroics of self-denial and self-control which have been left her

---

[21] It could be objected that she would then have been financially dependent upon him, and in the position of selling sexual favours. However, she is never explicitly given this reflection in the text and when she was proposing to live with Rochester as his wife, prior to legacy, she would have been just as financially dependent upon him.

by religion, and which she sees caricatured in the episode involving St John. When she has wrung herself clear of this legacy
('You are killing me now', Jane tells him), she hears the voice of
her mate, and true equal, calling her. For Rochester has sinned
against convention on several scores (girls in three countries, at
least). Why, in the era of the Great Family he doesn't even like
children – 'I'll have no brats! – I'll only have you.'

Furthermore, he was tricked into marrying Miss Mason
('cheated into espousing'), as women were tricked into marrying
men: 'a marriage was achieved almost before I knew where I
was . . . a nature the most gross, impure, depraved I ever saw,
was associated with mine, and called by the law and by society a
part of me.' As against Bertha Mason's 'pigmy intellect' he finds
Jane's elflike, aesthetic, temptingly free of the moral machinery.
Recounting his secret to her after the abortive attempt at marriage,
he tells her of his wife ('as you term that fearful hag') that 'it is
not because she is mad I hate her. If you were mad, do you think
I should hate you?' At Jane's affirmative he goes on, 'Then you
are mistaken, and you know nothing about me, and nothing about
the sort of love of which I am capable. Every atom of your flesh
is as dear to me as my own: in pain and sickness it would still be
dear. Your mind is my treasure, and if it were broken, it would
be my treasure still.' A lesson she learns, in inverse, at the end.

In short, Charlotte created two inequal characters – a girl of
eighteen, small, plain and poor, against a man in his forties, large,
Byronically handsome (viz. ugly), and rich – and showed that it
is the spark of the spirit in the human being which is the soul's
true equality. From the very start of their relationship Jane
pluckily reads Rochester a lesson in such: 'I don't think, sir, you
have a right to command me, merely because you are older than
I, or because you have seen more of the world than I have; your
claim to superiority depends on the use you have made of your
time and experience.' Jane arrives at Thornfield 'weary of an
existence all passive', and by the time she leaves it for good has
told Rochester quite a bit about the marriage contract: when he
buys her fine dresses, her cheek burns 'with a sense of annoyance
and degradation'. Rochester chuckles, delighted.

'The eastern allusion bit me again: "I'll not stand you an inch in the stead of a seraglio," I said: "so don't consider me an equivalent for one; if you have a fancy for anything in that line, away with you, sir to the bazaars of Stamboul without delay; and lay out in extensive slave-purchases some of that spare cash you seem at a loss to spend satisfactorily here."

"And what will you do, Janet, while I am bargaining for so many tons of flesh and such an assortment of black eyes?"

"I'll be preparing myself to go out as a missionary to preach liberty to them that are enslaved – your harem inmates amongst the rest. I'll get admitted there, and I'll stir up mutiny; and you, three-tailed bashaw as you are, sir, shall in a trice find yourself fettered amongst our hands: nor will I, for one, consent to cut your bonds till you have signed a charter, the most liberal that despot ever yet conferred."'[22]

Rochester, of course, loves all this. He sharpens her tools for her so that when she eventually meets St John she can stand her ground and resist the moral blackmail – 'Again the surprised expression crossed his face. He had not imagined that a woman would dare to speak so to a man.' Her lover can now call her back to his side via the telepathic cry. Now they are truly equal and she can say to him, 'I love you better now, when I can really be useful to you, than I did in your state of proud independence, when you disdained every part but that of the giver and protector.'

It could finally be said, and should finally be said, that *Jane Eyre* is therefore and thereby a profoundly and healthily s-m fiction.[23] By this we do not mean merely to refer to the scene of

[22] The *bashaw* was a Pasha. It is a fairly unusual spelling, Fielding giving us a *basha*.

[23] I am more than happy to adopt this new, snappy Americanism for *sadism*, clogged with fear and opprobrium as the latter term has become. Robert Anton Wilson tried *Sadeanism* in order to distinguish the gold of this creative erotic transcendence from the mud of the clinics, but it does not seem to have stuck. An s-m liberation movement would seem some sort of contradiction in terms, but in fact 'The s-m relationship is the most democratic that exists' (Terry Kolb, 'Masochist's Lib'. *Village Voice*. 13 May 1971). Feminists pleading for 'polymorphous perversity' need go no further.

Helen Burns being birched (though it is not without significance that in Lowood Charlotte strongly exaggerated the discipline of her model, Cowan Bridge School – the Brontë Society having usefully reprinted the 1830 Report of this establishment 'for Clergymen's Daughters'). The story is in fact full of non-functional allusions in this vein: the bullying scene at the beginning is pure s-m (until the brutal book-throwing episode) with the red room closely anticipating the celebrated *La Chambre jaune* of Jacques Desroix, a furiously best-selling Carrington title.

The whole semantic is shot through with s-m, from the initial use of the schoolboy term *fagging* (Jane's for John Reed) to the visit to Mrs Reed's bedroom 'to which I had so often been summoned for chastisement . . . I looked into a certain corner near, half-expecting to see the slim outline of a once-dreaded switch; which used to lurk there, waiting to leap out imp-like and lace my quivering palm or shrinking neck.' Bessie, meanwhile, has described girls' school to Jane 'as a place where young ladies sat in the stocks, wore backboards . . .' Jane is then sent to Lowood, sees Helen birched, and goes for walks on which the wind 'almost flayed the skin from our faces'. Indeed, the semantic carries Charlotte too far, well into Gothic appellation, making her confer names like Scatcherd and Harden ('a woman . . . made up of equal parts of whalebone and iron')[24] on severe mistresses, and Temple on the mild one.

Yet there is considerably more than this. Rochester is the classic 'dominant'. Jane early reflects that his 'sternness has a power beyond beauty'. In contrast with the guests at the party, some in positions of command, he stands out for Jane as follows:

> 'I compared him with his guests. What was the gallant grace of the Lyons, the languid elegance of Lord Ingram, – even the military distinction of Colonel Dent, contrasted with his look of native pith and genuine power?'

'Am I cruel in my love?' he asks her at the church door. At the start of the book, after Jane has turned on young John Reed,

[24] The imagery is exact. The dreaded *soko* birch was made of whalebone.

the lady's-maid Abbot holds her arms and reproves her for striking 'Your young master.' Jane blurts back, 'Master! How is he my master? Am I a servant?' Yet later at Thornfield she muses, 'it had a master: for my part, I liked it better.' And she peppers her dialogue with this term thereafter.

Such becomes particularly apparent when she returns at the end to the blind and maimed Rochester who is by now anything but her master. Indeed, there is the hint of the reverse. Then – 'I can single out my master's very window', she gloats to herself as she approaches the house; and when she finally sees him we read, 'it was my master, Edward Fairfax Rochester'. What is more, I know of no other novel even of this era which includes so many *sir's* from a young lady of refinement . . . even to her employer. The 'sense of power' Jane had first felt over Rochester now makes it possible for her to be the submissive, the Helen Burns she had earlier envied, since he has accepted her as his intellectual equal. No kinematograph picture made of this novel, and there have been several, including both Orson Welles and George C. Scott as lowering Rochesters, has got any slightest grip on this, the heart's core of the fantasy. That God is love . . . and he is always right.

Chase understood it well, even once calling Rochester 'sadistic'. In the best sense, as a sensitive male, he is. And Charlotte had of course played with this fantasy in her Angria juvenilia (whose hero, the Duke of Zamorna, is referred to as His Sublimity). The acknowledged expert on these 'legends', Fanny Elizabeth Ratchford, shows us how, with the possible collaboration of her extraordinary brother Branwell, Charlotte fantasized a certain Lady Zenobia Ellrington[25] who seems to storm straight out of the small ads of our underground press ('Dominant Female Seeks . . .'', etc.). The Lady Zenobia was a furious farrago of passions, subject to 'fits of rage in which she

[25] The odd acquisition, by first name, of reference to the third-century AD Queen of Palmyra strikes another feminist note. The name of this brave woman, taken chained to Rome by Aurelian, occurs again in Mrs Wharton's *Ethan Frome* (abbreviated to Zeena) and in Henry James's immaculate little story 'The Pupil', where the lady so named was a *governess*.

shrieks like a wild beast and falls upon her victim hand and foot', with the considerable advantage that she could also box as well as any man. The interesting point is that Zenobia was also an intellectual. And a Creole. Thus, as Chase was the first to observe, she was both Bertha Rochester and the little blue-stocking Jane Eyre:

> 'May not Bertha, Jane seems to ask herself, be a living example of what happens to the woman who gives herself to the Romantic Hero, who in her insane suffragettism tries herself to play the Hero, to be the fleshy vessel of the *élan?*'

We may not all agree that such suffragettism is any more insane than the male-dominated society which brought it forth. But the bifurcation images certainly lend support to Chase's view – the split chestnut tree, the ripped bridal veil. Jane is ambivalent to Rochester. Her society forces her to be so. She is fascinated by his physicality – the amatory adventures in other countries have to stand in for what today would be undoubtedly repellent detail – and desires to submit to him, but her rational side revolts. Woman must not be 'submissive'. That is an injustice. No one of Jane Eyre's intelligence can allow feminine subservience.

The evidence of the senses all but betrays this 'unregenerate and undisciplined spirit', as Lady Eastalake called her. The poems could go further, and do, allowing fantasy larger rein. They are accordingly replete with wives or women dominated by semi-tyrannical men, one of whom (Gilbert) descends to his spouse 'like a God'. Another tyrannical husband slaughters himself with an axe.

And so too with the well-imagined Rochester, who makes Jane sob 'convulsively', who 'took my feelings from my own power and fettered them in his' (observe the metaphor), and who pinches her for caresses. Whose rudeness she adores and in whom, finally, she 'could not . . . see God for his creature'. Her love for him is 'an earnest, religious energy'. Indeed . . . for he is God. And God is always right.

The whole marvellous understanding of this book suddenly

comes together. The Gothic can be released into the real. When reason wins, and Jane declines Rochester's offer, 'I abhorred myself . . . I was hateful in my own eyes.' Robert Heilman's admirable essay on 'Charlotte Brontë's "New" Gothic'[26] brings out what is purely there in the novel, that if you release one pattern of feeling you will uncover another. 'The supreme happiness of the woman in love is to be recognized by the loved man as a part of himself; when he says "we", she is associated and identified with him, she shares his prestige and reigns with him over the rest of the world; she never tires of repeating – even to excess – this delectable "we". As one necessary to a being who is absolute necessity, who stands forth in the world seeking necessary goals and who gives her back the world in necessary form, the woman in love acquires in her submission that magnificent possession, the absolute. It is this certitude that gives her lofty joys; she feels exalted to a place at the right hand of God.'[27] De Beauvoir's words remind us that Montague Summers's *The Gothic Quest* gets read for the wrong reasons, as low-grade vampire films are seen. We smile at what Summers calls the 'emotionalism' of such fiction. But we can also learn from its understanding of the psyche. Rochester may be 'a kind of lost nobleman of passion, and of specifically physical passion' (Heilman) but, as the same author writes:

'Aside from partial sterilization of banal Gothic by dry factuality and humor, Charlotte goes on to make a much more important – indeed, a radical – revision of the mode: in *Jane Eyre* and in the other novels . . . that discovery of passion, that rehabilitation of the extra-rational, which is the historical office of Gothic, is no longer oriented in marvelous circumstances but moves deeply into the lesser known realities of human life.'

True – and that rehabilitation was effected by a profound

[26] Robert B. Heilman, 'Charlotte Brontë's "New" Gothic', in *From Jane Austen to Joseph Conrad*, edited by Robert Rathburn and Martin Steinmann, Jr., University of Minnesota Press: 1958.
[27] De Beauvoir, p. 614.

knowledge of feminine psyche. For woman's nature, in the power relationship put on her in a male world, must be ambivalent, often cripplingly so. 'On the one hand she must retain her sources of real instinctual gratification and on the other, find ways of satisfying her need for prestige and esteem. Thus she stands, Janus-faced, drawn in two directions at once, often incapable of ultimate choice and inevitably penalized whatever direction she chooses.'[28] It is the governess governed.

So the whole rhetorical structure of *Jane Eyre* is enormously creative. If the dominant training of women was for dependence, and impregnation, any desires to emulate or rival will drive all the deeper roots, since disallowed. It is for this reason that we see here the s-m relationship as so impelling, and healthy, in this generous vision; for, by corollary, when women have achieved positions of dominance and are encouraged by their culture to take on other-directed norms, and traits of aggression and independence, then their unconscious exertions may drive toward another pole for gratification – tenderness, femininity (in the cliché sense of the term), and submission. Let us remember that for Emily the vampire image was male, for Charlotte female!

This passionate plea for liberation of the personal self in women now, by the latter, finally excuses all the coincidences, awkward shifts of points of view (evidently induced by Anne's *Agnes Grey*), and a whole deposit of sheer native prejudice – of Adèle we finally hear that 'a sound English education corrected in a great measure her French defects' while 'the British peasantry are the best taught, best mannered, most self-respecting of any in Europe' (how does nineteen-year-old Jane Eyre know?).

Despite such minor blemishes the life of the heart is what lives in these immortal pages, the fulness of free individuality. It is for this very reason that Charlotte could confidently allow herself the 'heresy' (as she herself called it) of criticizing Jane Austen who, for her, 'does her business of delineating the surface of the lives of genteel English people curiously well', but who was also 'a very incomplete, and rather insensible (*not senseless*) woman'.

[28] Lundberg and Farnham, p. 241.

In Jane Eyre Charlotte depicted the complete equal. For when the wife is such with her husband as Jane was at the end with Rochester, she forms part of a mutual imagination, and can create herself as submissive if she so desires and requires. 'To pluck the mask from the face of the Pharisee', as Currer Bell forever put it, 'is not to lift an impious hand to the crown of thorns'.

4

EMMA BOVARY
The Usurper

With a Coda on Luiza of *Cousin Baʒilio* by Eça de Queiroz

'It is in vain to say human beings ought to be satisfied with
tranquillity: they must have action: and they will make it if they
cannot find it. Millions are condemned to a stiller doom than mine,
and millions are in silent revolt against their lot. Nobody knows how
many rebellions besides political rebellions ferment in the masses of
life which people earth. Women are supposed to be very calm
generally; but women feel just as men feel; they need exercise for
their faculties and a field for their efforts as much as their brothers do;
they suffer from too rigid a restraint, too absolute a stagnation,
precisely as men would suffer; and it is narrow-minded in their more
privileged fellow-creatures to say that they ought to confine
themselves to making puddings and knitting stockings, to playing
on the piano and embroidering bags. It is thoughtless to condemn
them, or laugh at them, if they seek to do more or learn more than
custom has pronounced necessary for their sex.'
Charlotte Brontë, *Jane Eyre*

Flaubert's vision of bourgeois woman's lot was one of the most
perceptive of any novelist's. It is said to be hard to recognize
ourselves in mirrors – a thesis used at times to rationalize the
complexities of the more arcane contemporary philosophy – but
Flaubert, who never married, was cosseted by his mother, spent
his last pennies to keep a sister out of bankruptcy court, and
probably died of syphilis, produced at least one work so completely feminine in all senses it has even been derided as male
chauvinist in the Fem Lib press of modern America.

When Emma Bovary is expecting her first child, and after her doting husband has passed hands over her face, calling her 'little mamma' and other endearments reminiscent of Torvald Helmer's in *A Doll's House*, she fervently hopes the baby will be a boy:

'he would be strong and dark, she would call him George; and this idea of having a male child was like an expected revenge for all her impotence in the past. A man, at least, is free; he can explore all passions and all countries, overcome obstacles, taste of the most distant pleasures. But a woman is always hampered. Being inert as well as pliable, she has against her the weakness of the flesh and the inequity of the law. Like the veil held to her hat by a ribbon, her will flutters in every breeze; she is always drawn by some desire, restrained by some rule of conduct'.[1]

The passage is fully Flaubertian, uniting as it does the two sides of his nature and his times, that hybrid between realism and romance to haunt the century in its more sensitive art, and finally find itself summarized in something like Thomas Mann's *Tonio Kröger*. But unlike Tonio, Flaubert was far from inhibited by the bifurcation, he was impelled by it. The third of his works in order of composition, *L'Education sentimentale* (later known as *La première Education sentimentale*), written between 1843 and 1845, contrasts a 'cynical', realistic character called Henry with a dreamy, romantic Jules. There is a long letter Flaubert wrote to Louis Colet in 1852 clearly distinguishing the two aspects in his own personality. Tempting to cite here, yet almost untranslatable in the subtlety of its nuances, this document contrasts the twin

---

[1] I have throughout used the excellent new translation by Professor Paul de Man, 'based on the version by Eleanor Marx Aveling' (i.e. based on the original), to be found in Gustave Flaubert, *Madame Bovary*, London: Dent 1960. 'A Note on the Translation' is provided to this scrupulous edition. 'George', by the way, was certainly strong and dark. . . only female – George Sand. As Juliet Mitchell, author of *Women's Estate*, well puts it: 'A woman is a woman before she is born. The hands that knit in pink or blue, the midwife's tone of voice, the joy or disappointment of the parents, "tell" the fetus or newborn infant what it is to expect from life.'

sides of the author of *Madame Bovary*, as of the century, the one lyrical and ideological, and the other forcing a reluctant nose down hard into facts.

The polarity is particularly feminist. Until recently woman has been held in a 'romantic' mould by man. She is lyrical, ideal, the 'little mamma', and so on. This masculine conception has been called a tool for domination and in some cases has clearly been so, serving woman ill in practice (women commit suicide more often by poisoning than any other way, though this may be due to a reluctance to disfigure, one of the 'principles' of the Suicide Club of Flaubert's time). As Madame de Merteuil saw so well, all the imagination utilized to ensnare or 'catch' a man has to be thoroughly down-to-earth.

The lady of the château, even the county doctor's wife who calls her daughter Berthe because she heard the name at an aristocratic ball, has to go through the same disgusting labour pangs as the most deprived peasant; a brief follow-up of the birth of Berthe to Emma shows Flaubert sedulously insisting on this – Emma faints when she hears it's a girl, goes to see the wet-nurse, a carpenter's wife, before the prescribed six weeks of the Virgin are out, does so in company of her lover-to-be, Léon, and the infant promptly throws up all over her collar. Flaubert insists on this point – he has the wet-nurse come forward and complain altogether of the child's incontinence ('I always seem to be sponging her off'), then ask for some brandy for her husband. It is caustic enough.

It was too much so for Sainte-Beuve who, in his weekly book review put a point of view repeatedly met in the contemporary classroom – 'Why did Flaubert not include a single character who, by the spectacle of his virtue, would have offered some comfort, some repose to the reader and become a friendly presence?' Flaubert was 'too cruel'. Even in the provinces there were surely some 'good and beautiful souls'. Even conceding the new realism, it could not be said 'that truth resides entirely with evil'. In a word, Flaubert's book was loaded, cold, and inhumane.

It was indeed. That was partly why it was so revolutionary,

and why it was prosecuted. Yet it could have been the reverse of what Sainte-Beuve desiderated, and still not art. *Castigat ridendo mores*. All Sainte-Beuve could do was to offer the pharmacist's apprentice, Justin (Emma's go-between to Rodolphe and the inadvertent source, and observer, of the literal poison that kills her body just as surely as the 'romantic' poison of her reading had killed her mind) for the one pleasant personage in the book, 'the only devoted, disinterested character'. He might have added the pharmacist's unnoticed spouse, Madame Homais, 'the best wife in Normandy' of whom her husband 'never thought that she might be a woman to anyone, or that she possessed anything else of her sex than the gown'. Sainte-Beuve did not emphasize the unsparing picture of Emma herself, saying of Flaubert that 'He denounces without pity the overrefined tastes of her childhood, the coquettish little girl, the dreamy schoolgirl overindulging her fancies. Shall I confess it? one often feels more tolerant towards her than the author himself.'

Matthew Arnold was in accord. Flaubert's attitude to his material must not be confused with his mission (as it was by the voluble feminine liberationists we heard in New York in 1972). Flaubert's hatred made him observe carefully. Whether the result is a more or less 'likable' book is another matter. So Sainte-Beuve is understandably echoed by Arnold, for whom *Madame Bovary* was a novel of '*petrified feeling;* over it hangs an atmosphere of bitterness, irony, impotence; not a personage in the book to rejoice or console us'. Once again Flaubert is too cruel to his heroine – 'he pursues her without pity or pause, as with malignity; he is harder upon her himself than any reader even, I think, will be inclined to be'. One can but rejoin – Naturally.

We do have in Theodor Fontane's German *Effi Briest* of 1895 as in Eça de Queiroz's Portuguese *O Primo Bazilio* of 1878 adulterous heroines depicted with much warmer authorial 'feeling'. Particularly is this the case in the latter, to which we will revert below, and the social determinants guiding the leading woman in it are altogether other. This is true too, though in a different way, of Zola's early *Thérèse Raquin* (the novel, not the play). Flaubert simply had to be hard to Emma.[2]

In fact he was so to most of his realistic women characters, just as he was to himself. Such can be tested over shorter stretches of Flaubert, as in the story already mentioned, 'A Simple Heart', where he punishes the poor *vieille fille* of a servant, Félicité, both by ill luck and male betrayal, far more than he needs to make his point. Her name itself, picked up from that of Emma's maid who runs off with her wardrobe after she has died, is an irony akin to calling the smooth Yonville usurer-pawnbroker Lheureux – puns that seem unworthy by contemporary taste. Flaubert was bound to punish his principal characters since he was so unsparing of himself, and – '*Madame Bovary, c'est moi*'. If we believe his own claims, he physically vomited his dinner when the arsenic went into Emma's belly on the written page.

'I know of no other equally pathetic case in which a literary success could be achieved only at the cost of a secret undoing', writes Albert Béguin. The new Rouen manuscripts show what a constant ordeal, self-torture, it must have been to write '*un livre sur rien*', as Flaubert defined it to Louise Colet in the famous letter of 16 January 1852. One day inventing and creating, followed by weeks of cutting himself down – averaging about twelve small pages a month for most of the time – no wonder our author grows somewhat dyspeptic, loses teeth and hair, feels nauseous and finally fulminates, 'What a look Rouen has – is there anything more heavy and depressing? At sunset yesterday the walls were oozing such ennui that I was almost asphyxiated as I passed!'

The mistreatment Flaubert inflicted on himself throughout the writing of *Madame Bovary* was hardly calculated to make for a sunny disposition. He wanted to write a book (he went on in the same letter to Louise Colet) in which style was vision, 'a book dependent on nothing external, which would be held together by the strength of its style . . . a book which would

---

[2] All the same, he is bitter to Charles, enlisting our sympathy rather than antipathy for him by the thick jeer which closes Section XIII of Part Two – 'And, on top of all this, the poor fellow had money troubles!'

have almost no subject, or at least in which the subject would be almost invisible, if such a thing is possible.' He punished himself brutally to this end.

It is for this reason that Flaubert was able to sympathize with the woman he punished on the page, whose life was so empty and devoid of love, and to whose fate – *ennui* – he had to constrain his language, always longing to take flight, in the manner of some brilliant couturier with a gown that has to be made mediocre at a client's request. Paradoxically, then, it was for this reason that Sartre, in an extended essay on the novel, marvelled that the author 'was able to metamorphose himself into a woman'. For Flaubert's alienation in this composition *was* woman's – '*Madame Bovary, c'est moi*'. Developing the ideas of Joseph de Maistre, Baudelaire saw woman as artist over and over again ('Woman is quite within her rights, indeed she is even accomplishing a kind of duty, when she devotes herself to appearing magical and supernatural'). Artistically, Flaubert felt a world being stolen from him daily when writing *Bovary*, and he ended up with a masterpiece on his hands since he hit a bull's-eye of history's dialectic. 'Just what must that period have been in order that it should demand *this* book', Sartre wonders, 'and mendaciously find there its own image?' We shall try to see.

To start with, then, it is invalid to ask that the agony of emancipation that *Madame Bovary* represented in the writing should serve us up 'a friendly presence' or 'good and beautiful souls' as well as bad. Warmth is not a literary norm. In a fictional character it may or may not represent an artistic achievement . . . it depends. With almost identical subject matter Flaubert was cold . . . and liberal, Eça de Queiroz was warm . . . and reactionary. That it gives pleasure may well be beside the point (so can rage and fury). It has often been pointed out that Tolstoy is a far warmer portraitist than Flaubert – 'Tolstoy (unlike Flaubert) is unable to portray a single character as wholly unloveable' (J. P. Stern) – and we are willing to wager that *Madame Bovary* will nearly always lose at the box-office to any *War and Peace*. But this is not a matter of literary degree. Tolstoy's Natasha type, the adorable adolescent (all the more adorable now we have eliminated adolescence, perhaps), does not represent realistic observation of the 'witness' kind proffered by Flaubert and Zola. It is genial incantatory description, springing from an abundant belief in moral good.

Similarly, in Thomas Mann, who tends to continue the Tolstoyan girl stereotype, there is usually an appealing and winning warmth underlying (at times undoing) all the irony afoot. Turgenev softens yet further. There, indeed, was an author who refused to portray unpleasant characters. In *Fathers and Sons*, for example, Paul Petrovitch is, if you think the facts through, the representative of a thoroughly detestable philosophy, repressive to women and which Turgenev himself, whose mother was a tyrant, opposed in his own life to his cost. Yet at the end of the book Turgenev cannot let this character alone, mellowing him into a dear old gentleman doing spa duty 'on the Brühl terrace at Dresden'.

There is by now a library of criticism on *Madame Bovary*, and several on Flaubert's *oeuvre* as a whole. It is impossible to advance on such a broad front all at once, and our task here has been first to inspect something of Flaubert's attitude to his material in his major work. For as Erich Auerbach has put it, life is there for art to go to work on in Flaubert and 'in his total picture of the times, there appears something like a concealed threat: the period is charged with its stupid issuelessness as with an explosive'. This 'issuelessness' was particularly woman's and he chose a woman to express it. Baudelaire was in agreement. 'Good is always the product of some art', he wrote in his essay on make-up. Flaubert made a famous summary of all this: "89 destroyed royalty and the nobility, '48 the bourgeoisie, and '51 the people. There is nothing left but a bestial and imbecile rabble, and the only way to live in peace is to place yourself above the whole of humanity, to be a simple spectator. Yes, I am becoming a furious aristocrat.'

There was nothing left but to be a 'simple spectator' of that most oppressed class of all – women. To say as much is not to claim that any novel of adultery of the time was automatically authentic art. There were many failures. But the theme was in the air, for it was one of betrayal. Champfleury, whose un-enlightened realism Flaubert so disliked, gave us one of these adulterous *livres sur rien*, but in Flaubert all hope, all longings for anything beyond the self are cut down in the woman as they are in the society. A woman, a member of that class which is deceived daily, was the perfect vehicle for Flaubert's vision, then. Yet the book does not end with Emma's death; it is framed in Charles, the betrayed. The true subject of this book with 'no subject' is betrayal itself.

So our first step in the recognition of the feminist content of *Madame Bovary* must be to see that in writing it Flaubert mutilated himself as society was mutilating women. A diagram of the architecture of the story can be made to represent it as a sexual tumescence and detumescence, without difficulty.[3] Hence the author's empathy could be high in making his structure respond to psychological verity. Sartre posed the obvious psycho-logical question – why no one had wondered much that a trucu-lent Norman doctor's son, the 'cynic' who boasted of taking a prostitute with a cigar clamped between his teeth at each year's end, and who wrote 'The most beautiful woman is scarcely beautiful on a table in the dissecting room, her bowels draped over her face, one of her legs peeled to the bone, and a half-extinguished cigar lying on her feet', could project himself in Emma Bovary, 'a masculine woman and feminized man' (to Sartre as to Baudelaire before him).

The truth is social, as much as psychological. Emma loathed provincial mediocrity. So did Flaubert. She found Yonville dull, boring, stupid, peopled with clod-like knuckleheads. So did Flaubert its original. *Bovarysme* (a term first coined by Jules de Gaultier) is the recognition of this reality, of the sameness of the provincial pattern of experience – which, it has been shown, Flaubert's reiterative use of the imperfect tense cleverly under-lined, making the chronic futility of daily life permeate his prose. It is difficult to describe boredom without boring, but Flaubert

[3] See, for instance, the chart given in the Introduction to: *Oeuvres complètes de Gustave Flaubert: Tome premier: Madame Bovary*, Paris: Société Les Belles Lettres, 1945, p. CXXIII.

succeeds magisterially. The firemen, the schoolteacher, the old *retraité* fashioning his useless napkin rings, all rotate around the main square like the puppets on some Swiss barometer. The anaesthetizing routine is imported into the houses which become the coffins of dead illusions . . . and Charles's weekly letters to his mother are sealed with the same three wafers. Finally, Emma cannot bear it any longer, this endless simulacrum of a woman's lot. Nor can Flaubert. Harshening his own sister's, he makes Emma's burial a triumph of complacent monotony, a summum of received ideas, or clichés, of which he compiled his 'dictionary'. Priest and pharmacist bicker about her death-bed and indirectly again, via the holy-water censer, at the graveside.

The spatial imagery itself provokes this longing for annihilation, or *'rien'*. Not merely those long flat fields around Yonville but the town itself. A paragraph like the following, so surely and carefully worked, knocks the nails into the 'casket' of every local hope:

> 'Beyond this there is nothing to see at Yonville. The street (the only one) a gunshot long and flanked by a few shops on either side stops short at the turn of the high road. Turning right and following the foot of the Saint-Jean hills one soon reaches the graveyard.'

One does indeed. But by now we are trespassing on affairs of style, on Flaubert's method for expressing his vision, and should pause to consider such briefly here.

* * *

It is by now a platitude to point out that Flaubert arrived at a particular point in the history of fiction, as in the general European literary consciousness. Symbolism – and most notably, for us here, in the setting and relationships of things about women – gave his work an especial resonance at the time, and makes it still seminal today.

Now of course almost everything the human does is symbolical. 'Because we are in the world', the French philosopher

Merleau-Ponty put it in a famous formulation, 'we are condemned to meaning.' R. N. Anshen phrased it equally suggestively: 'man is that being on earth who does not have language. Man *is* language.' Every day a woman gets up and puts on clothing she has chosen in a shop; this is supposed to have expressed her particular personality – 'just you', as the saleslady says who has probably known her for all of four minutes. Woman passes messages in the way she sits, uses her fingers, lifts an eyebrow, and the like; so in his *Theory of The Leisure Class* of 1899 Thorstein Veblen instanced corsets and hobble skirts as clear cultural requirements, making women as helpless and frail as men wanted them to be. The halls of the Victoria and Albert Museum, and the many books of C. Willett Cunningham, testify to this elementary form of human symbolism in which the second Flaubert of the letter to Louise Colet mentioned, the patient researcher into facts, showed himself expert.

But he did so with full understanding of the whole motive force behind the symbolic process. The long article by Baudelaire on Constantin Guys, and the iconography of his world, written from 1859 to 1860 though appearing in the *Figaro* later, presents woman adorning herself in the manner of an artist – that is, with intimate understanding of the subject, or sitter (herself). The reverse direction can briefly be seen in American dolls (Barbie, Crissy, Dawn) which come supplied with outfits that are supposed to bring personalities with them, as it were. There is a deep breach in symbolic assumptions here, and Baudelaire and Flaubert both sensed it coming; as Kenneth Burke has put it, 'to say that man is a symbol-using animal is by the same token to say that he is a "transcending animal".'

Unfortunately, the study of literary symbolism threatened for a while to run amok in America. Students were set texts like so many Christmas puddings in which the cleverest child was the one who found the most charms.[4] Thus in an early story by

---

[4] The 'pudding' analogy is suggested, indeed, by W. K. Wimsatt's *The Verbal Icon* where we read, 'Judging a poem is like judging a pudding or a machine. One demands that it work.' For some correction of these excesses, see: Harry Levin, 'Symbolism and Fiction,' in *Contexts of Criticism*, Harvard

Joyce a character goes into a bar and orders some ginger beer and a plate of peas.

A leading Joyce critic, interpreting this story as a parallel to the Esau-Isaac legend, informs us that the peas stand for a 'mess of pottage'. But they do not first and foremost stand for anything – they *are*. And they represent internal compulsions and elements of social sequence. Did or did not the character concerned order a plate of peas? Joyce's first observation was that he did so, in common with others who visited Dublin pubs of the day. You could not order peas in most Irish pubs today, and that you could do so then is evocative commentary of the kind Flaubert perfected – almost everything everyone eats in *Bovary* is social or psychological history, down to the arsenic at the end by Emma. At the start of this century Dublin pubs were often also grocers (the publican's assistants known as 'curates'), and a plate of peas was a cheap dish to fill a stomach with, just as the caraway seed consumed by another Joycean tippler was used to hide the smell of liquor. That such a drinker may make a pun with Esau, or Isaac, or Nebuchadnezzar, is extremely secondary and perhaps even unnatural symbolism, though Joyce, in common with the later Henry James, and others, undoubtedly used it as so much ornamentation on his reality.

The mode of transcendence, present in primary symbolism, is absent in secondary. Indeed, Flaubert mocked our 'new' critics in advance. To such Bouvards and Pécuchets beavering over our contemporary texts it ceases to matter much what a fictional character does. The structure of his actions might be that of a madman, with delusions that he was Esau. Mary McCarthy puts it concisely when discussing *Anna Karenina*:

University Press, 1957. I. A. Richards gave us some hilarious examples of of American symbol-hunting in his 'Poetic Process and Literary Analysis' (available in *Style in Language*, edited by T. A. Sebeok), while in England, when Robert Conquest led a spoof symbol-chase through *Lucky Jim*, he was evidently deluged with letters from students, seriously contesting his 'findings'. There is more of the same to be found, too, in Mary McCarthy's 'Settling the Colonel's Hash', which first appeared in *Harper's Magazine* for February, 1954.

'At the beginning of the novel, Anna meets the man who will be her lover, Vronsky, on the Moscow-St Petersburg express; as they meet, there has been an accident; a workman has been killed by the train coming in to the station. This is the beginning of Anna's doom, which is completed when she throws herself under a train and is killed; and the last we see of Vronsky is in a train, with a toothache; he is being seen off by a friend to the wars. The train is necessary to the plot of the novel, and I believe it is also symbolic, both of the iron forces of material progress that Tolstoy hated so and that played a part in Anna's moral destruction, and also of those iron laws of necessity and consequence that govern human action when it remains on the sensual level.'

The train is here a particularly appropriate symbol, nor does Tolstoy have to force any secondary significance upon it. Clearly, the peasants looked up from their fields, as in *Middlemarch*, and saw this new titan of technology hurtling over their immemorial soil. It was a symbol of – if you wish, a metonymy for – industrialism and the scientific mind. Yet the railway gave certain new freedoms, which Carlyle felt in his first ecstatic train-rides, and in which Anna Karenina shared.

Moreover, one could here continue the symbolic content. T. H. Huxley (perfecting La Mettrie) and Samuel Butler reminded us that we are in a way biological mechanisms, subject to certain laws. The attempt to aestheticize the machine, from Carlyle and Turner to Whitman and Hart Crane, has generally been made by those writers like Wells and Zola for whom there was nothing over-promising in their own country's immediate past. This ambivalence – that science would provide a new limb for man and thus paradoxically give some kind of 'answer' to Darwin (and his economic outriders) – lies at the heart of the American civilization, of course, with its anthropomorphized motor-cars, and is brilliantly summarized in Zola's *La Bête humaine* (of which there is no English translation in print as I write). There Lantier's love of his locomotive says a lot about our civilization, for an engine like a girl suggests a girl like an engine. Des Esseintes parodies the insight – 'Does there exist, anywhere on this earth, a being conceived in the joys of fornication and born in the throes of motherhood who is more dazzlingly, more outstandingly beautiful than the two locomotives recently put into service on the Northern Railway?'

We have lingered on these elementaries of symbolism here as so many warnings for the reading of Flaubert who, with Baudelaire, disliked photography but employed high focus on objects. Thus he anticipated recent cinema and *chosisme* in the novel. For if woman is no more than a social digit, then the digitary elements of which she disposes are going to characterize her closely, as well as comment on the moral climate in which she is set. There is indeed high focus on all the objects around Emma, though the intensity of concentration varies. And of all the many critical catalogues of such functional details in the novel that by Professor D. L. Demorest correctly observes that these details are generally predicated on the thing-like nature of men for Emma.

When you are a sexual object, men become – to the recipient of the attitude – sexual subjects. Charles wears boots whose 'upper part continued in a straight line as if stretched on a wooden foot' (Hippolyte's peg-leg, for which he is responsible, is still to come). Emma later 'saw all his platitude spelled out right there, on his very coat' – just before she sees him take a knife from his pocket 'like a peasant'. The rigidity of attire of the men in Yonville reduces them to the *pantins*, or puppets, of Bergson's *Le Rire*; and basically, as Demorest points out, this is an *attitude* for Emma, one with which Flaubert himself can again side:

'Like Flaubert, Emma lives entirely in memory and by dreams. The viscount ceases to be a person and becomes a center of love-dreams. The same is true of the cigar box, for to Emma, objects and men soon become symbols, in the same way that lovers only exist for each other as incarnations of love. This binds the heroines even more tightly to the author. . . .'

It also differentiates Flaubert's book *toto caelo* from repeats of it like *Cousin Baʒilio*, charming as these often are.

The critical catalogues of symbols surrounding Emma Bovary have been several, and often exceedingly astute, possibly too much so – there is *mud* on her boots after the first illicit rendez-vous, her little plaster *statue* of a priest starts to flake off (loses a foot and develops scabs on the face like the beggar at the end and, of course, like religion), Bovary's cheap *dog-cart* contrasts tellingly with the elegant carriages at the Vaubyessard ball, Léon's *cactus* pricks Emma's finger, she breaks Charles's *barometer*, and so on. The list could be long. You can veritably stake out the story of the book by the symbols, Charles's aspiration to science in the form of the blue phrenological head being replied to by the stag's-head in the seducer Rodolphe's château.

Nor does the fulness of this symbolism stop there. It merges into . . . anticipates expressionism. The blind beggar, a probable syphilitic who panhandles coach travellers with a repulsive little pantomime, and is heard singing love ballads as Emma writhes in agony on her deathbed, moves into another kind of characteri-zation, is almost an emblem, like Sorge in *Faust II*.[5] On one level, that is, the beggar exists as a literal person who has evidently groped his way to Yonville for a cure from Homais, the pharma-cist (caught out, under a law of the nineteenth Ventôse, practising medicine on the side), for his venereal ills – Homais eventually has the man committed. On another level, needless to say, the beggar parodies Emma's own state, shows the other side of her illusions ('It all comes down to syphilis in the end', bemoans Des Esseintes, who is 'Spellbound by Flaubert's wonderful prose'), her fate for having contravened the code of a man's world.

So the beggar is both more and less than a symbol, he is a true example of what Schopenhauer called emblems, 'which might also be defined as short painted fables with obvious

[5] I purloin the suggestive parallel from: Walter H. Sokel, *The Writer in Extremis*, Stanford University Press, 1959, pp. 31–3. Here Sokel pushes it into Strindberg's *To Damascus* of 1898 which he calls 'the first fully Ex-pressionist drama ever written', and where a beggar also appears.

morals'. And in common with Baudelaire's feelings about Emma, which we study below, it is interesting that Schopenhauer, who was interested in the Flaubertian artist who 'more or less conceals himself behind his representation, and at last disappears altogether', wrote lengthily on suicide as an assertion of what he called Will. Flaubert's beggar, then, begins the tradition of depicting a character's inner state by an 'objective correlative', much as the demons of Joyce's 'Circe' section advance the subconscious of Bloom.

Emma, however, is there. She is positively and superbly and (I think) movingly real. When she stands at a window or by a fire, she exists. After all, a fire is a fire. We cannot say it is really Esau or Isaac. The most natural thing in the world for a woman, the wife of the local *officier de santé*, who has just posted to the inn of a new town where her husband will take up his duties, would be to go to the fire and warm her limbs after the chilly drive.[6] Cannot we leave it at that? I am afraid that with Flaubert we cannot:

> 'When Madame Bovary entered the kitchen she went up to the fireplace. With two fingertips she caught her dress at the knee, and having thus pulled it up to her ankle, held out her black-booted foot to the fire above the revolving leg of mutton. The flame lit up the whole of her, casting its harsh light over the pattern of her gown, the fine pores of her fair skin, and even her eyelids, when she blinked from time to time. A great red glow paseed over her with the wind, blowing through the half-open door.'

It is not simply that Emma's future *Innerlichkeit* is dramatized by this, her initial entry into Yonville where she will raise her skirts with a vengeance. No, surely any reader starts to get alerted by the degree of focus. We then realize that her wedding bouquet, which had pricked her finger, had just been put on the

[6] Of course, there were more fires and fireplaces then than now. One industrious scholar has counted that *Jane Eyre* contains eighty-five references to domestic fires, plus a dozen others to 'hearths'. Flaubert, however, nearly always shadows his literal descriptions with figurative overtones.

flames in her old house, like her old dreams. When Charles first goes to the Bertaux farm where the Rouaults live, to mend Emma's father's fracture, he passes through a kitchen 'where a large fire was blazing'. Later, married and already bored, Emma 'confided many a thing to her greyhound. She would have done so to the logs in the fireplace. . . .' In the first intensity of *ennui* she feels herself 'fainting with the heat of the hearth'. And when she first reflects that Léon might be in love with her, the leitmotif of 'the fires of passion' (to continue the clichés) replies at once: 'The flame of the fire threw a joyous light upon the ceiling.' Zola repeats this rather heavily in his early *Thérèse Raquin* (again, the novel not the play).

As has been suggested, one could continue these games almost indefinitely, and some critics do. But one should only do so with the stern proviso that such touches are natural, *felt* symbolism; in the Mauriac canon, for instance, the reverse is the case, for the blazing forests of the Landes, near Bordeaux, are introduced first to show the aridity of desire and only second as a realistic element (indeed, we very rarely ever visit these pine forests in the narratives).

Thus when we first see Emma she is helping the pseudo-surgeon Charles. She then pricks her finger which she (rather naturally) puts to her lips to suck. After bidding farewell, Charles goes back for his riding crop which he has forgotten, and finds Emma leaning with her forehead against the window looking out; the sucking of the bleeding finger seems to be equated with sensuousness and the window reverie with a propensity to dream, Emma's twin characteristics.

Yet all this can get pretty fine. Flaubert himself later remarks in the narrative that all provincial girls of the day tend to stand looking out of windows – 'in the provinces the window takes the place of the theatre and the promenade'. So it still does in South Italian villages. Much, too, has been made of the waltz scene, since the first waltzes were surrogate flirtations, with the dancer's bodies unusually close (Emma feels her legs intertwine with those of her partner, the Viscount). The early waltz was a revolutionary dance. The sexual undertones are simply there, they are hardly symbolic: what country girl of Emma's age and upbringing would not feel something of a similar sensation whirled in the arms of a handsome aristocrat?

So for our purpose, in identifying Flaubert's true feminism, we should recognize the symbolic activity as standing for something else, and secondly we should be alerted by the focus on details functional to a woman's psychology, as well as to the social scene. For instance: in the passage cited it was hardly necessary to have Charles forget anything at all and then to return to the Rouault house to retrieve it. It was surely even less essential to have what he had forgotten be his riding crop. Yet as we live through the book, we find a statement of woman's position clearly staked out by this marker within it. Throughout the first two Parts, at least, there is a constant kinship made between Emma and whips, harness, bridles, curbs. These are all perfectly natural and logical in their settings but, set beside Emma, they speak to us of her and for her.

As Charles first arrives at the Bertaux, he stables his horse. Natural enough. But then he notices the whips around. Why? Nothing unusual there, surely? He next forgets his own. He is meanwhile, we note, married to a woman (his first wife, Héloïse) 'whose harness wasn't worth her hide', according to his father. Preparing to ask, further on, for Emma's hand from old Rouault, the farmer cuts in with a chuckle to give his daughter away like one of his sheep or cows – making, in the process, the male deference to 'manners' – 'Although, no doubt, the little one agrees with me, still we must ask her opinion.'

The guests arrive for the marriage to the cracking of whips; harness breaks as they leave. Extremely likely, once again, but brought to our attention. And the first thing Flaubert focuses on in the first house Emma inhabits as a wife is the door, and 'Behind the door hung a cloak with a small collar, a bridle. . . .' Once again, as Emma goes to the Vaubyessard estate for the ball, the Marquis doesn't let her leave without showing her his stables. Why should this amuse Emma? In the harness-room she sees hung up 'the bits, the whips, the spurs, the curbs'. On the way back Charles's own traces break. After recovering from her seduction by Rodolphe out riding, Emma looks up and sees him mending 'one of the two broken bridles'. Later still, she herself gives Rodolphe a riding crop with a silver-gilt top, an instrument he explicitly fondles after she lies back in bed, trembling from his love-making. Revisiting Rodolphe at the end to elicit his help, she sees his whips almost as himself.

Now this integrity of focus is truly symbolic, as is human life. Everything is perfectly natural, yet everything symbolizes Emma's state, one under the male whip. As a matter of fact, it is all the more explicit since Flaubert, so careful over what has now been vulgarized as 'body language', has Charles feel his first tactile desire for the girl via his own whip. This had fallen between some sacks and the wall. Emma bends over the sacks. Out of politeness Charles makes to recover it also, 'and as he stretched out his arm, at the same moment felt his breast brush against the back of the young girl bending beneath him. She drew herself up, scarlet, and looked at him over her shoulder as she handed him his riding crop.' The pose is no accident. It recurs in the blood-letting scene, as Emma stoops to put a basin of blood under the table, her dress pulling taut across her body as Rodolphe watches.

Significance of this nature can never be exaggerated in *Madame Bovary*, and for that reason we have dwelt upon it. Minutiae are functional in the Flaubert of this text. The intimacy of a foot placed on the bar of Emma's chair, by young Léon at the communal inn dinner-table, is felt in the fact. When Emma says good-bye to the same character, for the first time, she is once more standing with her face pressed against a window-pane; then she turns and the clerk holds out his hand. She hesitates, but takes it with a forced laugh, saying 'In the English manner, then' ('*A l'anglaise donc*'). Thus the hand-shake, out of a more frigid, less tactile culture, is here more intimate than touching the back of a hand with the lips – 'Léon felt it between his fingers, and the very substance of all his being seemed to pass into that moist palm.' Then there is some fairly categoric tactile communication by hands later, in the scene between Emma and Rodolphe at the agricultural fair, and between herself and the notary, Guillaumin, at the end.

Similarly, at the Vaubyessard ball, scholars were puzzled by the reference to the placing of gloves in glasses by ladies. Gloves in those days were fitting and are seen by Emma at the ball 'outlining the nail and tightening on the flesh at the wrists'. It was found that it was evidently local custom for girls to refuse champagne by rolling up their gloves in their wine glasses; so Emma revealed her provinciality to company and reader alike by this observance, among society ladies who did not mind swilling wine.

Virtually everything about Emma contributes something to our understanding of her – white nails, white skin, the tip of her tongue passing between small teeth, her irridescent parasol which curtains the sun from her face almost the first time we see her, while 'drops of water fell one by one on the taut silk', the antiphon to which comes a few pages later when Charles sees her sewing with 'small drops of perspiration on her bare shoulders'. Already by these tactful tics or traits, knowing authorial nudgings, she becomes the victim, in harness, under male bridle and curb, soon to feel the chauvinist's sexual whip and snare – Emma is actually juxtaposed with so much cattle in the scheming Rodolphe's mind at the fair.

So it is interesting when we find that, at the same time, several of these character symbolisms define her as male. When Charles first sees her we read, 'Like a man, she wore a tortoise-shell eyeglass thrust between two buttons of her blouse.' Soon after, when she is married, she alters her hairstyle – 'she parted it one side and rolled it under, like a man's.' Later, just before her seduction by Rodolphe, she is seen wearing a 'man's hat'; like Anna Karenina, she smokes boldly, wears a man's waistcoat (unusual for her) and dresses in breeches as a man for the masked ball in Rouen. Surely Flaubert 'insists' somewhat. We are back to Sartre's sense of astonishment that Flaubert could so thoroughly metamorphose himself into a woman, a feeling shared by – borrowed from – Baudelaire, who (it is often said) called Emma Bovary a man.

Baudelaire did not quite do so; but he did write that Flaubert had given Emma 'all the qualities of manliness'. Baudelaire's criticism of the novel first appeared in *L'Artiste* for 18 October 1857, by which date he himself had written his major symbolist poems (including 'Correspondances', little noticed at the time). His own great poem collection *Les Fleurs du Mal* was, of course, to come under prosecution by the same attorney for the Ministry of the Interior, a gentleman given to writing spicy verses himself, in the year that *Bovary* was hauled into court (Flaubert, as is well known, won and the Ministry, out for blood, made certain Baudelaire did not do so). But the latter's somewhat diffuse and disorganized review carried, for Flaubert, the deepest possible perception. 'You have penetrated the inner mystery of the work as if you and I shared the same mind', was what he wrote to Baudelaire. 'You have felt and understood me entirely.' What was this 'inner mystery'?

It was nothing less than the sense of being a woman locked in a man's world:

> 'When all is said, this woman has real greatness, and she provokes our pity. In spite of the author's systematic tough-mindedness, in spite of his efforts to retreat entirely from the stage and manipulate his characters rather like a puppeteer handles his puppets, endowing them with a talent for dreaming as well as for calculating – a combination that constitutes the perfect human being – he has elevated the female species to new heights, far above the realm of the animal and close to the ideal realm of men.'

Such was Baudelaire's encomium. It is worth reading closely, so full of implications is it for the feminist. It tells us that Emma has aspired to be an artist ('the perfect human being'). She has declined merely to remain that jelly of emotions her male world wanted of its women; nor has she simply – in the conveniently facile high school sort of reading of her predicament – tried to translate Sir Walter Scott into modern dress, romance into reality. She cannot be said to have been satisfied with simply copying a 'male pattern' – it is true she does so in the final adultery with Léon where her behaviour is masculine and dominant (she undresses 'brutally', rips off her corset 'like a gliding snake', while the young man kneels before her), but this is like so much prophetic parody of the present fever over woman's clitoral orgasm. Emma is not merely aspiring to be a man: the examples in her society would not conduce her to do so. It is more a matter of introducing volition into sex – thought, imagination. Borrowed behaviour is shown, via Léon, not to be worth it. A woman's sexuality is far more refined than this. Emma wants to find an equal, a superior being, above all one with imagination.

Thus Baudelaire was right once more: 'As another proof of the masculine qualities which she carries in her arteries, one should notice that she is much less incensed by the obvious physical shortcomings of her husband or by his glaring provincialism, than by this total absence of genius, his intellectual ineptness forcefully brought home by the stupid operation of the clubfoot.' What woman, married to a humdrum husband . . . which sister in sexist chains . . . has not echoed these words at some time or another? Charles is not a man. Pushed on by her imaginative ambition he fails at the brink.

And so it is with both Rodolphe and Léon, too, alternate aspects of her psyche, men who attract her *through herself* and to whom she is thus vulnerable. They lack her own energy, and idealism (in the zeugma of all time Flaubert remarked of the latter at the end, 'He admired the exaltation of her soul and the lace on her petticoat'). It is the realization of Zola's Nana – men are nothing things, fit merely to be bestridden and ridden around the room like donkeys. It is only too well known that intellectual men are physically attractive to women; the stud is soon a bore.

In this pattern, brilliantly observed by a Flaubert who had fornicated his way through Cairo, woman emerges as someone of superior vision and perception. Intellect is power, and woman is trained to recognize power. She admires true superiority – 'the perfect human being' – and does so as an equal. It is part of a defensive male disdain to code intellect as less 'turning-on' a trait; the locker-room guffaw – 'I didn't go to bed with her for her brains' – makes of the bluestocking a figure of fun, rather than of attraction, and we have witnessed its correction in *Jane Eyre*. The fuddy-dud professor with the burlesque or chorus-girl 'anima' – or the sophisticated Humbert Humbert enslaved by a gum-chewing American teener – is essentially an exaggeration of male chauvinism, drawn in clear lines in Heinrich Mann's *Professor Unrat* of 1905. Thus for Henry James both Rodolphe and Léon 'are pictures that pass; they solve nothing, they lead to no climax'.

In his analysis of this issueless *ennui* for woman Baudelaire listed three characteristics or qualities which the male world called manly. Let us look at them and then pass on to reconsider, more closely, how his judgement is examplified by the Flaubertian text:

> 'In order to complete his exploit to the full, it remained for the author to relinquish, so to speak, his actual sex and make himself into a woman. The result is miraculous, for in spite of his zeal at wearing masks he could not help but infuse some male blood into the veins of his creation; the most energetic and ambitious, but also the most imaginative part of Madame Bovary's personality have definitely remained masculine in kind. . . .
>
> Let the reader carefully consider the following characteristics:
>
> 1. The imagination, the highest and most tyrannical of faculties, takes the place of the heart or what is called the heart: that from which reason is generally excluded; most of the time, women, like animals, are dominated by the heart.
>
> 2. Sudden forcefulness and quickness of decision, a mystical fusion of reason and passion typical of men created for action.
>
> 3. An unlimited urge to seduce and dominate, including a willingness to stoop to the lowest means of seduction, such as the vulgar appeal of dress, perfume and make-up – all summarized in two words: dandyism, exclusive love of domination.

And yet, Madame Bovary gives in to her lovers; carried away by the sophistry of her imagination, she gives herself with magnificent generosity, in an entirely masculine manner, to fools who don't begin to measure up to her, exactly as poets will put themselves at the mercy of foolish women.'

* * *

Famous stories can too conveniently be converted into legend, from which state they fall into cliché. Let us round out Emma's lovely outlines a moment, lest symbol-chasing may have caused us to lose sight of symbol-making. Flaubert liked to banter that he never saw a lovely lady without thinking of her skeleton, and that of his best book was ineluctably pro-feminine.

Emma Rouault is the daughter of a farmer in the Seine In-férieure. Her father Théodore is a coarse peasant, though neither too badly off (he has servants) nor especially cruel. He was the son of a simpler *berger*, or shepherd, thus, with Emma's subsequent ascent, showing that social mobility which was becoming a feature of an industrialized society. The novel stood to document this, in general.

Emma marries an *officier de santé* (he is so named in the original) of the district, called Charles Bovary, who failed his medical exams and occupies a licensed position, now vanished, in between pharmacist (Homais) and doctor (Larivière). Here Flaubert, a physician's son – the latter character was founded on his father – was very sure of his ground. Charles lets blood, extracts teeth (with tremendous strength), pokes 'his arm into damp beds' (after eating country omelettes), sets legs, like Rouault's, but should never have attempted the clubfoot clap-trap on Hippolyte. The last movie made of the novel to date in fact refrains from having him do so.

The marriage soon stagnates, in every way. Charles's love-making becomes 'one habit among other habits'. Emma asks herself repeatedly, 'Why, for Heaven's sake, did I marry?' Sensing his young wife's dissatisfaction, intensified after a ball at a nearby château, Charles moves from Tostes to Yonville where his predecessor, a 'former Polish refugee' evidently called Yanoda, had vanished, run away. The couple arrive at Yonville l'Abbaye sometime during the winter of 1840. Exegetical attempts to date the action exactly (Emma's reading to the rescue here) generally agree on at least this year in the book, thanks to Flaubert's allusion to the catastrophic Rhône flooding of the time – Homais mentions 'the victims of the Lyon floods' on the night the Bovarys arrive. The point about some precision as to the date of the novel's action here is to emphasize that Emma lived before the Third Republic restored elements in the divorce laws established by the revolutionaries and adopted in the Napoleonic Code, but abolished at the Bourbon Restoration.

Emma gives birth to a girl she calls Berthe (she later 'sent wood to women in childbirth'), and senses attraction for the notary's clerk, Léon Dupuis, a moment that turns to ashes in her hands as he leaves for Paris, and law examinations. A rich bachelor and philanderer who has just bought into the area next attracts Emma, Rodolphe Boulanger de la Huchette (our author here bearing a sarcastic eye, perhaps, on the easy ennoblement, via small farmsteads, of bourgeois writers, e.g. Gérard de Nerval). Thirty-four, shallow and handsome, Rodolphe reminds Emma of the Viscount with whom she had waltzed at the ball; at an agricultural fair Rodolphe cleverly externalizes Emma's 'romantic' sentiments for her and finds his way into her mind as, later, her heart. 'Madame Bovary!' he exclaims, 'why, the whole world calls you thus! Moreover, it is not your name; it is the name of another!'[7] Emma yields to him out riding.

[7] 'The first thing that happened to us at the Registry Office, where we had gone to perform the legal garbage, was that I was asked by some clerk to sign the green form in my maiden name. My *maiden* name? I couldn't understand what the clerk was talking about. "You'll sign your maiden name here, deary", the clerk said, "and this is the last time you'll ever sign it." I couldn't believe him. Germaine Greer is my name . . . it's a known name, a name I made – when I sign it to a piece of writing, it has a certain value. Now I had lost my name just because I was marrying this schmo. So the clerk said I could have my passport endorsed to read that I was "trading as Germaine Greer". *Trading as Germaine Greer*!!! I told them immediately I would not agree to that and that I would keep my own bank account, pay my own tax, and conduct my own business affairs.'
Interview with Germaine Greer, *Evergreen Review*, October, 1971.
The first right demanded in 'The Utopian Marriage Contract', published

It is as well to clarify this. Emma does commit adultery before the clubfoot operation, on which Baudelaire set much store as her psychological turning-point. However, as Baudelaire well put it, after Charles has bungled the operation, 'Her fierce anger, pent up for years, suddenly bursts into the open; doors slam; the awed husband, who was never able to give his romantically inclined wife the slightest spiritual satisfaction, is relegated to his room; he is locked up in punishment for his guilty ignorance. . . .'

When Rodolphe ditches her as mistress, via a sanctimonious *Dear Joan* letter, Emma has what the French call a *crise*, is tempted to jump out the window, and retires to bed with amatory neurasthenia. Next, Léon re-enters her life, working for a Maître Dubocage in Rouen, and is taken on as her lover. The focus has now shifted somewhat from external scene to internal soul, and by this time Emma is our 'point of view' or Jamesian 'centre of vision'. The victim of '*Moeurs de province*' – as the book was subtitled – is in danger of becoming their example, in an almost perfectly reciprocal interplay of character and environment. Emma is on her *déchéance*, after sexual release, if you wish to view the book's structure as orgasmic.

The usurer Lheureux begins to foreclose, Emma appeals to the notary who is actually in collusion with him and slavers like an animal before her, imploring her favours on his knees in his dressing gown (a scene duplicated in *Cousin Bazilio*) at the moment he should have been trying to help her. When a despairing Emma then evidently offers herself to the town dummy and Army hero, Binet, Flaubert tactfully turns up the note of the man's silly lathe, and the scene gets reported to us indirectly by a sort of Greek chorus of crones, one the Mayor's wife, who would like to see her whipped.

Everyone Emma turns to boredly refuses to help. They are not all men, though most of them are (the priest, Rodolphe). The village nurse simply gets on with her spinning. Finally, Emma swallows her arsenic in front of the young and adoring

in the first issue (20 December 1971) of the feminist American *Ms.* magazine was: 'The wife's right to use her maiden name or any other name she chooses.'

Justin, whom she tries to scare into some sort of silence by a quasi-professional threat – 'Say nothing, or all the blame will fall on your master.' Charles reads her death-note, summons the pharmacist, but despite a last-minute emetic Emma dies in considerable agony (a childbirth duplication, amongst other allusions). A coda shows us Charles sprucing up after Emma's death, the horrible Homais prospering, and most of the complacent or frankly wicked successful. One sees Sainte-Beuve's point. Charles himself dies holding a hank of Emma's hair, on the garden seat where she had met a lover. Lacking all support, little Berthe is despatched by an aunt to sweated labour in a cotton factory, clearly destined to fall victim to the same male-dominated society.

It is when one compares the bare bones of this outline with what Flaubert worked on that one sees what he contributed to the cause of women everywhere. In truth, imaginative giants of his nature have so suffused the modern libertarian conscience that it is hard to describe where exactly they broke trail, and where they simply enlarged already nascent revolt.

The 'real' Madame Bovary – another subject to which archives have been devoted – was supposedly Delphine Couturier who, in real life, had married the local health officer, Eugène Delamare, of a village called Ry, near Rouen. Bored stiff with her undramatic husband, she too took lovers, overspent widly, and finally killed herself. René Dumesnil, in his valuable *La Vocation littéraire de Gustave Flaubert* (1961), sees 'little but anecdotal interest' in the Delamare source, and would rather draw our attention to a schoolboy manuscript by Flaubert, generally referred to as *Passion and Virtue*.

From the standpoint of radical feminism, however, Flaubert's changes from the Delamare story, which he had come upon through the visit of the man's mother to his own, the luckless health officer having been a devoted student of Dr Flaubert, stand out strongly. Two points should be emphasized here. But before making them, one must always bear in mind that Flaubert was writing a work of art, not a psychological case history, and that he well knew how permeated everything he had written in

Bovary was with a bitterly critical attitude. This he expressed in the celebrated letter that must make him beloved of every author, in which he wrote to Léon Laurent-Pichat, co-director of *La Revue de Paris*, that 'I will not suppress a comma', adding that he wouldn't mind in the least if publication were stopped:

> 'By eliminating the passage about the cab you have not made the story a whit less shocking; and you will accomplish no more by the cuts you ask for in the sixth installment.
>
> You are objecting to details, whereas actually you should object to the whole. The brutal element is basic, not incidental. Negroes cannot be made white, and you cannot change a book's blood.'

He might have added – Nor its sex.

*   *   *

Bearing in mind, then, that he was involved in a fiction rather than a sociology, it is still significant that he made such a strong departure from the otherwise rather faithfully followed Delamare story *at the start*. Emma is Charles's second wife. Delphine was Delamare's first. What is the point of introducing Héloïse, Bovary's shrew of a wife at the time he met Emma? Is she functional to the story?

No sooner put, the question makes one realize that Flaubert obviously introduced this first marriage in order to pillory the 'double-standard' attitude of a complacent husband. Héloïse is a bailiff's ugly widow, past her youth, who is selected more as a guardian-virago for Charles than wife – 'his wife was master; he had to say this and not say that in company, to fast every Friday, dress as she liked, harass at her bidding those patients who did not pay. She opened his letters, watched his comings and goings, and listened at the partition-wall when women came to consult him in his surgery.' Later she makes him swear, 'hand on the prayer-book', that he would go to the Rouault farm no more. Adultery, Flaubert observes, is a male privilege. When Emma 'gives herself with magnificent generosity, in an entirely masculine manner', to use Baudelaire's words, it is suddenly a crime.

Secondly, Flaubert was interested in the fact that Delamare went for nine years knowing nothing of his wife's infidelities. Here he met an aesthetic difficulty. Fiction is a concertina of fact, and uses time qualitatively rather than quantitatively. Because we see the time span of a novel only in its salient integers, Charles Bovary loses credibility as a cuckold. It is fairly absurd that he doesn't 'twig' when told of Emma's order of the elopement cloak and trunk, nor again when he meets Madame Lempereur, the music teacher (Nabokov obviously echoes sexual betrayal as music instruction at the end of *Lolita*).

Flaubert has to fix this up, as it were, by making Charles a fantastically, indeed unreally, stupid man. We may be judging by the standards of an advanced technology, with its compulsory pseudo-education, but a man who complains that the music interferes with the words at the opera, asks his wife to go on playing the same phrase she is stumbling over on the piano, and who can stand watching whist for 'five consecutive hours' (at the Vaubyessard ball) is pretty close to parody, at least for modern tastes, certainly more suited to the pages of *Don Quixote* than a novel by 'the father of realism'.

Yet we should remember that the French provincial bourgeoisie was far more brutalized a century ago than it is today. Longevity was also less – Charles always seems much older than he is (his father dies at fifty-eight). He himself has dirty nails, doesn't shave for days on end, and indeed only smartens up after his wife's suicide – another alteration of the real-life legend, since Delamare subsequently killed himself. On the contrary, Charles lives on for Emma's revenge – 'He waxed his moustache and, just like her, signed promissory notes. She corrupted him from beyond the grave.'

And such is the point. His 'love' *increases* with his stupidity, until Emma has to 'relegate him to a room on the third floor', like the pathetic little schoolboy with the absurd cap whom no one can understand at the start. But a schoolboy is not Emma's equal – 'Charles had no ambition . . . she felt a wild desire to strike him; she went to open the window in the passage and breathed in the fresh air to calm herself. '"What a man! what a man!" she said in a low voice, biting her lips.' In Flaubert's canon there can be no pity for stupidity.

When a woman is crushed to the core like this, her marital obligations cease. As in *A Doll's House*[8] the suffocated wife owes it to herself to abandon her children to save her soul:

HELMER To desert your home, your husband and your children! And you don't consider what people will say!

NORA I cannot consider that at all. I only know that it is necessary for me.

HELMER It's shocking. This is how you would neglect your most sacred duties.

NORA What do you consider my most sacred duties?

HELMER Do I need to tell you that? Are they not your duties to your husband and your children?

NORA I have other duties just as sacred.

HELMER That you have not. What duties could those be?

NORA Duties to myself.

Fantasying about the free lovers of literature just after she has given herself to another man for the first time in her marriage, 'Emma felt a satisfaction of revenge.' In such circumstances adultery indeed becomes a duty owed to identity, almost a matter of honour. But in a Yonville world this does mean borrowing a male pattern, rather than being able to eventuate the varieties of feminine response, and so of course 'Emma found again in adultery all the platitudes of marriage.' At the opera Charles asks her, puzzled, why one of the Lords is torturing the heroine, to which Emma retorts, 'he is her lover!' A moment later, bathing in the poetry and power of the piece, she empathizes with the hero – 'she tried to imagine his life – extraordinary, magnificent, notorious, the life that could have been hers if fate had

---

[8] There is a perhaps unnoticed premonition of Ibsen's *The Wild Duck* in the scene where Emma stumbles on the absurdly solemn Binet duck-hunting out of a barrel in a ditch at the side of the road (Part Two: X).

willed it.' Yet 'fate' had willed that she should be not merely a woman, but what is defined as a woman by men.

Furthermore, there is no trace in the Delamare story of the wife physically prostituting herself, as in both the *Bovary* and *Bazilio* redactions. In this suggestion – the scene with Binet – Flaubert comes close to our times, of course, jostling elbows with the Shaw of *Mrs Warren's Profession* who accused society of 'underpaying, undervaluing, and overworking women so shamefully that the poorest of them are forced to resort to prostitution to keep body and soul together', or, even more recently, with a Ti-Grace Atkinson asserting that 'prostitutes are the only honest women left in America, because they charge for their services rather than submit to a marriage contract which forces them to work for life without pay'.

Flaubert here touches on, anticipates, something that seems to have become crucial to contemporary feminism; he apparently sensed the shock of what he was saying by shifting his centre of vision in the scene between Emma and Binet, and having it told to us indirectly. It is, indeed, the only such break in that part of the book. Is Emma's position in marriage any different from that which Mrs Atkinson describes? Somewhat, since she has denied Charles her sexual favours. The question is further compounded by matters of volition or compulsion in the sexual act itself. We tend today to reject the idea that sex is chiefly a response to a biological need, seeing it rather as coloured and stimulated by what a culture considers to be arousing – in a word, psychological rather than physiological.

This was not so, of course, in Emma's day. Then it was widely considered that man was responding to an innate genetic structure with the most honourable aspect of sexuality therefore being the ejaculation of male semen. Woman's satisfaction was thus a dependency of man's (hence the 'myth' of the vaginal orgasm). Under such conditions it was rather natural to hear clarion calls for marriage to be an equitable, kind of Wollstonecraft 'contract' between the subsuming parties, as it might be between management and labour in industry. Jane Eyre makes it quite clear to Rochester that, if they marry, their charter will be 'the most liberal that despot ever yet conferred'. She goes on:

> 'I would have no mercy, Mr Rochester, if you supplicated for it with an eye like that. While you looked so, I should be certain that whatever charter you might grant under coercion, your first act, when released, would be to violate its conditions.'

A trifle perplexed, Rochester replies that 'I fear you will compel me to go through a private marriage ceremony, besides that performed at the altar.' (More or less what American feminists are trying to provoke today.) He asks what terms she would stipulate and Jane replies, in effect, those of perfect equality ('Your regard: and if I give you mine in return, that debt will be quit'). Given its context, that of female sexuality being generally considered subservient to male, this sort of thing is thoroughly understandable. But it seems a little anomalous today. Leonard and Virginia Woolf are said to have pooled their incomes, shared expenses and divided up any surplus equally; their contributions to the marriage were probably pretty equal. But something like the alleged marriage contract between Jacqueline Bouvier Kennedy and Aristotle Onassis, with one hundred and seventy bristling financial clauses, seems more to advance the idea of the prostitute-wife than correct it. Flaubert said that he learnt a lot from prostitution.

When he was writing *Bovary* Paris was beginning to seethe with prostitutes. The big new boulevards Haussmann was to drive through the city were going to teem with little Nanas and Berthes, whose holiness both Baudelaire and Dostoevsky apostrophized, and whose pathos Constantin Guys conscientiously recorded – for Baudelaire 'The Painter of Modern Life', in truth. Emma herself sees the new whores thronging the Rue Nationale in Rouen.

In the light of what prostitution represented then and now attempts by women's groups to 'liberate' hookers (presumably from madames, as well as pimps) border on the comic, and have indeed come unholy croppers. Poe, Baudelaire, Flaubert, Dostoevsky – it is usually said that such alienated writers found kindred spirits on the streets (Dostoevsky's Sonya and Liza).

Baudelaire represents this view in his article on 'Women and Prostitutes' where he calls the courtesan 'a beast of prey', adding, 'She is a sort of gipsy wandering on the fringes of a regular society', in common with the lesbians who also intrigued him. But there is more to it than this. Flaubert saw no less than a synthesis of our civilization in the activity.

It has been said that he was a sexist because he admired prostitution. But he did not admire it as such. He admitted that he was attracted by prostitutes and analyzed his own lechery as a symptom of our times (Marie of *Novembre* is a vampira). Mario Praz tells us that 'Flaubert's feminine ideal is, naturally, a woman of infamous character, a prostitute, an adulteress.'[9] If left unqualified, this is a serious misunderstanding, by a great scholar, of a great writer. Flaubert suggested, rather, that these were the types of our times. To Louise Colet he confessed:

'It is perhaps a depraved taste, but I love prostitution, and for itself, too, quite apart from what there is underneath. My heart begins to pound every time I see one of those flashily dressed women walking under the lamplight in the rain, just as monks in their corded robes have always excited some deep, ascetic corner of my soul. The idea of prostitution is a meeting point of so many elements – lust, bitterness, complete absence of human contact, muscular frenzy, the clink of gold – that to peer into it deeply makes one reel. One learns so many things in a brothel, and feels such sadness, and dreams so longingly of love!'

The true fracture of modern sexual consciousness was illustrated in the opprobrium thrown on the whore. The composite Magna Mater figure, proliferating in the Near East (where Flaubert incidentally seems to have enjoyed his intensest sexual moments), succoured in all senses, bestowing fertility. 'These deities', writes Rattray Taylor, 'were not decomposed; so that the same goddess could represent both virginity and fulfilment, both mother and prostitute. This is why Ishtar, the mother, can

[9] Praz, pp. 155–6.

say of herself "A prostitute compassionate am I."[10] In the nineteenth century the side of the mother that is the prostitute (or all-comforter) becomes intensely taboo, with a resultant detestation and persecution of whores well rendered in *Nana*, as also in the many stories of dying prostitutes (*Manon Lescaut*).

Nor did Baudelaire 'admire' prostitution. He simply saw it in front of him ('If by chance anyone should be so ill-advised as to seek here an opportunity of satisfying his unhealthy curiosity, I must in all charity warn him that he will find nothing whatever to stimulate the sickness of his imagination'). But in his time, before every second whore was an addict supporting a habit, the prostitute was a little artist, a person 'of artifice', a 'Protean image of wanton beauty', for was not selling your body in this sense also ultimately controlling it? So he could greet another *révolté* beside him:

> 'In that vast picture-gallery which is life in London or Paris, we shall meet with all the various types of fallen woman-hood – of woman in revolt against society – at all levels.'

Thirdly, while Flaubert was hardly the first to depict the Christian (notably the Catholic) religion as a carrier of male supremacy, substituting the new whore for the old witch, he did succeed in pushing forward pro-feminist insights in this connection. Long an opponent of abortion reform, the Roman Catholic Church, with its all-male hierarchy and male priesthood (not to mention its stress on the 'spiritual' significance of motherhood-virginity), fails Emma at every point.

Throughout *Bovary* you could list the points at which ritualistic religion is directly or indirectly derided: the 'baptism' with champagne by Bovary *père*, the convent lesbianism, the eating of meat on Friday, destruction of the plaster curé, violation of the six weeks of the Virgin, and so on. You could then cut them all out. The book would still share in that secularism which spurred on the novel in general. In fact, this feature attracted the attention of both the government and Baudelaire, the latter

[10] G. Rattray Taylor, *Sex in History*, New York: Ballantine Books, 1954, p. 216; London: Thames and Hudson, 1952.

citing the callous idiocy of Father Bournisien who, consulted in despair by Emma, refers her to (*a*) St Paul ('we are born to suffer'), and (*b*) her husband ('a doctor of the body'). As Baudelaire astutely commented, 'Thus absolved by the ineptness of the priest, what woman would not wish to immerse herself in the swirling water of adultery . . .?'

Religion, then, is yet another betrayal. Bournisien's recalcitrant catechism choristers cannot complete, we notice, the answer to the good priest's question, 'What is a Christian?' Nor can Emma find something here called 'love', that *Amor nel cor* or eternal carrot which has been used both to urge women on and keep them in harness. As she pushes her inept husband into the club-foot operation, 'She only longed to lean on something more solid than love.' Lucie de Lammermoor is her alter ego.

This thirst in the soul which produces Emma's agony, as that of countless women denied an outlet for their creative selves, is provoked rather than appeased by religion. Given communion 'at the height of her illness', Emma 'fainted with celestial joy as she advanced her lips to accept the body of the Saviour presented to her', a hideously blasphemous but purely apposite kiss she inflicts at the very end, just before the priest's *Indulgentiam*, on 'the body of the Man-God' in 'the fullest kiss of love she had ever given'.

La Merteuil would have understood. The church had made religion so much substitute sex. Flaubert's scene in the Rouen cathedral likened to a boudoir is a supremely desecratory metaphor (incidentally given again in Kafka's *The Trial*). So is the comparison of 'betrothed, husband, celestial lover, and eternal marriage' in Emma's earlier mind. There is no room to go into the complexities and vagaries of this well-known psychological trickery, but the location of Flaubert's sympathy here may be seen in a passage from Part Two where we read of Emma:

'When she knelt on her Gothic prie-Dieu, she addressed to the Lord the same suave words that she had murmured formerly to her lover in the outpourings of adultery. She was searching for faith; but no delights descended from the heavens, and she arose with aching limbs and the vague feeling that she was being cheated.'

This crystallizes in the parody of Extreme Unction with which Flaubert presages Emma's death, and of which he wrote to Madame Schlesinger that it was 'nothing but a page from the *Rituel de Paris*, put into decent French' (14 January 1857):

'Then he recited the *Misereatur* and the *Indulgentiam*, dipped his right thumb in the oil, and began to give extreme unction. First, upon the eyes, that had so coveted all wordly goods; then upon the nostrils, that had been so greedy of the warm breeze and the scents of love; then upon the mouth, that had spoken lies, moaned in pride and cried out in lust; then upon the hands that had taken delight in the texture of sensuality; and finally upon the soles of the feet, so swift when she had hastened to satisfy her desires, and that would now walk no more.'

Obviously our sympathies are here enlisted on the side of the senses, rather than their repression. 'I hate your God', shouts Charles at the priest, when Emma is dead (an imprecation left out of all motion pictures I have seen made from this book). For Flaubert saw that the whole of our society is founded on repressive structures, of which sex personifies a kind of amalgam. 'Every notary bears within him the débris of a poet.' The harness breaks and Emma 'puzzled her head to find some vow to fulfill'. At which point we should perhaps pass to Dumesnil's *Passion and Virtue* source for *Madame Bovary* and finally identify Bovarysme as a prime sickness, as well as illusion, of our times.

The fascinating thing about Flaubert's early manuscript – a 'philosophical tale', as he termed it – is its strong sympathy with woman on the part of a fully sexed schoolboy of sixteen. In this draft of the masterpiece to come Emma is Mazza, and Rodolphe an engineer (cp. *Bazilio*) called Ernest. Of Mazza (who, like Emma, kills herself by poison, though by drinking it) we are told, 'She sees life as one long cry of pain.' Here Ernest writes to Mazza the same letter Rodolphe was to send to Emma, laden with French absolutes – 'cease to love me. Love Virtue and Duty instead'. These failed Emma, too – '*bliss, passion, ecstasy, that had seemed to her so beautiful in books*'.

The extraordinary thing about this early document is that (as Baudelaire cleverly identified of the later) woman really wins. In the Extreme Unction section we surely all long to let Emma's senses – her eyes, nostrils, mouth and hands and feet – succeed. But the truncation of aspiration expressed by the syntax alone[11] reverberates strongly thanks to its harmony. This is not to obfuscate. Far from it. As Erich Auerbach summarizes, 'The novel is the representation of an entire human existence which has no issue.' In a male supremacy woman knows she 'has no issue'. She cannot *result* in anything. Another critic neatly puts it, 'The indulgence and the mortification of the body are inseparable for Flaubert, even as they are for Baudelaire: chastity is liable to corruption, even as prostitution is compatible with holiness.'[12]

So this interminable *ennui* or failure of hope, falling from its leaden skies, really strengthens Flaubert's portrait of Emma and directly answers Dorothy Richardson's charge that no male novelist can fully represent the feminine psychology. All alienation, or exclusion, will awaken in us longings; we expect that what our language represents should to a fair extent accord with what actually passes before our sensory perceptors. When it does not do so, we get that betrayal of the human contract which leads to suicide; Emma thus rises high above the presentation of woman as the flighty, unpredictable, supposedly erratic and whimsical sprite of the Strindberg-Hamsun-Lawrence axis, notably that in Hamsun's early *Pan* (Edvarda), *Victoria, Hunger* and *Mysteries* (Dagny).

Any student of nineteenth-century literature must at some time wonder at the intensity and spread of the term *ennui*. Baudelaire

[11] I refer again to the telling use of the zeugma, a union in grammatical equality of two disparates, which Flaubert turns into a sublime-to-ridiculous trick: Emma 'wanted to die, but she also wanted to live in Paris', etc.

[12] Harry Levin, *The Gates of Horn*, Oxford University Press, 1963, p. 242.

made of the emotion (or lack of it), which is only roughly translated by boredom or tedium, the cornerstone of his world-view. It stares out at us, provided with a capital letter like some cardinal sin, at the end of the epigraph to his one collection of poems. Dostoevsky used it, in French, to denote the sickness of his underground man, as Tolstoy of his Ivan Ilyich. Why was it so powerful? To what did it correspond in the social *Geist* to make it reverberate so powerfully?

Ennui is certainly a form of Emile Durkheim's *anomie*, the gap between social aims and achievements, and it is one of the most dangerous and damaging. It is a kind of profound psychological emptiness resulting from a final lack of trust in language, personified in Emma and modern America. Flaubert, of whom Théophile Gautier said that his every line was 'the coffin of a dead illusion', dedicated his five years of writing *Bovary* to the characterization of this loss of faith both in language and in life. When all the social directives fail, all the promises and catchwords turn out to be empty, the human animal sinks into apathy, an *accidia* of the soul where (as for the later Flaubert) everything becomes boring almost before it is uttered. According to Eugene Kinkead, author of *In Every War But One*, GI prisoners in Korea suffered acute losses from an otherwise almost inexplicable form of 'give-up-itis'. We recall, via Maigron, the celebrated Suicide Club of Baudelaire's day.

So Emma's adulterous *ennui* is a whole social issue. As she tells Léon, her second lover, 'you too, you will leave me! You will marry! You will be like all the others.' He asks, 'What others?' She answers, 'Why, like all men', adding, after a moment, 'You are all of you wretches!' Flaubert's *L'Education sentimentale* ends on the same note of erotico-social apathy – 'We were better off then.' Once more we remember, ''89 destroyed royalty and the nobility, '48 the bourgeoisie, and '51 the people.' The social directives seem destined to fail just as (in Levin's suggestion) chastity exists to be corrupted.

For there is finally a kind of sexology of *ennui*. Emma grows up in a culture which patterns frailty and reticence as feminine traits. She attempts the male norms, only to realize the enormity of her offence . . . woman is supposed to be the passive partner of the sex act, and Emma infringes violently upon this view. Only a prostitute does so in actuality. What Flaubert is saying here is summarized by Ruth Herschberger, in a delightful little book well worth all the Betty Friedans and Kate Milletts put together:

'It is precisely because women do nothing that they get so tired doing it. The cure is not rest and sedatives but the freedom to participate.

What is frequent in unhappy sexual relations? Fatigue. What can relieve fatigue? Adrenalin. What stimulates adrenalin? Excitement. Who is the notorious Tired One of marriages? The woman. For whom is excitement supposed dangerous? She.'[13]

The resultant erotic *ennui* is shown by Baudelaire, Flaubert and Zola alike as the product of dependency. The prostitute enjoys what de Beauvoir well calls a 'negative' liberty.[14] A long passage in *Nana* exemplifies this. Nana herself could have all the men in Paris, but she still feels like yawning. Emma exchanges one male, Charles, for another, Léon, but the barter only brings her more boredom. The point is that she is still being exploited by another. Berthe Morisot did not kill herself; Marilyn Monroe did. The Hollywood woman star of the past was the living martyr to Baudelairean *ennui*. Her freedom was wholly factitious. She was told how lucky she was, how free, but in reality she was still a disposable object. She had not become independently creative.

*　　*　　*

Thus the most resonant aspect of *Madame Bovary* for a woman – to which Flaubert organized structure, style, syntax – is its vision of the failure of erotic alongside social hope. For over one half of the human race this is the great betrayal, and the revenge for

[13] Ruth Herschberger, *Adam's Rib*, New York Harper and Row, Har/ Row Books, 1970, p. 151 (first published in 1948).
[14] De Beauvoir, pp. 539.

love that Emma must enact on herself. It is that 'bitterer poison' which rises to her mouth beside the bile of her death-bed.

Women, Flaubert is saying, are allowed to dream, that is to imagine – only to have the dream, the activity, denied them in real life. This fissure in our consciousness, the gap between the intensity of aspiration and the possibility of its achievement, can be that most damaging kind of social disease, or narcosis, which Durkheim termed *anomie*. We all know we won't inherit the world of the television screen, and the yawn of deception these hopes elicit deprives us of social energy, anaesthetizes us to injustice. 'You all die at fifteen', was what Diderot wrote to Sophie Volland. Emma puts it touchingly:

> 'But suppose there existed somewhere someone strong and beautiful, a man of valor, passionate yet refined, the heart of a poet in the form of an angel, a bronze-stringed lyre, playing elegaic epithalamia to the heavens, why might she not some-day happen on him? What a vain thought! Besides, nothing was worth the trouble of seeking it; everything was a lie. Every smile concealed a yawn of boredom, every joy a curse, every pleasure its own disgust, and the sweetest kisses left upon your lips only the unattainable desire for a greater delight.'

Here Emma stands squarely beside Hedda Gabler, though she has neither the latter's gifts nor opportunities. We may not be able to live as other than we are, yet we ought to be allowed to live *as we are*, that is as intelligent human beings contributing fully to society. Alas, "89 destroyed royalty and the . . .', etc. Opposed to this, 'all is liberty in a world of fictions', as Flaubert also wrote.

So *ennui* is more than boredom; it is an endemic of the century, like silicosis for miners. Thomas Mann was to give it a chapter as such at the end of *The Magic Mountain*. For Emma Bovary 'ennui, the silent spider, was weaving its web in the darkness, in every corner of her heart'. The image seems picked out of one of Baudelaire's '*Spleen*' poems, and to lend itself later to the phraseology of an Ibsen character. For the end of *ennui* is

Baudelaire's outburst of *spleen*; by aligning woman with the imaginative dreamer such writers make her the artist, the creator of unity. The increasing casualty list of artist-suicides of the time (Borel is mentioned in Baudelaire's review of *Bovary*) muster behind Emma's death-bed. As a fine critic puts it:

> 'If woman, in Baudelaire's work, is not just the other sex, but the Other, absolutely, she is also – at least figuratively – primordial Unity whose way this Other blocks.'[15]

* * *

When Emma's daughter is sent off to the cotton-mill at the close of the book, Flaubert leaves us with an open end – to further oppression of womanhood. Zola was to conclude *L'Assommoir* on the same '*j'accuse*', with little Nana wandering from her drunken mother's side onto the streets, and formal prostitution. Perhaps the saddest story in the legacy of *Madame Bovary*, one Flaubert might have considered ironically characteristic of our male society, was the fate of the novel's first English translator, Karl Marx's youngest daughter Eleanor.

'Tussy', as her famous father called her, translated Flaubert's book as a teenager and, though her version is flawed by contemporary standards of precision, it was for generations through her over-abused eyes that English readers came to the text. And Eleanor Aveling appears to have been a signal sacrifice on the altar of caricatural male chauvinism.

She grew up as a sort of skivvy to the founder of communism, as tyrannous a parent in his way as Freud seems to have been in his, and one afflicted with nauseating boils. From domestic slavery to Marx she passed to total dependence on Edward Aveling, a pseudo-socialist or plain scoundrel who kept her as mistress, refrained from divorcing his wife, and addicted her to opium. On the side he slept with her socialist friends and defrauded the party of funds.

[15] Pierre Emmanuel, *Baudelaire: The Paradox of Redemptive Satanism*, translated by Robert T. Cargo, University of Alabama Press, 1967, p. 45.

With astonishing stoicism 'Tussy' continued to stand by this arrant rascal till his wife died and, though he then married an actress, she still stayed faithful to him, finally poisoning herself, like Emma, at his suggestion and leaving him all her money. The gentleman was good enough to name prussic acid as the preferred poison.

Gustave Flaubert would have nodded.

* * *

In America, at any rate, there usually comes a point in almost every discussion of *Madame Bovary* when someone objects: If Emma had had the necessary money, she wouldn't have had to kill herself.

In common with Balzac, Flaubert wanted to show the intrinsically corrupting power of the cash nexus, with the result that both have drawn praise from Marxists. We then note that Charles virtually finances his own cuckoldry and that Emma pays off her bad conscience in the form of the beggar, much as Aschenbach, in Mann's *Death in Venice*, pays his dues to the mountebank entertainer in lieu of the gondolier who had ferried him over to Thanatos.

Although the Portuguese master José Maria Eça de Queiroz (1845–1900), a consul and lawyer as well as writer, explicitly admired Flaubert in his correspondence, modelled his *O Primo Bazilio* of 1878 on *Bovary*, his *A Relíquia* on *Salammbô*, while his character Jacinto (in *A Cidade e as Serras*, his last work) echoes Des Esseintes, the intensity in the symbolism is by now lacking. The book opens with a cuckoo clock striking, but this is more an anticipatory pun rather than a symbol. Eça's debt to Flaubert is acknowledged in Joaquim Ferreira's *Historiada da Literatura Portuguesa* (2 ediçao), and *Cousin Bazilio* closely follows the general outlines of *Bovary*. Too closely – for the comparison from the point of view of feminism becomes a fascinating postscript underlining the importance of the latter.

It would be both a tedious and totally unnecessary task of documentation to list blow-by-blow the likenesses in the two stories, outside their similarities of style. Eça's lovely (albeit blonde) Luiza deceives her adoring husband, an engineer, during one of his business absences. She does so with a cousin, Bazilio de Brito, who has come to Lisbon primarily for this purpose, to seduce her; his is far more a silhouette of Don Juan than Rodolphe, being an idle hedonist ('we must pass through this valley of sorrow with the greatest of comfort') who yawns at bullfights and, though but twenty-five, frequently laments his old age. He is, in short, a *macho* and Luiza a victim of *machismo*. And for this reason alone Eça has to portray her husband as a 'true man', even if one interested primarily in 'papers, pistols, linens, and his beard'. The author establishes the depth of their love early on, before dismissing Jorge to Beja, south of the Tagus. In *Madame Bovary* the adultery must take place under Charles's very nose.

Like Emma, Luiza is abandoned. With the heroine of twenty-one years previously, too, she tries to borrow money – in her case to silence a blackmailing maid who has intercepted her letters. Emma went to Guillaumin, Luiza goes to a banker called Castro, who also falls on his knees and makes a bid for her favours, whereupon Luiza, in a fine scene, beats him up. On Jorge's return, with attendant fury, Luiza lapses into a coma and, her lovely hair chopped off, dies of a so-called cerebral fever. Both lovers are indifferent to the fates of their mistresses.

Though there are close similarities, even textual[16] (as in the speeches of Bazilio and Rodolphe), it is the differences which stand out, and concern us here. For example: Homais and the Dickensian Councillor Accacio (whose bald head, in Eça's novel, Doña Felicidade finds so exciting) represent the same values. A beggar opens the coach door for Luiza at the theatre, and so on. In fact, one soon finds that the Portuguese writer has really reversed the theme. Provincial Portugal has firm values. Middle-

[16] The death-bed scenes are very close, e.g. 'The doctor took Luiza's pulse, and he felt the last tremor of it flee away from him as though it were the broken string of a guitar' (*Bazilio*); 'her pulse slipped beneath the fingers like a stretched thread, like a harp-string about to break' (*Bovary*). I take Roy Campbell's translation of the Portuguese on trust.

class they may be, but they are far from static and self-reflexive, as in Flaubert's France. Jorge is active, Charles passive. And the erotic betrayal is by a shallow cosmopolitanism in the form of Bazilio (or the Viscount Reynaldo), one imported from Paris where Eça himself had been a disgusted diplomat. 'Rape her, damn you, and kill her if she resists', Reynaldo counsels Bazilio, over a copy of *The Times*.

Both Emma and Luiza devour romantic novels,[17] and both become obsessed with the idea of elopement (each book features a love scene in a carriage), one paralleled or parodied by the Flaubertian Félicité running off with Théodore, which Eça duplicates by having his cook, Joanna, make assignations with her Pedro by suspending a carpet from a window. But the more Luiza is captivated in her little love nest (nicknamed 'The Paradise') by Bazilio, the more she really loves Jorge. In the original, of course, the reverse obtains – the more Emma dotes on Rodolphe, the more she hates Charles and the entire institution of marriage. It is significant, too, that Luiza has no children.

Bazilio is thus a sort of anti-*Bovary*. Eça gives us a thirty-year-old washout called Juliao Zazarte who pines to be a surgeon. But the man is a failure as a man, before being one as a doctor, whereas Flaubert is excoriating false scientism in Homais's opinions, and the hold they have on Charles. Luiza suffers degradation in the course of her decline, both in the servant-mistress ratio as in the wife-prostitute relationship; yet she is invariably charming and retains her feeling for her husband throughout – 'It was really absurd having a husband like Jorge and thinking about another man. . . .'

In the final death scene, therefore, the desperation is lacking since it is not socially oriented. After all, the servants in *Bazilio* appear to be treated with extreme cruelty, their dormer rooms being stiflingly hot and infested with rats; we observe that none of this seems to bother Luiza unduly. Indeed, the reader is accordingly tempted to feel that she gets something of a come-

[17] Luiza soaks herself in *La Dame aux Camellias*, another dying-whore story, for which Emma was too early.

uppance from Juliana, the blackmailing back-stairs shrew, for such harsh treatment and general lack of consideration. 'Out of pride and dread of dismissal', we read of Juliana, 'she had never offered herself as so many had done, either to an employer or a fellow servant.' Our sense must be of pity for the woman. Eça's defence fails.

This is the crux of the comparison. If Eça's Luiza had genuinely loved her Jorge in a society of any mutual sexual equality, she would have simply told him that she had made a slip. But the society presented so lovingly in these pages is still curiously feudal and sexually decadent, so that the effort to shore up the sexual values of Hispanic culture becomes ineffective. Directly we have asked ourselves why Luiza cannot tell her husband of her 'lapse' (it was not such a gross one, after all, given Bazilio's abilities), the whole edifice collapses and we see sexism rampant – in all senses.

So Eça ducks the issue of what adultery means. His Luiza feels remorse for what she has done. Her sufferings turn into a penance. Needless to say, Emma feels none of this. Her hatred merely intensifies, and the burden of this examination of her condition has been to show it as that of her author for a sham society also, the 'bestial and imbecile rabble' by which Flaubert came at the end to designate almost everyone but himself. 'She was eaten up', we read, 'with rage, with hate.' Thus Flaubert could write, 'Though I have never suffered, thank God, at the hands of man, and though my life has never been lacking in cushions on which I could curl up in corners and forget everything else, still I detest my fellow-beings and do not feel that I am their fellow at all.'

While it has not been our intention, then, to present the author who could also plainly write that 'Equality is slavery' as a modern radiclib, still Flaubert's sense of *saeva indignatio* deepened his search into the injustices of the 'incomplete man', as a woman was considered in his day, and so often still is now. In Emma Bovary, as Baudelaire saw, he gave us a usurper, one who took the male world about her by the throat and shook it like a dog. Baudelaire paid tribute to her courage in these telling terms:

'Trapped finally within the narrow confines of a village, this bizarre Pasiphae, now a poor exhausted creature, still pursues the ideal in the country bars and taverns. But does it matter? Even then, we must admit, she is, like Caesar at Carpentras, in pursuit of the ideal!'

5

TESS OF THE D'URBERVILLES
The 'Pure Woman'

'Woman is truly less free today than ever she has been since time
began, in the womanly sense of freedom. Which means, she has less
peace, less of that lovely womanly peace that flows like a river, less
of the lovely, flower-like repose of a happy woman, less of the
nameless joy in life, purely unconscious, which is the very
breath of a woman's being.'
D. H. Lawrence

Hardy asks – What is love? In *Tess of the D'Urbervilles*, his
thirteenth novel in order of composition and possibly his first
in emotional commitment, we have the heroine as victim, 'a
visionary essence of woman – a whole sex condensed into one
typical form'.[1] She is perhaps the most firmly fleshed-out person
in these pages, as also the most fully sexed. What is more, Hardy
takes pains to present her as both a living, breathing, individual
woman and one trying hard to defer to the models in her culture.
In short, she exemplifies what one feminist has defined as modern
woman's true tragedy – 'the sad thing for women is that they
have participated in the destruction of their own eroticism'.[2]

It is important to be clear about Hardy's intentions here from
the start. For his own reticences, compounded with those of his
time, sometimes obscure – certainly for the contemporary student
steeped in libertine literature – what shimmers through the

---

[1] The text used here is the Wessex edition of 1912.
[2] Susan Lydon, 'Liberating Woman's Orgasm', *The New Eroticism*,
edited by Philip Nobile, New York: Random House, 1970, pp. 225–6
(reprinted from *Ramparts* magazine).

imagery, in a manner in which of course it does in life. Tess liked sex.

In the serial publication in the *Graphic*, for instance, Tess's account to her mother of her own seduction by Alec d'Urberville is wholly changed; in it Tess is deceived into a false marriage ceremony in a 'private room' with Alec. This sop to contemporary bias (the term morality can barely be used), apparently echoing the similar deception of Thomasina in *The Return of the Native*, was reinforced by the expunging of all references to Tess's child from the serial story, including the whole of Chapter XIV. The first episode involving the text-painter, whose fire-and-brimstone hortations Tess instinctively felt to be 'Crushing! killing!', was also omitted.[3]

While Hardy was no Flaubert in this respect – after all, he had had Harper's American offer for *Tess* in his pocket for over a year before British serialization – he nevertheless went about faithful thematic restoration for eventual book publication, letting Angel Clare carry the dairymaids in his arms over the flooded lane where his magazine editor had successfully suggested his transporting them by wheelbarrow . . . and, above all, restoring the famous, eloquent subtitle 'A Pure Woman', which estimate, as he himself put it in his Preface to the Fifth and Later Editions, 'was disputed more than anything in the book'.[4]

So between Phase The First ('The Maiden') and Phase The Second ('Maiden No More,' explicitly enough) there is an interval or lacuna during which Tess must be conceived as having been carried away by her sexual side, to which she obviously yielded with a degree of pleasure. Alec's initiation into sex – bully

[3] The composition of *Tess* and the concessions Hardy had to make for an illustrated weekly newspaper have been thoroughly covered by two works: Richard Purdy, *Thomas Hardy: A Bibliographical Study*, Oxford University Press, 1954, and Ian Gregor and Brian Nicholas, *The Moral and the Story*, London: Faber and Faber, 1962. *Tess* appeared in the *Graphic* in twenty-four illustrated weekly instalments from 4 July to 26 December 1891. Both books show what happened to odds and ends of the original conception.

[4] Hardy complained at the omission, in the first American edition, of 'the second title, which is absolutely necessary to show its meaning'.

though he is – was not, in short, wholly unpleasant. She was, in Hardy's words, 'stirred to confused surrender awhile . . .', and, in her own to Alec, 'My eyes were dazed by you for a little, and that was all.' He, meanwhile, was the kind of man who makes James's Dr Sloper exclaim in exasperation, 'You women are all the same! But the type to which your brother belongs was made to be the ruin of you, and you were made to be its handmaids and victims.'

We must establish all this securely at the start since it influences so much later on. The structural response comes in the pivotal confession scene with Angel, whom Tess realizes she could at this point win over by the wiles of sex yet refrains from so doing, sensing that (in a shame-culture for women) seduction can be no solution – 'she might have used it promisingly', we read here, 'it' being 'her exceptional physical nature'. Hence Tess hates herself for her initial weakness, really a little rape when we compare its similarity with that of the dying pheasants later on when she again sleeps outside. So at the very beginning of her destiny she turns with flashing eyes on Alec to cry, 'My God! I could knock you out of the gig! Did it never strike your mind that what every woman says some women may feel?'

We now know, or think we know, very much more about Thomas Hardy's private life and it may be that his liaison with Tryphena Sparks, who probably bore him the only child he ever had, urged further reticences on an already inordinately shy author. Sue Bridehead of *Jude the Obscure* and Tryphena are indeed astonishingly alike, and Hardy himself said that 'some of the circumstances' of this book were suggested by the death of a lady in 1890, the year in which Tryphena herself died. *Jude* was written not long after *Tess*. The model for Tess herself was apparently a dairymaid called Marian, four years older than himself and 'one of the few portraits from life in his works' (Florence Emily Hardy).

Appearing in 1895, *Jude* was the last novel Hardy ever wrote, so far as we know. 'A man must be a fool to deliberately stand up to be shot at', as he put it, splitting an infinitive, in a diary entry of 15 April 1892. He had already been astonished at, and soured by, the extraordinary reception of *Tess*, and *Jude's* was worse, the *Pall Mall Gazette* heading their review 'Jude The Obscene', while the Bishop of Wakefield bragged that he had thrown the book into the fire. According to his second wife, Florency Emily Dugdale, Hardy hated even to be touched. Yet his reticences may have been a protective persona, or mask – we note Ezra Pound's high estimate in his *ABC of Reading*, while quite independently Virginia Woolf saw the public stance of the late Hardy as a kind of self-protective pose. He liked to touch his vast bevy of cats, at any rate.

Surely the man had to grow some self-protection in a culture which constantly took offence at the reading of erotic betrayal as prototypical of religious betrayal, and/or vice versa. In view of the reception of his novels, to which we will return below, then, Hardy can scarcely be called hypersensitive if he soon reverted to poetry, which he deemed his 'more instinctive kind of expression'. Indeed, the best of his novels are pure prose poems.

And actually, a lot of Hardy's reticences are what might be called semantic hang-ups of his time (see his article 'Candour in English Fiction', first published in *The New Review* for January, 1890). The marvellous metaphor in *Tess* of the mechanical reaper making a noise 'like the love-making call of the grasshopper' – marvellous in that the two arms of the image comprise so much of our time – is revised for first publication to 'the love call of the grasshopper'.[5]

As with *Jane Eyre*, an initial (anti-familial) breach with convention starts out others. In Tess's case, of course, for she is surely one of the most charming heroines in literature, this breach of convention is based on obeisance to another. For if it had not been for her father's egregious infatuation with aristocracy, Tess would never have been urged forward by her mother in the first place (pimped by her maternal parent would be the less polite, if more accurate, term). Flatteringly described

---

[5] For a brief but enlightening review of Hardy's revisions of *Tess* in manuscript (now in the British Museum), see the relevant chapter in Wallace Hildick, *Word for Word: A Study of Authors' Alterations*, London: Faber and Faber, 1965, pp. 109–25.

as 'foolish', her mother blames her oldest daughter for not having got Alec to marry her, later chides her again for telling Angel the truth about the resulting bastard ('christened' Sorrow, in book form), and can still round on her at the end for not having practised general sexual deception as a life principle – 'O, Tess, what's the use of your playing at marrying gentlemen, if it leaves us like this!'

Finally, the 'maternal' Joan Durbeyfield is responsible for pressuring Tess to marry Angel, and so sets in train the eventual tragedy. In fact, Hardy's ironies can become a shade heavy-handed in these contexts, at least for modern taste, as when he has Alec d'Urberville, who has watched Tess tortured by treadmill-like labour on the steam thresher all day long, tell her – the woman he himself had seduced – 'You have been the cause of my backsliding.'

But a novel, as Hardy wrote in a Preface to this one, is 'an impression, not an argument'. As a young critic has put it, 'Nobody thinks of T. S. Eliot or D. H. Lawrence as model democrats, or of *The Waste Land* or *Women in Love* as being about good citizenship. But both *are* about the impact of modern civilization on the finest, keenest, most intelligent, most serious minds involved in it.'[6]

Hardy has here seen that a moment has come in our civilization when meekness and humility are no longer values in the true sense . . . and all the less so since we pay such loud lip-service to them in church. We talk a lot about the virtues of humility but, in America at any rate, encourage our sons to be aggressive, 'tough', to 'flay' and 'whip' their opposition in sports, to make a 'killing' on the market. We give meekness few emotional rights any more. So the two strands of our culture are being unravelled in different directions, as it were (one of Tess's sisters is called Modesty). Flaubert anticipated this important feminist insight in his late story *Un Coeur simple*. Gogol also comes to mind.

Male sexual aggression, incarnate here in Alec d'Urberville,

[6] Martin Green, *Science and the Shabby Curate of Poetry*, New York: Norton, 1965, p. 82; London: Longman, 1964.

is thus virtually half of the Puritan conscience. James's Dr Sloper had said as much. 'The man submits', in the words of another writer, 'to the force of nature; the woman submits to the man. Sex is an act of aggression with which she complies only because she is physically the weaker.'[7] So Alec can cry out, 'You have been the cause of my backsliding.' Forever Eve! As a woman, it must seem, at times, that you cannot win. For, as Hardy brilliantly if indirectly demonstrates, to put woman on a pedestal is to take the defence of her honour out of her own control, to tie her hands behind her back. Man is then encouraged to attack purity *per se* . . . as does Alec d'Urberville (or Dostoevsky's Svidri-gaïlov). I am suggesting that in another culture Tess could take care of herself very well, thank you.

In so doing, however, one must also confess that Hardy considerably loads the dice by making Tess, an unlettered country girl, after all, 'quite a Malthusian towards her mother for thoughtlessly giving her so many little sisters and brothers' (a reflection from Hardy rather than Tess) and by having her, in her teens, think of her siblings as 'six helpless creatures, who had never been asked if they wished for life on any terms'. This unlikely consideration on the part of a teenage Wessex girl is almost immediately succeeded by a slighting reference to Words-worth and his belief in 'Nature's holy plan' (from 'Lines Written in Early Spring'). Almost the most violent authorial outbreak in the whole of *Tess* replies to this in the penultimate Phase The Sixth ('The Convert'), where we read:

'for to Tess, as to not a few millions of others, there was ghastly satire in the poet's lines –
    Not in utter nakedness
    But trailing clouds of glory do we come.
To her and her like, birth itself was an ordeal of degrading personal compulsion, whose gratuitousness nothing in the result seemed to justify, and at best could only palliate.'

Hardy is here advancing another sexological insight, namely that woman has laboured too long – in all senses – under the

[7] Herschberger, p. 27.

ban of the concept that sexual pleasure is a concomitant of reproduction. As Ruth Herschberger well puts it:

'In a very basic sense, a child is the only admission of marital eroticism that wins the approbation of society . . . It is of the utmost importance to make clear that reproduction and the sex act are far more closely allied in the man's case than in the woman's for in the normal man the sex act is by Nature's design specifically a reproductive act as well.'[8]

Intercourse must always have reproductive significance for the male. It does not do so for the female. A woman ovulates, sheds an egg, usually but once a month, and during the long child-bearing period of her life is generally infertile; furthermore, ovulation is not with her a response to copulation (as with horses and sheep).

It is far from far-fetched to bring this into a discussion of *Tess* for the imagery surrounding the heroine is so succulently suggestive of what sexual union is for a woman – 'The coordinated system of the male is merely the negative reflection of the positive features of the female. The male functions to produce sperm to give to the female' (Herschberger). As far as the sexual side of the book goes, this could have been Hardy's epigraph. It is another sense in which his heroine is a 'pure' woman.

Some of the sweetest pictures of Tess are tactful reinter-pretations of this 'woman's view' of biology; here is Tess on that June evening when she wanders out 'conscious of neither time nor space' and hears Angel's harp:

'Tess had heard those notes in the attic above her head. Dim, flattened, constrained by their confinement, they had never appealed to her as now, when they wandered in the still air with a stark quality like that of nudity. . . . The outskirt of the garden in which Tess found herself had been left uncultivated for some years, and was now damp and rank

---

[8] Herschberger, pp. 42, 76, with accompanying footnotes provenancing Amram Scheinfeld's *Women and Men*.

with juicy grass which sent up mists of pollen at a touch; and with tall blooming weeds emitting offensive smells – weeds whose red and yellow and purple hues formed a poly-chrome as dazzling as that of cultivated flowers. She went stealthily as a cat through this profusion of growth, gathering cuckoo-spittle on her skirts, cracking snails that were under-foot, staining her hands with thistle-milk and slug-slime, and rubbing off upon her naked arms sticky blights which, though snow-white on the apple-tree trunks, made madder stains on her skin; thus she drew quite near to Clare, still unobserved of him.'

This little still life of fecundity, reminding us in passing, perhaps, that of all our authors Hardy is the only considerable poet, is repeated again and again at this 'phase' in Tess's develop-ment. Living 'at a season when the rush of juices could be almost heard below the hiss of fertilization', she exhibits to Angel Clare 'a dignified largeness both of disposition and physique, an almost regnant power, possibly because he knew that at that preternatural time hardly any woman so well endowed in person as she was likely to be walking in the open air within the boun-daries of his horizon'. Again when he comes across her shortly after this, 'The brim-fulness of her nature breathed from her. It was a moment when a woman's soul is more incarnate than at any other time; when the most spiritual beauty bespeaks itself flesh, and sex takes the outside place in the presentation.'

*   *   *

Tess, then, is ironically enough Nature's 'holy plan', though strictly speaking, if she could comment about novel-reading as cited, it is unlikely she would have been familiar with Words-worth. 'She was not an existence, an experience, a passion, a structure of sensations, to anybody but herself. She simply existed.' It is a pity de Beauvoir did not study Hardy; and he, in turn, might have subscribed to much of what she wrote in *The Second Sex*, one passage of which could well be superscribed over much of *Tess*:

'Woman is the victim of no mysterious fatality; the peculiarities that identify her as specifically a woman get their importance from the significance placed upon them.'[9]

The existential sanguine is there again when Hardy – once more somewhat spuriously – attaches a little Sully Prudhomme to his heroine's reflections, and remarks that she could 'hear a penal sentence in the fiat, "You shall be born".' Then after Tess has been betrayed – that is, after she has 'fallen' – we are asked:

'In a desert island would she have been wretched at what had happened to her? Not greatly. If she could have been but just created, to discover herself as a spouseless mother, with no experience of life except as the parent of a nameless child, would the position have caused her to despair? No, she would have taken it calmly, and found pleasures therein.'

It is something of a pity Hardy felt he had to make Tess an aristocrat by birth, for the book is really unconcerned with class, except inasmuch as that through Alec a rural West Country girl is betrayed by common trade turned pseudo-squireen.[10] It is a pity if only since it led D. H. Lawrence into some maddeningly self-indulgent passages on the novel, in which, however, genuine insights lie buried.

Possibly not meant to be published, and only posthumously so (in the *Phoenix* collection edited by Edward D. McDonald), these pages are rendered almost unreadable by Lawrence's assumption that we will all share his love ethic, together with its attendant and highly arbitrary terminology. Tess is an aristocrat and, for him, 'has the aristocratic quality of respect for the other being'. What does this mean, if anything? We need a key. 'She could attend to the wants of the other person, but no other person,

[9] De Beauvoir, p. 685.

[10] I would maintain this despite the minor theme of the snobbery of the senior Clares – 'she *is* a lady, nevertheless – in feeling and nature', Angel objects to his mother of Tess, and again, 'Distinction does not consist in the facile use of a contemptible set of conventions, but in being numbered among those who are true, and honest. . . .', etc. Others have preceded Hardy here.

save another aristocrat – and there is scarcely such a thing as another aristocrat – could attend to her wants, her deepest wants.'

This is infuriatingly suggestive and, indeed, Lawrence nearly always strikes through to the marrow of some truth – Tess does respect the rights of others, only to have her own infringed. The 'embodiment of desire' is destined to be betrayed in this fashion. Meekness marries aggression. We shall return to Lawrence's critique below. It is a valuable one, well worth the tedium of having to plough through Lawrentian rhetoric at its most intolerable, e.g. 'The murder is badly done, altogether the book is botched, owing to the way of thinking in the author, owing to the weak yet obstinate theory of being. Nevertheless, the murder is true, the whole book is true, in its conception.' Which is really to asseverate that Lawrence's sex ethic differed from Hardy's.

For Lawrence's interest was chiefly in what he was forever calling the male principle. Hardy's was not, as Virginia Woolf well saw:

> 'For the women he shows a more tender solicitude than for the men, and in them, perhaps, he takes a keener interest. Vain might their beauty be and terrible their fate, but while the glow of life is in them their step is free, their laughter sweet, and theirs is the power to sink into the breast of Nature and become part of her silence and solemnity, or to rise and put on them the movement of the clouds and the wildness of the flowering woodlands.'

One thinks of the charming frieze of the three milkmaids always hovering behind Tess at the Talbothays farm in a real picture of feminist solidarity:[11] never spiteful nor vicious toward Tess, as well they might have been, only, as mortally dependent beings, gently envious of her good luck ('Such supplanting was to be'), and two of them serving to warn Angel at the end. In the dairy dormitory they twist in their beds at night 'under the oppressive-

[11] Cp. 'WSPers [members of Women Strike for Peace], wearing Vietnamese "coolie" hats made of newspaper, bearing black flowers and signs and tolling small bells, marched down Broadway reminding passers-by that "We're all POWs".' *WSP Peaceletter*, vol, II, no. 9, October, 1971.

ness of an emotion thrust on them by cruel Nature's law. . . .
The differences which distinguished them as individuals were
abstracted by this passion, and each was but portion of one
organism called sex.'

No wonder Lawrence railed at this book. He repeatedly called
it 'botched', though he repeatedly admired it. And his was
nothing to the venom expounded on it by the all-male chorus
of immediate contemporaries. On 5 December 1892, Robert
Louis Stevenson, for instance, wrote to Henry James, 'I was
mortally wounded by Tess of the Durberfields [sic]. I do not
know that I am exaggerative in criticism; but I will say that Tess
is one of the worst, weakest, least sane, most *voulu* books I have
yet read. But the style, it seems to be about as bad as Reynolds. . . .'[12]

James replied in kind on 17 February 1893: 'oh yes, dear
Louis, she is vile. The pretence of "sexuality" is only equalled
by the absence of it, and the abomination of the language by the
author's reputation for style. There are indeed some pretty smells
and sights and sounds. But you have better ones in Polynesia.'
Although James tempered this estimate later, it is typical of the
vituperation Hardy early met with, culminating in Chesterton's
famous personal gibe ('a sort of village atheist brooding and
blaspheming over the village idiot') as in Maugham's caricature,
Edward Driffield, in *Cakes and Ale*. It culminated, indeed, in an
eclipse of fame – no entry in the Cambridge *History of English
Literature* – until a generation brought up on Sartre and Camus
suddenly hears Hardy speaking closely to them, this time from
out of the English countryside. (In passing one could ask – Who
has lasted, Hardy or Chesterton . . . or even Maugham?) And so

---

[12] Stevenson is here referring to G. W. M. Reynolds, author of *Wagner:
the Wehr-Wolf* as of much other cheap fiction around the middle of the
nineteenth century. Ironically enough, Reynolds was a political radical, and
exposed the exploitation of seamstresses. There is a good chapter on him
('The Most Popular Writer of Our Time') in Dalziel, pp. 35–45. The
paradoxes implicit in 'liberal' trash of the time are also brought out in
Louise E. Rorabacher's *Victorian Women in Life and Fiction*, originally an
Illinois doctoral dissertation of 1942.

many of these attacks seem to have been on Hardy's style, or alleged lack of it. Even the relatively friendly F. R. Leavis, in *Southern Review* for Summer, 1940, alludes grudgingly to this – 'he has made a style out of stylelessness'.

The reception of Hardy's fiction has been considered here, at more length than in the case of our other authors, since it is important to be clear just what he was doing. He was not writing the conventional nineteenth-century novel, what Ford called the 'nurvole', as his contemporary critics appear to have been anticipating. He was writing for and on behalf of women and made, for his society, the ultimate trespass of what he himself called 'a full look at the worst' – not only in Tess, but also in Eustacia Vye of *The Return of the Native*, and (though somewhat differently) in Bathsheba Everdene of *Far From The Madding Crowd*. These heroines he saw as archetypes, essences. It was only parenthetically that he ventured into the sociology of his stories, though distinctions like this are hardly separable.

The picture of dairy farming, cleaning a field of garlic plants, of the first steam threshing (long before the coming of the combine harvester), are powerful adjuncts to the novel, as to Tess's inner life. Passages on the cheapness of female field labour (particularly in the section 'The Woman Pays') could be set beside the statistical findings reported at the start of de Beauvoir's *The Second Sex* (e.g. her Chapter V, 'Early Tillers of the Soil'), and parenthetically remind us that, for the Tesses of those days, the now much-despised housework would have been nothing less than a glorious treat.

But though Hardy was writing not long after Zola's *Earth* (mainly composed in 1887), he was not rewriting it. Some contemporary reviewers seemed to think he was: there is, after all, the same sexual determinism, the same tragic sense that all women can do until they revolt is endure. Hence Hardy was considerably judged by those standards of verisimilitude belonging to a kind of narrative in which he was uninterested. Improbabilities were early pounced on, in a way they would not be now. Andrew Lang's famous notice in his *The New Review* for February, 1892, points out, for instance, that 'The black flag would never have been hoisted as in the final page', though Hardy himself saw two executions, one of them of a woman, close to; in fairness, it should be added that Lang, replying in *Longman's Magazine* for November of that year to Hardy's own criticism of his review, spoke of *Tess* together with *Madame Bovary* (and also *Clarissa Harlowe*).

The debate about the coincidences in the book seems to have been rather pointlessly continued, therefore. Pointlessly because Hardy did not really need to have the Dickensian recurrence of characters like dark Car, once Alec's paramour, nor make Groby, 'floored' by Angel, crop up as the exploiting farmer later (though here the theme of male revenge contributes to the story, it is true). Hardy's coincidences have been variously explained, e.g. as 'the persistence of the unforeseen' (Samuel Chew) and thus an aspect of Immanent Will which hung over Hardy's whole view of life, or again as almost the reverse, no chance at all but rather a sort of miraculous element characteristic of folk feeling and literature (Donald Davidson). The reader must be left to himself/herself to sift through such suggestions and decide whether they are or are not so many rationalizations for a kind of writing Hardy merely inherited.

The reviews of the time, in fact, laid so much stress on Hardy's supposed lack of realism that Arnold Kettle's Marxist interpretation of *Tess* as 'the destruction of the English peasantry' seems somewhat falsely syllogistic. Almost any great novel about the English countryside of this date is likely to be about this. Moreover, Kettle carefully points out the realistic imperfections throughout. If, then, the novel is guilty of departing so from verisimilitude, how may we, in the same breath, trust it as a vehicle of social insight?

No, Hardy was moving into a far more symbolic sort of fiction. If Lawrence alleges that 'The murder is badly done', well, so in one sense it was. It is highly unlikely that Alec's blood would stain through the ceiling as fast as it does – 'Drip, drip, drip' (the parallel onomatopoeia may be found in the sad poem 'Beyond The Last Lamp' which Hardy wrote as a kind of companion piece to the scene of Angel and Tess debating what to do after her confession). It is even less likely that the blood-stain would appear – for the landlady, Mrs Brooks – as 'a gigantic ace of hearts'.

This shape is simply a symbolic response, the chance of cards is a leit-motif in the books, as in others by Hardy. It suited his way of thinking. In the early moonlight walk back from the market and fair, Car Darch is 'dubbed Queen of Spades' and her sister Nancy, evidently another of Alec's paramours, the Queen of Diamonds. And the treacle that oozes from the basket the former is carrying on her head is described as looking 'like a slimy snake in the cold still rays of the moon'.

Though such considerations, then, closely condition the manner in which we read *Tess*, they must be left on the sidelines here, to literary scholars, since it is time to pass on to a closer inspection of the worth of this work to the feminist movement.

* * *

Tess Durbeyfield grows up to a strong county girl, able to face a walk of twenty-five miles with equanimity and to write a long impassioned letter to her husband after stoically enduring a dawn-to-dusk thumping on the platform of a steam-thresher at Flintcomb-Ash (a Hardy name, if ever there was one). It is important to stress her physique since it is made much of, and is clearly meant to fit her character as a Gea-Tellus, Earth Mother. At the end she kills a strong man with evident ease with a table knife ('Fulfilment' is the title of this section, or Phase).

Now it is far from frivolous to suggest that a great deal of the present ranting about feminine inferiority in a pretentiously egalitarian world is a sort of tight-shoes syndrome . . . women are told, and therefore feel, they have inferior physiques. A firm way of classifying men, that is, appears to be by the fact that they are physically stronger. Our laws embed this distinction within them at points.

But is this a biological parentage or a social construct? It seems hard to discern. Professor Juliet Mitchell of the University of Reading asks, 'how can we tell whether there would be sexually

determined differences in a society not dedicated to their production?' The arguments here can become circular, if not frankly
self-contradictory. One school of anthropology would have it
that the vulnerable female breasts are ersatz buttocks, a rump-
presentation duplicated in the breastless chimpanzee and forced
on the human primate when he stood erect: 'The protuberant,
hemispherical breasts of the female must surely be copies of the
fleshy buttocks, and the sharply defined red lips around the
mouth must be copies of the red labia.'[13]

Surely . . . must be? As a layman I remain relatively uncon-
vinced by the bizarre theory. Anyone who has studied chimps
must concede that they are far more upright than researchers
report them to be, and indeed do know frontal genital exposure
(the cause of much of the bother here). And the theory relies
on, and strongly supports, the idea that the female orgasm is
originally 'borrowed' from the male, which we are now indus-
triously disproving.

Yet even within a short span of time woman seems able to
alter her physique to conform to social norms, unaided by corset,
hobble-skirt and bustle. It has been said, for instance, that the
sloping shoulders of the idealized Victorian heroine were more
an attempt to copy patterns of elegance to be found in fiction,
written largely by males, than a received reality. A section of
my own study of popular iconography, *Parade of Pleasure*,
tried to show that the size of women's breasts in America of the
early fifties followed fantasy rather then function (receiving
ultimate reductio in the early pages of *Playboy*). Women have
simply been assigned subordinate physique-roles for so long.
Lady athletes in the last Olympics, one dating a steady boy-
friend, were surprised and indignant to find themselves re-
classified males (sometimes on the mere basis of testes concealed
in the labia major). Such sex tests indeed provoked one British
doctor to declare, in 1966, 'There is no definite line between
male and female.'

Margaret Mead had told us this years ago, showing how

[13] Desmond Morris, *The Naked Ape*, New York: Dell, 1969, p. 63;
London: Corgi, 1969.

certain societies institutionalize types and traits in both men and women:

'No culture has failed to seize upon the conspicuous facts of age and sex in some way, whether it be the convention of one Philippine tribe that no man can keep a secret, the Manus' assumption that only men enjoy playing with babies, the Toda prescription of almost all domestic work as too sacred for women, or the Arapesh insistence that women's heads are stronger than men's. In the division of labour, in dress, in manners, in social and religious functioning – sometimes in only a few of these respects, sometimes in all – men and women are socially differentiated and each sex, as a sex, forced to conform to the rôle assigned to it. In some societies, these socially defined rôles are mainly expressed in dress or occupation with no insistence upon innate temperamental differences.'[14]

In her valuable *Adam's Rib* Ruth Herschberger starts off with a denunciatory dissection – indeed a 'ribbing' – of the famous findings made by Robert M. Yerkes with his Yale chimpanzees, on which so many 'norms' of male dominance have been based, norms already intensionally present in the all-too-male experimenters – desiderata. Female chimps of the same weight as male seem to be far more aggressive in almost every activity, including and especially mating:

'If a mother discovers her young son and daughter wrestling, she usually feels there is something vaguely indecent about it. Even though the little girl may on this occasion have established a half-nelson and be about to pin her brother to the ground, the mother's injunction will be the same; "Junior! Don't hurt Joan! You know girls aren't as strong as you!" As the children get shamefully to their feet, obedient to their mother's note of horror (and it *was* pleasurable), Joan really believes she was about to be hurt in some uncalculated way, and Junior thinks he was about to forget his strength and

[14] Margaret Mead, *Sex and Temperament in Three Primitive Societies*, London: Routledge, 1935, pp. xix–xx.

wound a lady. Already pleasure begins to smack of the harmful.'[15]

This was not always so. Certainly not in the pre-agricultural period. 'We do not even know whether woman's musculature or her respiratory apparatus, under conditions different from those of today, were not as well developed as in man.'[16] Tacitus reports that notions of feminine inferiority are basically physical, since women have had leading roles as prophetesses and priestesses without disfavour. In France we have recently seen male writers promoting a veritable cult of the muscular woman, ranging from Henry de Montherlant's poems on thousand-meter women runners to Jacques de Lacretelle's *La Bonifas*, the portrait of a masculine woman haunted by fatality. And in contemporary America we can observe the distortions and difficulties being created for women by introduction of the muscle rhetoric into their lives. The desire for women to compete in men's sports is doubtless laudable, and has worked in swimming, but it can be dangerous as well as ridiculous in other games.

It is natural that 'Masculine arrogance provokes feminine resistance', as de Beauvoir puts it. Male demands are met symmetrically. If we look at the dominant-subordinate polarity between the sexes as one partially originating in physique, we at least fight free of some of the silly squabbling that has lately been obscuring reality. And we can come to agree with Mrs Herschberger when she suggests that 'Some woman scientist ought to start passing it around that males must be unnatural because they don't have cyclical changes during the month.'[17]

In view of woman's superiority in sensitivity – of skin, breasts, nipples and of course the clitoris, capable of extraordinarily varied response – it must rank as a tragedy of our times that something called penis envy came to be regarded as even an idea. Who said that women suffer from penis envy? His Embarrassing Eminence from Vienna. It is experientially untrue and has vulgarized and degraded women. Who said that boys have secret

[15] Herschberger, p. 139.   [16] De Beauvoir, p. 56.   [17] Herschberger, p. 9.

envy of their father's sexual organs? Do they? Did they? None that I ever knew. Nor do many women seem notably galvanized by the idea of penis envy on the part of their sex:

> 'Authorized to test her powers in work and sports, competing actively with the boys, she would not find the absence of the penis – compensated by the promise of a child – enough to give rise to an inferiority complex.'[18]

There is probably no such thing as penis envy at all, except in the eyes of adults like Freud. De Beauvoir elsewhere hints as much:

> 'Thus, far from the penis representing a direct advantage from which the boy could draw a feeling of superiority, its high valuation appears on the contrary as a compensation – invented by adults and ardently accepted by the child – for the hardships of the second weaning.'[19]

The conception of the boy child being in constant fear of castration at the same time as envious of his father's penis is, in other words, only a baffling absurdity until you recognize it as an adult rationalization for a repressive male society.

This of course is the hub of most of D. H. Lawrence's unfortunate verbal dervish-dancing about something called the phallus. We notice his prose – as in the *Fantasia of the Unconscious* – becoming unreadably rhetorical directly he touches on this subject. For if the universe can only be apprehended through the phallus, woman is deprived of all rights at the start of the game. Man is saying, Come and play tennis with me, but only I am allowed a racquet. Significantly, therefore, Lawrence keyed his love ethic to monogamous relationships in which woman discovers her derivation in man. Perversions of this plan generally proved disastrous.[20]

---

[18] De Beauvoir, p. 683.   [19] *Ibid.*, p. 253.

[20] The classic pro-Lawrentian view on these matters, one which takes all the posturing at face value and reduces it to exposition, must be read to be believed: Mark Spilka, *The Love Ethic of D. H. Lawrence*, Indiana University Press, 1955. It is studied in university courses.

Now this is not surprising in a sensitive male. For at times the phallus does seem to act rather like some existential 'Other'. Maddeningly so. It erects itself whimsically, will refuse to perform at will, and then goes and ejaculates at night without permission. Surely it must be a god. What man of middle age, who has made love regularly all his adult life, would deny, on the threshold of paradise, that the clitoris is a far more reliable, and sensitive, organ? 'Feminine sexual excitement can reach an intensity unknown to man',[21] writes de Beauvoir; but it is not only intensity that is at issue here, it is *variety*. To admit as much, however, would be to topple Lawrence's entire love ethic, or mis-ethic.

It is ironic that America should discover the clitoral organism in the laboratories of the Masters-Johnson sex research team, aided by a US government grant, when every second page of the uncharted sea of Victorian pornography tells the same story, and far more organically. Laboratory lovers are the electroded robots of sex. And it will be more than ironic, it will be tragic if the public consciousness accepts the aggressive, self-seeking role placed on the clitoral orgasm by so many noisy, and sometimes noisome, feminists in our midst today. It will be to play directly into the hands of the dominant technology to objectify this experience, seal it off and code it as some sort of independent rival of the male ejaculation. Why make the mistakes of a masculine society all over again? As Susan Lydon puts it:

'female sexuality is subtle and delicate, conditioned as much by the emotions as by physiology and sociology. Masters and Johnson proved that the orgasm experienced during intercourse, the misnamed vaginal orgasm, did not differ *anatomically* from the clitoral orgasm. But this should not be seen as their most significant contribution to the sexual emancipation of women. . . . As they wrote, "With orgasmic physiology established, the human female now has an undeniable opportunity to develop realistically her own sexual response levels." Two years later this statement seems naïve and entirely too optimistic. Certainly the sexual problems of our society will

[21] De Beauvoir, p. 367.

never be solved until there is a real and unfeigned equality between men and women. This idea is usually misconstrued: sexual liberation for women is wrongly understood to mean that women will adopt all the forms of masculine sexuality. As in the whole issue of women's liberation, that's really not the point.'[22]

Equality, in other words, doesn't mean sameness, and I for one think Hardy was trying to show this. Women's sexuality is immensely varied and delicate, and literature – even the sub-literature of pornography – may be a better guide to it than the clinics. It is currently a sort of platform with American feminists to attack pornographies as 'encouraging rape and other forms of sexual sadism and exploitation. They are an insult and a crime against women'.[23]

Such writers have probably not read the pornography they are so bitterly attacking and which, in fact, contains more than a modicum of completely enfranchised and extremely dominant women, all thoroughly enjoying the sexual experience. America has been the first country to mass-produce pornography (in the last century it was, in England, a prerogative of the elite); I am not suggesting that *pornos* replace sex manuals, but they have certainly given lower-class people in America lately a new rhetoric of sex and one that does not show it as a response to a biological need alone. Clitoral orgasm is invariably enjoyable, in such pages, and sometimes even linked with affection, tenderness and awareness. Once more, Fem Lib contradicts itself. To lock up pornography is to work for just those forces of repression that have kept women down so long. Herbert Marcuse has a whole theory of sexual liberation in which Eros and Agape are conjoined:

'The regression involved in this spread of the libido would first manifest itself in the reactivation of all erotogenic zones and, consequently, in a resurgence of pregenital polymorphous

[22] Lydon, pp. 226–7.
[23] 'BOYCOTT ALL Newsstands Selling Pornography', *Woman's World*, 15 April, 1971, p. 1.

sexuality and in a decline of genital supremacy. The body in its entirety would become an object of cathexis, a thing to be enjoyed – an instrument of pleasure.'

Certainly it was so for Tess.

For women are in a majority, and they have several superior faculties, including that of memory.[24] Monique Wittig, in her recent novel *Les Guérillères*, played amusingly on a reversal of our assumptions of male physical superiority. Undoubtedly these assumptions were spurred on by Puritan capitalism. In *Patriarchal Attitudes* Eva Figes makes this indictment: 'The rise of capitalism is the root cause of the modern social and economic discrimination against women, which came to a peak in the last century.' When Angel Clare, by this time married to Tess, makes his proposal to Izz Huett to come to be his mistress in Brazil, he footnotes the offer as follows: 'But I ought to remind you that it will be wrong-doing in the eyes of civilization – western civilization, that is to say.' The accent is on western, and it is the man he meets in South America who shrugs his shoulders at Angel's erotic problem.

Under Roman law, at the end of the Antonine jurisconsults at any rate, women were legally equal with men in most matters, a position of which the matrons seem not to have profited. As we know, the troubadour period later perfected a form of matrism which, while it undoubtedly turned men's minds to the Virgin Mary in another world, concomitantly civilized their behaviour to the Lauras and Beatrices of this. 'It may be questioned', Burckhardt wrote of the Holy Virgin, 'whether, in the north, a greater devotion was possible.' Under such matrism women certainly began to emerge more as fellow-beings than they had for some while before, thus making the Portias and Rosalinds of a later century possible. 'The period soon became one of enhanced status for women. They were given an education similar to that

[24] Viola Klein, *The Feminine Character: History of an Ideology*, with a foreword by Karl Manheim, New York: International Universities Press, 1949, p. 99; this book was first published in 1946, reviews various writings on women, and here resumes the theories of Helen B. Thompson. American women are 106 millions strong in 1972.

of men, and were regarded as their equals, even if it was held to be proper for them to work by influencing men rather than to engage directly in politics.'[25]

Such is stressed here since Hardy has been called, by Lord David Cecil, one of the last of the heroists. Two strains meet in Tess, the Gea-Tellus or all-powerful fecundator (*queen* in the original sense, one shared with *quim*) and, of course, the all-too-human equal and companion of man. For it is likely that Bachofen's famous study overstressed the feminine quotient in the alleged early matriarchies of the Mediterranean basin. De Beauvoir shows herself uncomfortable with the Bachofen view:

> 'These facts have led to the supposition that in primitive times a veritable reign of women existed: the matriarchy. It was this hypothesis, proposed by Bachofen, that Engels adopted, regarding the passage from the matriarchate to the patriarchate as "the great historical defeat of the feminine sex". But in truth the Golden Age of Woman is only a myth. To say that woman was the *Other* is to say that there did not exist between the sexes a reciprocal relation: Earth, Mother, Goddess – she was no fellow creature in man's eyes; it was *beyond* the human realm that her power was affirmed, and she was therefore *outside of* that realm.'[26]

With Molly Bloom, Tess very much wanted to be within that realm; she earnestly longed to be a fellow creature in man's eyes here and now. By this route we can come logically back to Lawrence and his twin insights concerning her plight. For she is very strong physically and quite unafraid of Groby at the end: 'To have as a master this man of stone, who would have cuffed her if he had dared, was almost a relief after her former experiences.'

[25] Rattray Taylor, p. 131: Maurice Valency's *In Praise of Love* (New York: Macmillan, 1958) beautifully complements this text from the literary side.

[26] De Beauvoir, pp. 64–5.

Tess's physicality has been thoroughly insisted on since she is the flower of her sex and race: so much so that it sometimes suggests her as older than she is. She is thoroughly natural, a 'pure' woman, and 'her exceptional physical nature' causes her to ask Angel to marry her sister after she has been hanged, as if she were some generous tree, giving off another branch of life. By this request, too, to which Angel evidently accedes, she urges him to join her on the other side of convention: of her own crime Hardy had at once commented, 'She had been made to break an accepted social law, but no law known to the environment in which she fancied herself such an anomaly.'

It must be clearly established, too, that Angel Clare was far more anti-conventional than a modern reader (certainly a modern American reader) might assume. Dairyman Crick tells us that he is 'one of the most rebellest rozums you ever knowed', he is described as 'un-Sabbatarian' and 'preferred sermons in stones to sermons in churches'. At one point the adverb 'communistically' is used of him, the word only having acquired English currency around 1850. But Angel fails at the brink and can only go the whole way 'Too late, too late!' (in Tess's terms before the murder).

The story is archetypally simple. A young country girl is seduced, has an illegitimate child which dies in infancy, marries another and tells her husband the truth before consummation of the wedding. The latter cannot tolerate the idea and abandons her to go to Brazil. Now at this turn in the narrative we may, in fact, tend to judge Angel too harshly. But his identity and whole relationship with the world depended on things being what they were. Tess tells him she has a child by another man. As James Baldwin puts it of another regional writer, William Faulkner, 'Any real change implies the breakup of the world as one has always known it, the loss of all that gave one an identity, the end of safety.'

Pestered by her first lover, Tess gives in to live with him since he will then support her family – the words 'He bought me' in the 1892 text were expunged by Hardy from the later Wessex edition. On her husband's return and subsequent discovery of her new ménage, Tess kills her paramour, has a few days' elegaic happiness with her new-found husband and is apprehended for her crime lying, like a sacrificial victim, on an altar at Stonehenge, an episode of overcrude symbolism for many critics. She is hanged.

We see that Hardy carefully arranged for chance to interfere with Tess's first confession of her supposed fault and then for Angel, before the marriage consummation, to see fit to make his own admission of sexual 'backsliding'. Overjoyed, Tess then makes hers 'because 'tis just the same'.

But of course it isn't, given the society. Convention intervenes and though 'nothing had changed since the moments when he had been kissing her', ignorant of her lapse, 'the essence of things had changed' – the essence, not the existence. Tess slides to her knees and begs for forgiveness, saying 'I will obey you like your wretched slave', and asking, from the depths of her instincts, how he can suddenly stop loving her on the mere receipt of information – 'It is in your own mind what you are angry at, Angel.' In truth, it is. Angel's position is put in the following exchange:

> ' "In the name of our love, forgive me!" she whispered with a dry mouth. "I have forgiven you for the same!"
>
> And as he did not answer, she said again –
>
> "Forgive me as you are forgiven! I forgive you, Angel."
>
> "You – yes, you do."
>
> "But you do not forgive me?"
>
> "O Tess, forgiveness does not apply to the case! You were one person; now you are another." '

If we have been correct in tracing two themes working through Tess so far, fecundating Earth Mother and social and political equal, we can see that there is far more at stake here than a simple attack on the double standard of male convention. As with Emma Bovary, the characterization is saturated with civilization. And we can return to Lawrence's analysis.

For Tess is longing to be *whole* and neither man in her life will let her be so. Lawrence sensed the psycho-dynamics of this, writing of Angel Clare:

'He had no idea that there was such a thing as positive Woman, as the Female, another great living Principle counterbalancing his own male principle. He conceived of the world as consisting of the One, the Male Principle.'

Spattered as it is with capital letters, this statement is an unnecessarily over-complicated way of saying that Angel was the classic case of the Puritan. But Lawrence proceeds astutely to observe that you can't have the one without the other, the Puritan without the Cavalier; and his interpretation of the other social pole repressing sex by exploiting it, and also refusing full consciousness to woman, is extremely interesting.

For him Alec d'Urberville is the opposite of Angel Clare, he has 'killed the male in himself, as Clytemnestra symbolically for Orestes killed Agamemnon'. So his is really another way of hating the flesh (indeed Hardy writes, 'd'Urberville gave her the kiss of mastery'). 'It is a male quality to resolve a purpose to its fulfilment', Lawrence here claims, 'to receive some impulse into his semen, and to transmit it into expression'. Woman, that is, needs the mediation of the male, the reverse view, of course, of a feminist sexologist like Mrs Herschberger ('The male functions to produce sperm to give to the female'). Thus Alec 'seeks with all his power for the stimulus in woman. He takes the deep impulse from the female'.

Though Schopenhauer, of all people, could hardly be called pro-feminist, Hardy comes close to his thinking here, and indeed Helen Garwood's study of Hardy's work as an exposition of Schopenhauer's was published as early as 1911. What Lawrence is saying is structured to show the destruction of a woman's psyche: this happens in two ways – (a) Angel denies woman, (b) Alec identifies woman and destroys her by betrayal. The result is death since in neither case is the woman left whole. In short, 'The female is the victim of the species.'[27]

*　　*　　*

[27] De Beauvoir, p. 18.

Thomas Hardy was one of the last great heroic writers – 'Eliza-bethan' for Cecil – lodged in a time that was running down. His God, or anti-God, was Immanent Will, President of the Im-mortals, The Spinner of the Years, a purblind Doomster (the diffidence of specification, in Hardy's semantic here, is itself an 'ironic' acknowledgement of taboo). Once more, Lord David, in his admirable little book on *Hardy The Novelist*, comes to our rescue and can be brought to the feminist bar in evidence.

For, as he observes, when the black flag moves up the prison pole as Tess drops to her death, we are given to read, ' "Justice" was done, and the President of the Immortals, in Aeschylean phrase, had ended his sport with Tess.' The 'Aeschylean phrase' may be a literal translation of two words in line 169 of *Prometheus Bound*, but in the given context it has a sneering, sarcastic ring that is curiously insecure . . . 'strange terms for an atheist', as Lord David well puts it.

Precisely. With one side of himself (the rational) Hardy tried to adumbrate a universe of sheer fatality, chance, 'hap'. As the fields are cut in *Tess* rabbits and rats, friend and foe alike, cluster together in panic and misery, then run for their lives. Like humans, it is a matter of luck which of them is killed, and which escapes. We are all, that is, in the words of one of Hardy's best poems ('Neutral Tones'), 'Alive enough to have strength to die.'

There is a whole philosophy in that line, which seems to be Hardy's inheritance from those urns of Zeus of which the weary Achilles talks to Priam at the end of the *Iliad*.[28] Angel once confesses to his father 'that it might have resulted far better for mankind if Greece had been the source of the religion of modern civilization'. And again, after the chance but most important meeting with the stranger in Brazil, a cosmopolite who thought Tess's slip 'of no importance beside what she would be', Angel

---

[28] 'There are two urns that stand on the door-sill of Zeus. They are unlike
    for the gifts they bestow: an urn of evils, an urn of blessings.
    If Zeus who delights in thunder mingles these and bestows them
    on man, he shifts, and moves now in evil, again in good fortune.'
    Homer, *Iliad*, Book Twenty-Four, ll. 527–30
    (translated by Richard Lattimore).

reflects that he had himself 'persistently elevated Hellenic Paganism at the expense of Christianity, yet in that civilization an illegal surrender was not certain disesteem'.

This is all very well, but Hardy proceeds to people his fiction with omens, and his poetry with ghosts. Intuitions, hauntings, spectral voices usually have a habit, with Hardy, of coming true. Cecil pinpoints the difficulty:

> 'You simply do not get a dyed-in-the-wool rationalist writer employing omens to increase his effect in a serious work. As a matter of fact, Hardy was not altogether consistent. Though his intellect accepted rationalism and materialism, his imagination never did. . . . Intellectual inconsistency, however, is often aesthetic gain.'

Tess may be part of nature, but she *has to be* part of society. 'Thus Tess walks on, a figure which is part of the landscape. . . .' This is the existentialist Hardy who could write, with some fervour in his prose:

> 'Tess was no insignificant creature to toy with and dismiss; but a woman living her precious life – a life which, to herself who endured or enjoyed it, possessed as great a dimension as the life of the mightiest to himself. Upon her sensations the whole world depended to Tess; through her existence all her fellow-creatures existed, to her. The universe itself only came into being for Tess on the particular day in the particular year in which she was born.'

This could be straight Camus, and in fact it really is for, as Cecil suggests, Hardy's mnemonic side had to concede what the Greeks called a human nature. We can, after all, talk about persistence beyond death; rabbits and rats cannot. 'Despairing literature', as Camus once put it, 'is a contradiction in terms'.

So society executes Tess, as it did Camus's Meursault, and for not entirely dissimilar reasons. In neither case is the murder the guilt; the revolt against convention is the real guilt. Meursault is decapitated 'in the name of the French people'. Tess is hanged in the name of male society. And yet her touching, tentative revolt against inhuman laws affirms something irreducibly human, and makes us all her murderers, as well as her fellow-condemned.

Of course, the great difference, aesthetically, between Hardy's brand of existentialism and Camus's is that the latter writer could already locate his in a social situation where the values of solitude, alienation, revolt (during German occupation) were normatively heroic. As a matter of fact, there may even have been an artistic penalty for this; however sympathetic Camus's fiction was, he was again giving testimony, acknowledging public truths, rather than (or just as much as) writing out of private discovery, apart. We feel he is as honest as Hardy all the way, but does he maintain the same creative energy over long stretches (his best work is short)? As Irving Howe once put it, 'Camus has not yet given himself irrevocably to the powers of art, he has not yet taken the final step that would bring him from the realm of reflection to the realm of imagination.'[29] Yet Camus's tragic optimism replies to, rounds out, Hardy's ironic pessimism. Surely he would have agreed with Camus that 'a human nature does exist, as the Greeks believed. Why rebel if there is nothing permanent in oneself worth preserving?'[30]

So Tess, this 'mere child of the soil', is also a child of our time, a truly delicate organization of appetencies. No wonder Tolstoy approved her (at least in serial shape). She is 'Alive enough to have strength to die', all right, and cannot imagine no further life for the true lovers of this world. She speaks closely to women since she lives 'under an arbitrary law of society which had no foundation in Nature'. For although we may all be pawns in the hands of the purblind Doomster, there is a sense of joy in the very copiousness of nature: as we read in *Tess*:

'The "appetite for joy" which pervades all creation, that tremendous force which sways humanity to its purpose, as the

[29] Irving Howe, 'Between Fact and Fable', *New Republic*, 31 March, 1958, p. 17.
[30] Albert Camus, *The Rebel: An Essay on Man in Revolt*, with a foreword by Sir Herbert Read, translated by Anthony Bower, New York: Vintage Books, 1959, p. 16; Harmondsworth: Penguin, 1969.

tide sways the helpless weed, was not to be controlled by vague lucubrations over the social rubric.'

Nature itself is guiltless, and Tess a sample of its innocence. For, if not the first, Hardy is certainly one of the best of our writers to use landscape as psychic state, and sometimes one of the most daring (in *Tess* there is a lengthy description of the Vale of the Var as a vaginal cleft). So Hardy makes his 'pure' woman cry out for all women when, exhausted by field labour, she lashes at Alec with her glove, then sinks on the straw, on which his blood is dropping, to cry out in agony, 'Now, punish me. . . . Whip me, crush me; you need not mind those people under the rick! I shall not cry out. Once victim, always victim – that's the law!'

6

TONY BUDDENBROOK
The Fall of the Family

'The greatest woman is she who has the largest family.'
Napoleon, to his brother Lucien.

It may seem somewhat paradoxical – a sort of irony of ironies –
that a writer like Thomas Mann, author of that celebrated
'reactionary' autobiography, *Betrachtungen eines Unpolitischen*
of 1918, as of the Berlin speech four years later, should figure
here as a feminist. Man's inhumanity to Mann, indeed.

Yet it should not truly seem so. The German language con-
served (some say, carried) within it strongly familial and anti-
feminine values,[1] and from the start of his career Mann evinced an
extreme refinement in nuances of stylistic tone, often lost in
Mrs Lowe-Porter's plodding, ultra-'British' and now thoroughly
old-fashioned translation, one that gives us *ennui* as 'the dumps'.
Mann's semantic sensitivity alone compelled him to act as
interlocutor to social change, and so to represent, if not exactly
champion, women's rights. Philosophic fiction is bound by its
nature to be pedagogic, seeking values of conduct and interested
in *Bildung*, that much used, and abused, German word which
has the sense of 'becoming' built into it.

That many of Mann's ideas are today so well-known and
widely accepted as to appear platitudinous hardly denigrates
their inception. Mann undoubtedly inherited insights from earlier

---

[1] See Dolf Sternberger's *Aus dem Wörterbuch des Unmenschen* of 1945,
followed up by Cornelia Berning's brilliant *Von "Abstammungsnachweis"
zum "Zuchtwart"* of twenty years later.

German minds, notably those of Schopenhauer and Nietzsche,[2] but his application of such to social action is most suggestive and conferred on him a kind of prescience.

We are not thinking merely here of the obvious political anticipations (verging on outright Kafkaesque prophecy) made by a work like 'Mario and the Magician' of 1929, but rather of profound semantico-social insights into nascent Fascism in the early drama *Fiorenza* of 1905, or even the even earlier *Tonio Kröger*, with its anticipations of Aryan blondness as a physiological ideal turning into a political value, and of the 'dark' Jew, later to be the cliché of Streicher's *Der Stuermer*, as outsider and enemy.

Alongside work by Musil and Hesse, we meet the same self-worshipping of an inbred elite parodied, by way of Wagner, in 'The Blood of the Walsungs', also of 1905. Georg Lukács, anything but a Marxist at the start of his career, caught glimpses of the underside of this German *Geist* in a work as rigorously 'un'-political as the 1911 *Death in Venice*.[3] The Apollonian side of Mann may have admired Kaiserian Germany – he often alluded to the quasi-martial nature of aesthetic control[4] – but his Dionysiac side saw it coming.

We must admit, however, that the former half of Mann inherits, and imports into fictive literature, a certain stiffness of semantic also. The neo-classical movement around the turn of the century effected a virulent and very nasty little cultural war that finally resulted in a real war. Mann remains, when all is said and done, remarkably unstained and uninfected by these coeval ideas. It is not so much a matter of Stefan George (who mildly resisted

[2] Gerhard Jacob's University of Leipzig doctoral dissertation *Thomas Mann und Nietzsche* was written in 1926.

[3] The celebrated Hungarian Marxist (who subsequently dropped the von from his name) published in the same year as *Death in Venice* a work entitled *Die Seele und die Formen*, an intensely anti-democratic opus which includes an enthusiastic essay on a German 'classicist', neo-Greek dramatist, and male chauvinist to boot, Paul Ernst.

[4] 'To me at least it has always seemed that it is not the worst artist who recognizes himself in the image of the soldier.' (Cp. the role of Joachim in *The Magic Mountain*.)

Hitler's blandishments at the end) and the celebrated George-Kreis which might have taken for their motto, and, for all we know, possibly did, Goethe's classic '*Classisch ist das Gesunde, Romantik das Kranke*'. At least, it is not *only* a matter of that 'Mallarméan Parnassian', as Jethro Bithell so properly dubbed George. It is more in others like Paul Ernst, Wilhelm von Scholz, Rudolf Pannwitz, Samuel Lublinski, and even Karl Joël that we find the virus, of sexual and racial chauvinism, in full bloom.

Curiously enough, this latter wing rounded on France as the seat and source of wicked 'romantic' ideas (and idea-mongers like Baudelaire), though France itself was throwing up a healthy, or unhealthy, 'classical' movement of its own. Maurras, Massis, the Baron de la Seillière, Lasserre, to a lesser extent Benda and even Péguy participated in an attitude towards culture which found its final voice in a political party, the Action Française, two seats in the Chambre prior to the first world war, and several places in prisons after the second, for varying forms of collaboration with the enemy. We are not concerned here with literary historiography, but there are affinities with Mann in the supposedly 'classical' presentation of women as Faustian, 'musical' (Frau Klöterjahn), Dionysiac, and the like.

Yet he took the course of Hesse rather than of the hotheads, and feared the general swamping of European intellect principally from the Slavic East. It is arbitrary to the point of monotony to equate, as Mann did again and again, Dionysiac and anarchic values with Polish or Russian characters, something for which today we have to make a concession, or 'suspension of disbelief'.

Thus Aschenbach dreams of savagery and chaos in the East, is magnetically attracted to the European city which has traditionally traded with the East, and dies of an Eastern disease. What Mann here called 'the triumph of drunken disorder over the forces of a life consecrated to rule and discipline' is, of course, effected in the story by a boy who is – quite needlessly – Polish. The same corruptive lethargy and indulgence is repeatedly brought on, as mental and moral slackness, by Slavic characters, or those Russian elements which were so feared before the Bolshevist revolution (as, indeed, after it). The apogee of such stereotypes in Mann's fiction is to be found in *The Magic Mountain* and to an extent summarizes, even parodies, the emotional woman of neo-classical legend.

Clavdia Chauchat, the warm cat (we note she can't spell), is laxity and indiscipline personified, culminating in sickness and disease – she becomes interested in Castorp when he first runs a temperature. With her 'Tartar physiognomy' she is somewhat reminiscent of Tonio Kröger's 'artistic' friend in Munich, Lisaveta Ivanovna (the name taken, presumably, from *Crime and Punishment*), and reminds us at once of Russia, the door through which disorder and darkness are to be let in, for Mann as for Hesse. 'Up here', says Settembrini, 'there is too much Asia.' It is not without significance that the place is full of Muscovite and Mongolian types.

It is not without significance, indeed, that Mann should represent this commonplace yielding to the 'feminine' as a sort of deck-chair (later sick-bed) renunciation of effort, resulting in the capitulation of all intelligence to barbarism. It was in the air at the time. Hans Castorp's first real look at Clavdia is in terms of such indiscipline; she lets doors bang behind her and 'How badly she held herself! Not like the ladies of Hans Castorp's social sphere, who sat erect at their tables, turned their heads towards their lords and masters, and spoke with mincing correctness.' The sarcasm is even stronger in the original.

Such women as Clavdia are pre-Eves, Liliths[5] or Lolitas (the Faustian association is explicit in one instance), and martial Joachim finds himself attracted by another edition of the same element in his 'undisciplined' Marusja (he is himself, we learn,

---

[5] 'Adam and Lilith never found peace together; for when he wished to lie with her, she took offense at the recumbent posture he demanded. "Why must I lie beneath you?" she asked. "I also was made from dust, and am therefore your equal." Because Adam tried to compel her obedience by force, Lilith, in a rage, uttered the magic name of God, rose into the air and left him.' From an eighth-century Palestinian midrash quoted by Eva Figes in *Patriarchial Attitudes*.

studying Russian). Fictionally, however, it is one thing to have an uncontrolled Russian couple representing 'barbarians' (Joachim's own term), it is another to find repetitious Slavophobia percolating the symbolism, too. In *The Magic Mountain* there is the Light of Asia cigar, and in *Buddenbrooks* Thomas smokes innumerable Russian cigarettes in his decline. The symbolism becomes inelastically unireferential, virtually push-button, when *every* death figure in Thomas Mann has to have red hair as an obligatory signal, or character tick. The thorough reader, directly we first see 'Gerda, mother of future Buddenbrooks' with her face framed in red hair, knows she spells trouble.

Mann is such a great writer that his women characters cannot carry the neo-classical chauvinism; it turns to parody in his hands. In effect, therefore, he turns the flank of their anti-feminism. His sensitivity to language, let alone social values embedded in language, compelled him to do so. While Mann went one way, then, to enlightened liberalism, the neo-classic dream went exceedingly sour as it crossed the Channel to England, where we find it operated by T. S. Eliot, who praised Mosley, Pound, who championed Mussolini, and Wyndham Lewis who wrote in his book on Hitler of 1931, 'The Hitlerist dream is full of an imminent classical serenity'.

Before leaving the movement, we can see in Lewis its most sexually chauvinist apostle. Attacking throughout his career, with boring monotony, youth, women, and 'negro-worship' as reversing the values of experience, Lewis openly suggested that the extension of the franchise to women had dreadfully decreased the common political sagacity (whatever that was . . . it seemed to be leading to serial world war). In his arraignment of woman as a vehicle of 'romance', revolutionary humanitarianism, and general anti-authoritarianism Lewis's biasses far surpassed the wildest van of neo-classical writings, or ravings.

For this suspicion of woman is, it is true, also paralleled in the French anti-romanticists mentioned, men like Seillière, Maurras, and Lasserre, but Lewis let it have its head in a body of fiction, where its fantasy could be fully unleashed. 'As to women', he has his Nietzschean character, called The Herdsman, remark early in his own career, 'wherever you can, substitute the society of men' and, in fact, not only did he generally do so himself but he repeatedly cited Nietzsche's Zarathustrian advice to take a whip with you whenever you went to make love to a woman. His most interesting character Tarr remarks, 'Surrender to a woman was a sort of suicide for an artist.' The burden of the present book has been to propose the reverse . . . that, as Baudelaire saw, woman *is* an artist.

Forms of history come to seem commonplace, perhaps, after they have been enacted on the boards. Or 'History is the propaganda of the victor' (Malcolm Muggeridge). That art, culture, should work like disease on the fabric of bourgeois capitalism scarcely seems to us today such an epoch-shaking notion, but it is nonetheless one that received really lyrical twists in Thomas Mann's work. For, as he suggested in his famous essay on Dostoevsky, it matters not a little who is sick; when it is a Nietzsche or a Dostoevsky, then 'the disease bears fruits that are more important and more beneficial to life and to its development than any medically approved normality'.

Throughout *Buddenbrooks* Mann played with, and punned on, aesthetic transcendence via dentistry, a sturdy commercialism built on decay (almost needless to say, there are distant echoes of the same at the end of *Lolita*). 'What is lost in health and moral certitude', writes Kenneth Burke, 'is gained in questioning and conscientiousness, in social and æsthetic sensitiveness.' And Erich Heller, who sees *Buddenbrooks* as a fairly precise if hyper-subtle exposition of Schopenhauer, treats it as a Fall of Man. It certainly is a fall of male sexism in the absolute sense.

For the pessimism that is well-nigh musical in its reverberations throughout Mann's work is the result of our lost social innocence. We put on knowledge and lose our vigour. Perhaps we were wrong, after all. Perhaps knowledge is what it was for Aschenbach at the close of *Death in Venice* . . . 'it *is* the abyss', he reflects. All this means that we must look at Mann's treatment of the erotic relationship in an attentive, and qualified, way. For alongside his ideas he inherited also the ironic manner of communicating truths, that of a Kierkegaard or a Dostoevsky.

So, since there is no place in our society for a proper balance of sexual equality – that true union of 'the heart' we have seen Charlotte Brontë calling for – then there can be no fully eventuated love. There virtually is none in Mann's canon. There is erotic passion, Apollonian admiration, Dionysiac debauch; but there is no hope, within the 'realm of possibility', of a mature union between the sexes. Tony Buddenbrook, the Bovary *de ses jours* (and ours), marries scoundrels seriatim and is hopelessly impractical in the great world of affairs, yet her metaphysical vision is completely secure. *She* knew that Grünlich was a swindler, while her businessman father failed to do so. Her subjectivity turns out to be perfect truth. The ever so feminine 'little woman' was right all along.

Mann's early anti-decadent sense of aesthetic apartness, aloofness, then, turns into one of those self-consuming dreams, of great artists like Yeats, Joyce, Baudelaire, Flaubert; and in *Buddenbrooks*, probably the finest familial novel ever written if only since it is an anti-familial novel, we see him marrying it with that member of our species who has for so long been condemned to be the eternal pessimist – woman: the passages by Schopenhauer on negative happiness call out for quotation here:

> 'That all happiness is only of a negative not a positive nature, that just on this account it cannot be lasting satisfaction and gratification, but merely delivers us from some pain or want which must be followed either by a new pain, or by languor, empty longing, and ennui; this finds support in art, that true mirror of the world and life, and especially in poetry. Every epic and dramatic poem can only represent a struggle, an effort, and fight for happiness, never enduring and complete happiness itself. It conducts its heroes through a thousand difficulties and dangers to the goal; as soon as this is reached, it hastens to let the curtain fall; for now there would remain nothing for it to do but to show that the glittering goal in which the hero expected to find happiness had only disappointed him, and that after its attainment he was no better off

than before. Because a genuine enduring happiness is not possible, it cannot be the subject of art.'[6]

The passage is positively entitled to stand over the best art of our time. Robert Musil epigraphs his *Young Törless* with a variety of it he discovers in Maeterlinck:

'In some strange way we devalue things as soon as we give utterance to them. We believe we have dived to the uttermost depths of the abyss, and yet when we return to the surface the drop of water on our pallid finger-tips no longer resembles the sea from which it came. We think we have discovered a hoard of wonderful treasure-trove, yet when we emerge again into the light of day we see that all we have brought back with us is false stones and chips of glass. But for all this, the treasure goes on glimmering in the darkness, unchanged.'

The prototype of this aesthetic disillusion must be woman. Thus she is seen through tears in Thomas Mann. Lips cling, but fall away. Hope rises, only to fall and fail. In Yeats's pregnant lines:

'Everything that man esteems
Endures a moment or a day.
Love's pleasure drives his love away,
The painter's brush consumes his dreams. . . .'

This is no less than the erotic fate of woman in a society which prohibits proper equality, and it is interesting to think of the numbers of Mann's lovers who go through their agonized yearnings prone in bed or else semi-prone on some sickroom sofa or convalescent chair (from Aschenbach through Castorp to Leverkühn); this is, as Erich Heller neatly puts it, 'invalid love rising from the invalidity of life'.[7]

[6] Arthur Schopenhauer, *The World as Will and Idea*, translated by R. B. Haldane and J. Kemp, New York: Doubleday Dolphin Books, 1961, p. 331; London: Routledge, 1883; the passage cited is from the Fourth Book, dealing with the assertion and denial of the will to live.

[7] Erich Heller, *The Ironic German*, Boston: Little, Brown, 1958, p. 64: a perfectly coruscating study, almost a little work of art on its own, and extremely allusive.

It may again be objected that Mann's transvaluing here still lacks originality. The theme of cursed beauty was one that drew Baudelaire to Poe, as Nerval to several 'fatal' visionaries, and both men in their own lives to disastrous erotic liaisons. Mario Praz gives us a whole litany of ladies of pain, ranging from hunchbacks, dwarfs, amputees, to lovely epileptics, seductive hags, sensuous consumptives, delectable idiots and, of course, that epitome of social deformation, the prostitute.[8] De Sade, Kleist, Keats, Mérimée, Baudelaire, Hoffmann, Poe, Gautier, Ibsen even (whose Rebecca West, after all, 'kills' the man who loves her), and of course Strindberg and D'Annunzio – the list could be continued to Proust and Joyce, for Leopold Bloom's masturbatory fantasy, Gerty McDowell, is, we observe, lame. Why? She does not have to be. It is not her limp that turns Bloom on.

As a matter of fact, it is said that Mann did not know Zola[9] when he wrote *Buddenbrooks* (which was published at the end of 1900 with a 1901 date on the verso of title-page), but that, rather, the novel's origin lies in the Goncourts's *Renée Mauperin*, in which the heroine physically disintegrates – 'elle disait comme dans la maladie il y a dégagement et délivrance' – like the Buddenbrookian teeth. Looking at the seductive Clavdia Chauchat, Hans Castorp reflects, 'For a man to take an interest in a woman inwardly diseased had no more sense than – well, than the interest Hans Castorp had once taken in Pribislav Hippe.'

Cadaverous and/or androgynous beauty itself suggests a sort of *Liebestod*. Reflecting on the invalid girl to whom he had once been engaged, Dostoevsky's Raskolnikov declares, 'I really don't know what drew me to her then . . . she was always ill. If she had been lame or hunch back, I believe I would have liked her even better.' Thomas Mann peoples his fiction with 'invalid' lovers who are *au fond* dying of the poisoning of sexual relationships –

[8] See Chapter IV ('La Belle Dame Sans Merci') in Praz's *The Romantic Agony*, already cited.

[9] In one sense Mann really reverses Zola, the impetus of his work being almost wholly metaphysical. Zola got his revelations largely from research (for Henry James, he 'reasons less powerfully than he represents'); no question of aesthetic value inheres here.

Aschenbach, Castorp, Leverkühn, Frau Klöterjahn, the heroine of *The Black Swan*, consumed with both love and cancer. Victims, all.

Alone of Mann's major women characters, Tony Buddenbrook calls into question the whole 'motherhood' absolute of her society, that cruel abstraction which has overpopulated the world and received its spokesman in the world's greatest lover, of himself, Napoleon Bonaparte, author of that celebrated statement, 'women are made far too much of; they should not be regarded as men's equals, for after all they are nothing but the machinery for the turning-out of children'. For if every woman is born to be a mother by virtue of owning a womb, then everyone ought to be an opera singer, thanks to having been born with vocal cords. Despite the meliorative connotations our society has contrived to strew about the term *mother*, some mothers have been murderers.

Fortunately, Mann had an open-ended philosophy at hand for his writing of the mock-epic of the Buddenbrooks, namely that of Schopenhauer. As a result, aesthetic ambiguities are, if anything, strengthened within its protection, and contradictions converted into those of the times. Degas once made a nice comment – that perfection closes the door. When something has been completely understood and eventuated into art, there seems nothing more to say. *Buddenbrooks* is just such a perfect illision of fiction and philosophy, and it is time to take a closer look at it.

* * *

Buddenbrooks is a *Geistesgeschichte* or, in Albert Thibaudet's classification for *War and Peace* and *Les Misérables*, 'le roman brut qui peint une époque'. It begins with tiny Tony perched on her grandfather's knee and asking a truly Schopenhauerian question, 'And – and – what comes next?'

Life comes next, of course, and another meal, and then death. The world of old Johann Buddenbrook is conceived as a blind Schopenhauerian *Wille*, uselessly and mechanically repeating itself. Reading the family genealogy, Tony is later absorbed, mesmerized, by the monotony of this confidence, that, as trees produce trees, roses more roses, so Buddenbrooks must produce more Buddenbrooks:

> 'What she read were mostly simple facts well known to her; but each successive writer had followed his predecessor in a stately but simple chronicle style which was no bad mirror of the family attitude, its modest but honourable self-respect, and its reverence for tradition and history.'

Her own importance, as her father informs her, is 'as a link in this chain'. Such significant insignificance is challenged early on when, as a little girl, she muddles up the order of thunder and lightning and is crossly corrected by old Johann. In his semi-delirium at the end her brother Tom (whose cuckolding during music sessions pays due tribute to *Bovary*[10]) has a dreadful vision of the senselessness of this repetition, paralleled as it has been all his life by cash-register arithmetic. And directly *Idee* questions this merciless rote of blind *Wille*, the cycle is doomed.

'I shall live!' Tom cries, as sheer Will becomes spiritualized by suffering, by love, and incidentally by his reading of Schopenhauer: 'This is the revelation: that I shall live! For *it* will live – and that this *it* is not I is only an illusion, an error which death will make plain.' His reflections flicker to his son – 'He is I, myself, soon, soon; as soon as Death frees me from the wretched illusion that I am not he as well as myself.' Then, before he dies after the botched extraction of a badly abscessed tooth, he walks with Tony who 'would repeatedly emphasize the independence and equality of all human beings', and has his rapturous vision of the sea as a force transcending himself, and thus a little Schopenhauerian eternity.

If we seem to have strayed from the paths of radical feminism, we have not truly done so since, as Heller well reminds us, the

[10] There is an echo of the Vaubyessard ball when Tony talks to Tom about a society where 'if a gentleman picks up a lady's fan it is supposed to be a love-affair'. Further, Tom spruces up near his end, when it is too late, like Charles Bovary, and the maid Severin runs off with her employer's clothes, in common with Flaubert's Félicité.

chapter from *The World as Will and Idea* which Tom has been perusing is Schopenhauer at his most pre-Freudian. There the Will is defined as 'a blind incessant impulse . . . the thing-in-itself, the inner content, the essence of the world'. To enslave sex to the Will, as the Freudian system does, is to murder the individual and break woman on the eternally rotating wheel of reproduction of the species. The Hannos of this world are then 'abnormal'. And women . . . ?

Tony Buddenbrook, farcical as she may seem in her rigorous dignity, represents Mann's Germanic contribution to the sex-war, for she has made an effort to stand apart and resist; the book ends with her beaten to her knees enveighing against all those values she has inherited from the family, by now lying in ruins about her. Like Ibsen's Hedvig, she possesses 'eidetic' knowledge, and we know that such is given only to the aristocracy of the race. Her values, and those of Hanno, marked out by sickness and fatality in a society of sheer Will, stand for true life and are the only hope of rejuvenating the world that lies ahead.

Antoinette, Antonia or Tony Buddenbrook, then, is the first-born daughter, and third-born child, of Consul Johann (Jean) Buddenbrook and his Frau Consul Elizabeth, née Kröger, a lady who dies in some pain at the end – as perhaps she should, having borrowed her name from another famous fiction by her author. Tony's comes to her from her grandmother, née Duchamps. Her own life runs through the book which roughly circumscribes the period 1835–75, an era of European upheavals and rising mercantilism – the narrative is punctuated, in another sort of pun, with deaths and meals ('One must eat', Tony's mother reminds her, and a merchant Senator dies with cake in his mouth). It is a very historical novel, for the history is ours. Tony marries two rogues, Grünlich and Permaneder, and her daughter by the first marries a third, Hugo Weinschenk, later jailed.

It is true that Tony may be 'a parody of "life" ' (Heller), notably in her unfailing optimism, which is a bit absurd. But then if pessimism is the rather natural effect of observing Will, and biology becomes a sort of business cycle, such optimism is courageous, to be cherished. It is too easy to dismiss Tony as another Emma Bovary, and in her dressing-gowns a simple spoof of Wagner – 'You are romantic, Fräulein Buddenbrook', her one true soul-mate, the revolutionary Morten Schwarzkopf, tells her. 'You have read too much Hoffmann.' She has. But the reading in the romantic century has aroused the Dionysiac, and she is easily able to recognize the 'operator' Grünlich in a way no one else in the rest of her family seems to have been able (Christian *in absentia*).

By being an imposter Grünlich is something of an artist. He is a real swindler and devil figure – 'Ceaseless activity is a condition of my being', he declares in a Mephistophelian echo. So he squanders the dowry, and little Tony – 'Madame' Grünlich – who misjudges so absurdly on the business level has his number from the first, we find. 'Of course', Tony has said, 'I shall marry a businessman. He must have a lot of money, so we can furnish elegantly. I owe that to my family and the firm.' She brings chaos to both, but they have brought it to her first in their pressure on her to marry a con-man.

We must further remember that Tony had judged correctly before her marriage to Grünlich, at the only point at which it really counted for her, namely during the Travemünde episode. With Morten, the young lover of freedom, she 'suddenly felt herself one'. She should have married Morten, of course, but it was as unthinkable that she could as it was for Tom to marry his 'little flower-girl with the Malay face' called Anna. As Tom tells his shopgirl *grisette*, they have to be 'reasonable'. Even in unreason.

Which is of course what the devoted evolutionary determinism of the Buddenbrooks is. Such is brought into brilliant focus in the scene when Tony's Consul father questions her about her true feelings for the rascally Grünlich:

' "Listen, my dear child," said the Consul, stroking her hair. "I want to ask you something very serious. Tell me: you love your husband with your whole heart, don't you?"

"Of course, Papa," said Tony with a face of child-like hypocrisy – precisely the face of the child Tony when she was

asked: "You won't tease the old doll-woman again, Tony?"
The Consul was silent a minute.

"You love him so much," he asked again, "that you could
not live without him, under any circumstances, even if by
God's will your situation should alter so that he could no
longer surround you with all these things?" And his hand
described a quick movement over the furniture and portières,
over the gilt clock on the étagère, and finally over her own
frock.

"Certainly, Papa," repeated Tony, in the soothing tone she
nearly always used when any one spoke seriously to her.'

Here she stands beside Catherine Earnshaw, parroting accept-
able and presumably desirable answers when asked about something called love. But the Consul continues. Tony learns that
her husband is bankrupt financially, as well as emotionally.' "Ah,
Papa," she said softly, almost without moving her lips, "wouldn't
it have been better –"?' But it seems undutiful to say what she is
thinking and she shuts up. Her father prods her on, but she
merely answers 'Oh, nothing'. After a moment she kisses him
and he continues:

' "Yes, I have bad days behind me. I have had much to try
me. These are all trials sent from God. But that does not help
my feeling a little guilty toward you, my child. Everything
depends on the question I have already asked you. Speak
openly, Tony. Have you learned to love your husband in these
years of marriage?"

Tony wept afresh; and covering her eyes with both hands,
in which she held the batiste handkerchief, she sobbed out:
'Oh, what are you asking me, Papa? I have never loved him –
he has always been repulsive to me. You know that." '

She concludes as if to say, Surely you have instincts too. This
is precisely in the spirit of Tom's reflections on his Uncle
Gotthold's death – 'Did you know one can be a great man, even
in a small place; a Caesar even in a little commercial town on the
Baltic? But that takes imagination and idealism – and you didn't
have it, whatever you may have thought yourself.'

Tony has both. But she cannot eventuate them in her male-dictated environment which regards reproduction as a stock market in all senses, and so she goes and makes one more disastrous marriage, anticipating the divorce rate of modern America (three out of five marriages, with the figures rising). Indeed, after she has run away from Permaneder, she talks to Tom in the family spirit, by the values she has been given to inherit and pass on, with human feelings laid out like cash ledgers:

> ' "Clean and open dealings must be the rule. Why, you can open your books any day, for all the world to see, and say, 'Here they are, look at them.' We should all of us be just the same." '

The scene with her father is thus duplicated between herself and her daughter, Frau Erica Weinschenk, later on. It is a little parody of Will.

For a writer then in his early twenties Mann seems immensely penetrating. The Will of the species, now served by Freud instead of Consul Buddenbrook, crushes and irons out all true life. Tony's brilliant brother Christian, returning from exotic Valparaiso with his stick with the bust of a nun for handle, is an erotic misfit, aberrant. He is one who won't come to 'reason' and so ends in an insane asylum. With 'a beautiful, clean double line diagonally across the entire page' Hanno closes the family book because he rightly thought 'there was nothing else coming'.

There is nothing else coming. What else can come? The whole rhythm of the novel wonderfully responds to its ideological errand, the book breaking up into parties, deaths . . . functions, like sex. For Schopenhauer genius was an objectivity and originally the order imposed by the Buddenbrooks on affairs was quasi-aesthetic, Apollonian; this has degenerated into Will when we meet them, so much repetition. Such is underscored at the start by mention of the previous owners of the Buddenbrooks mansion, a 'brilliant family who had built and lived in the house and then, broken and impoverished, had left it'.

Tony Buddenbrook indeed represents 'life'. And her passionate cry at the close of the book must surely be every woman's until society is reformed, which means seeing it through the other end of the sexual telescope. If you want to breed businessmen, don't talk about love, and fidelity, and the rest of the erotic absolutes. Simply set up something called *motherhood* or *normality* and you will easily achieve that apotheosis of sexism represented, not in 1869 but in 1969, in the frail figure of Gabrielle Russier mentioned, gassing herself because her love of a minor could not be understood by others. That most of her opponents of the more vituperative kind, including her lover's parents, were Communist is almost the main point. Hell hath no fury like a Marxist sexist scorned. Writing to Clara Zetkin Lenin stated unequivocally:

> 'Questions of sex and marriage are not regarded [by you] as part of the principal social question; but, on the contrary, the main social question itself appears as a part of, or an appendix to, the sex problem. . . . This attitude can disguise itself in as many subversive and revolutionary forms as it wants; the fact remains that it is a purely bourgeois attitude. . . . There is no place for such an attitude in the party, among the militant proletariat which is conscious of its spirit of class distinctions.'

In Tony Buddenbrook Mann shows us someone who sees life from the other end of the telescope, what might well be called the receiving end. As her brother is about to leave for Amsterdam, Tony remembers Morten and is overcome with grief. 'Naturally one forgets', her brother chides her. To which she makes hot retort – ' "But I don't want to forget", Tony cried out in desperation. "Forgetting – is that any consolation?" '

The outburst is intensified at the very end, by which time she knows there is no place in this world for her passionate spirit to lodge, no small attic for her wild duck, or, to give her own words for such metaphoric sanctuary: 'Tom, when we were little, and played war, there was always a little spot marked off for us to run to, where we could be safe and not be touched. . . .' Now it has gone. The Lenins of this world were to subordinate 'questions of sex and marriage' to 'the main social question', as if one weren't the other. There would indeed have been no Lenin without 'questions of sex and marriage'.

For Freud joins Marx at the male end of the telescope. It is sometimes almost a question as to which was the better novelist. You make a myth of childhood and of woman as 'the incomplete man', then direct both child and woman into 'normal' genital sex by a system of self-created repressions. Shulamith Firestone summarizes it as follows:

> 'radical feminism does not accept the social context in which repression (and the resulting neurosis) must develop as immutable. If we dismantle the family, the subjection of "pleasure" to "reality", i.e. sexual repression, has lost its function, and is no longer necessary.'

Tony does dismantle the family. Christian, her gifted brother who can imitate the swallowing of a peach-stone so as almost to convince himself he has, refuses the family, and is put into a mental home. Dr Thomas Szasz succinctly describes the horror chamber called normality into which most women are driven:

> 'In our society the words "good" and "bad" are swiftly becoming obscured by notions about mental health and mental illness. And what is "mental health" anyway? Ask six different psychiatrists what "normal" means, you'll get six totally different answers. And if you asked me, I'd say normality is either a four-sided triangle or a square circle. So how do psychiatrists decide who is, and who isn't, "healthy"? Well, Disraeli was once asked to define an agreeable gentleman, and he said, "A gentleman who agrees with me." '

So Tony is a little outcast or aberrant like her brother Christian, and she is so because she is a woman, a voice of feeling in a world of Will and 'reason'. She leaves her second husband for a word, one which 'shall never pass my lips', and rightly so for, while it comically offends her exaggerated dignity, it all too tragically describes the capitalist wife, and mother.

It is a very pure cry of protest she is driven to at the very end of this very considerable book, one that epitomizes, too, much of what we have tried to pursue through our own modest pages. Hanno has died and Tony, now Frau Permaneder, bursts into scalding tears:

' "I loved him so much," she sobbed. "You don't any of you know how much – more than any of you – yes, forgive me, Gerda – you are his mother. – Oh, he was an angel."

"He is an angel now," corrected Sesemi.

"Hanno, little Hanno," went on Frau Permaneder, the tears flowing down over her soft faded cheeks. "Tom, Father, Grandfather, and all the rest! Where are they? We shall see them no more. Oh, it is so sad, so hard!"

"There will be a reunion," said Friederike Buddenbrook. She folded her hands in her lap, cast down her eyes, and put her nose in the air.

"Yes – they say so. – Oh, there are times, Friederike, when that is no consolation, God forgive me! When one begins to doubt – doubt justice and goodness – and everything. Life crushes so much in us, it destroys so many of our beliefs –! A reunion – if that were so –" '

This 'melancholy understanding' of which another tragi-comic figure created by Mann was to speak in 'Tristan', when 'An ancient stock, too exhausted and refined for life and action, stood there at the end of its days', can seek comfort in art when the individual is gifted. And when the individual is a woman.

Yet sometimes one wonders if in women's eyes the tears have stood too long. . . .

Index